VERÖFFENTLICHUNGEN
DES INSTITUTS FÜR EUROPÄISCHE GESCHICHTE MAINZ
ABTEILUNG FÜR UNIVERSALGESCHICHTE

HERAUSGEGEBEN VON HEINZ DUCHHARDT

BEIHEFT 53

VERLAG PHILIPP VON ZABERN · MAINZ

2002

COASTAL SHIPPING
AND THE EUROPEAN ECONOMY
1750–1980

EDITED BY

JOHN ARMSTRONG

AND

ANDREAS KUNZ

VERLAG PHILIPP VON ZABERN · MAINZ

2002

XI, 263 Seiten mit 25 Abbildungen, 32 Tabellen

Bildschirmsatz: Giuliana Taborelli (London) und Christine Weil (Mainz)

Die Deutsche Bibliothek – CIP-Einheitsaufnahme

Coastal Shipping and the European Economy 1750–1980 / ed. by
John Armstrong and Andreas Kunz. – Mainz : von Zabern, 2002
(Veröffentlichungen des Instituts für Europäische Geschichte Mainz ;
Beiheft ; 53 : Abteilung für Universalgeschichte)
ISBN 3-8053-2943-1

CONTENTS

LIST OF TABLES, FIGURES, AND DIAGRAMS

Chapter 13

Chapter 16

LIST OF MAPS

LIST OF ABBREVIATIONS

£	pound sterling
AFB	Archivo Foral de Bikaia
AHL	Archiv der Hansestadt Lübeck
ANF	Archives Nationales de France
BM	building materials
ch	chapter
CL	Commerzlast
DP&L	Dundee, Perth & London Shipping Company
DS	domestic shipping
ed., eds	editor, editors
ff.	following
FS	foreign shipping
GDP	gross domestic product
GSA	Stadtarchiv Greifswald
HAPAG	Hamburger-Amerikanische Paketfahrt Aktiengesellschaft
HNA	historical national accounts
kg	kilogramme(s)
km	kilometre(s)
kml	(kommerz)lasts
MZA	Madrid Zaragoza & Alicante Railway
no.	number
nrt	net register tons
OFFICEMA	Oficina Central Maritima
p., pp.	page, pages
ptas	pesetas
PRO	Public Record Office
RA	Rigsarckivet Copenhagen
RENFE	Red Nacional de los Ferrocarriles Españoles
rt	register tons
SAHS	Stadtarchiv der Hansestadt Stralsund
ser.	series
SMC	Servicios Mancomunados de Cabotaje
SRC	Scottish Record Office
ton-km	ton-kilometre(s)
vol.	volume
ZPB	Zaragoza Pamplona & Barcelona Railway

1

INTRODUCTION: COASTAL SHIPPING AND THE EUROPEAN ECONOMY

JOHN ARMSTRONG AND ANDREAS KUNZ

These papers originated in a workshop held at the Museum for the History of Hamburg between 4 and 7 June 1997, which was funded largely by the Fritz Thyssen Stiftung, and organised by John Armstrong of Thames Valley University, London; Andreas Kunz of the Institute of European History, Mainz; Ortwin Pelc of the Museum for the History of Hamburg; and Lars Scholl of the German Commission for Maritime History. It followed on from the highly successful workshop which was held in Mainz in September 1993 on the topic of »Inland navigation and economic development in nineteenth-century Europe«. The proceedings of this workshop were published in 1995.[1] As was explained in the Introduction to that volume, this was one plank in the strategy to encourage the re-examination of the role of inland transport in economic growth, but on a European-wide basis rather than the narrowly national approach which has characterised most past research on this topic. The present volume is another step on that same road, and we hope by no means the last.

In preparation for the workshop in Hamburg, the organisers made explicit their aims for the meeting, and circulated some thoughts on what might be valuable topics to explore. The overall aim was to try explore the importance of coastal shipping in the process of economic growth and development experienced in Europe before the First World War. Again, like the Mainz workshop, it was accepted that papers could address this topic on a national, regional or local level. A rather ambitious list of possible topics was put forward by the organisers. This included the question of the definition of coastal shipping, in order to see if different European countries were talking about the same sort of trade; the availability of long runs of compatible statistics, collected by either national or regional governments or by port and harbour authorities, and precisely what details were collected (the number or tonnage of ships, or freight, or what), and the extent to which these were disaggregated to show different types of ship, trade or route; the trends dem-

---

[1] Andreas KUNZ/John ARMSTRONG (eds.), Inland Navigation and Economic Development in Nineteenth-Century Europe, Mainz 1995.

onstrated in any such statistics; and what they indicated about growth rates; the role of the coaster in urbanisation and industrialisation; the extent of competition among the coasters and between them and other forms of transport; technological change in coastal shipping over time and what effect this had; the most important commodities carried, routes served and how this changed over time. Obviously not all participants could address all of these questions but it was hoped these might illuminate the papers, and allow the beginning of a European wide view of the role of coastal shipping.

Inevitably it was not possible to recruit scholars to give papers on every European country with a coastline. One or two agreed to provide papers but then were unable to deliver. Despite our best efforts it proved impossible to find relevant researchers in some countries. We hope the publication of this volume may inspire scholars studying those countries not covered to remedy this omission.

In the course of the workshop it became apparent that there were some differences in what was understood by coastal shipping in different countries and hence what trades might be covered by this phrase. This introduction sets out to do three things on a European-wide basis. Firstly, to explain the definition and usage in each country of the various concepts and phrases with which we are dealing. Secondly, to outline the extent of government protection or subsidy for coastal shipping in each country. Thirdly to discuss the availability of long-run, consistent statistics on this topic in each country covered.

Definitions

In Britain coastal shipping is synonymous with cabotage or internal trade. This was laid down in various pieces of legislation dating back to the medieval period[2] and reinforced by common usage and more recent official definitions.[3] It is relatively easy to differentiate coasting from overseas trade in Britain, since it was in the nineteenth century a series of islands, and hence sticking to the coast meant staying in home waters and to go abroad meant leaving the coast and going into deeper waters. Short-sea shipping was used to denote trade in continental waters and therefore included journeys to the near

---

[2] For instance the port books, commonly kept from the sixteenth to eighteenth centuries, used separate volumes for coastwise and overseas trade.

[3] Coastwise traffic. Goods loaded or unloaded at ports in GB, or the UK, and transported to or from another port in the UK, in: Department of Transport, Transport Statistics Great Britain, HMSO 1996, p. 121.

continent, the Mediterranean and the Baltic.[4] This was not enshrined in legislation, but rather contributed one of the sub groupings of various ship–owners' trade associations, such as the UK Chambers of Shipping. A further phrase, which was enshrined in legislation, was the »home trade«. This included coastal shipping as internal trade but was wider than that, since it also covered trade to the proximate coastline of the mainland between Brest and the Elbe river. Thus some of both the French and German coastline was included and all of Belgium as well as the Netherlands.[5] This was sometimes designated grand cabotage in Francophone countries.

Although the definition of coastal trade as internal trade might seem peculiarly suited to the British case, in fact it was the most common definition in Europe. Thus Danish, German, Greek, Italian, Norwegian, Spanish and Swedish cabotage meant internal trade.[6] Obvious examples of this are Germany and Italy. Where the national definition of coastal trade does not equate directly to internal trade, three types of reason seem to occur. Firstly the country may include in its definition some or all of its colonial possessions. A clear example of this is Portugal, which included as coastal trade that from the mainland to Madeira, the Azores and its other Atlantic possessions, as well as between ports on the mainland. In similar vein, the Netherlands included in its definition of coastal trade some of the trade within its east Indian possessions. Great Britain, despite having the largest empire in the world, never included any of her colonial possessions within the definition of coastal trade. Then, secondly, some countries did not bother to distinguish explicitly between coastal and overseas trade. Thus Belgium had a definition of overseas trade and anything not included in this was deemed to be coastal trade. France had a third and similar approach to the problem, and that was to define foreign trade (*au long cours*) as any voyages going outside certain geographical limits (30° to 72°N and 15°W to 44°E) and then to relegate any activity inside that box as coastal. This was similar to Britain's definition of »short sea shipping« and the limits were almost identical. In addition France differentiated between *petit cabotage*, which was trade between two ports on the same coastline, that is along the Mediterranean shore or the Atlantic/Channel coast, and *grand cabo-*

---

[4] For instance the National Ports Council in 1973 defined the short sea trades as »Scandinavia and the Baltic«, »Iberia and western Mediterranean«, »Italy«, and »Central and Eastern Mediterranean«: National Ports Council, Digest of Port Statistics 1972, London 1973, p. 268.

[5] 1894 Merchant Shipping Act, articles 437 and 438.

[6] This and the next section are largely based on League of Nations publication (Communication and Transit): Enquiry into the Scope of the Idea of Coastal Shipping in the Various Countries, Geneva 1931, VIII 6. I am most grateful to Greta Devos for bringing this invaluable publication to my notice.

tage which was trade between the two seas, between Marseilles and Biarritz for example.[7]

A number of countries also used the phrase »home trade«. We have already mentioned it in connection with Britain. This was slightly wider than »coastal« but more restricted than »short-sea shipping«. In Britain it included the very near continental ports. It was also used in this way by Denmark for it included some of the coastline of Germany, Norway, Sweden and the Netherlands, as well as that of Denmark itself.[8]

What comes out clearly in this study of definitions of coastal trade in various European countries is that the vast majority equated coastal trade with that carried on within the state's borders. Thus, if we use it in the same way in this volume we will be doing no historical disservice.

Protection of the coastal trade

The second broad area to be explored is the extent to which the coasting trade in Europe was protected by the national governments. The most common outcome here was that a large number of European governments restricted activity in the coastal trade to the ships which were carrying the national flag and hence were registered within that country. The date at which this protection was introduced varied enormously but if we take a date around 1900 then France, Germany, Greece, Italy, Portugal, Spain and Sweden all restricted their coastal trade to their own ships. Again we have the problem of countries which had no separate existence before 1914, such as Finland, Poland and Ireland, but which were part of larger empires and thus subject to their laws. There is also the complication that some of the countries of 1900 or 1913 had no unified existence throughout the nineteenth century but only came into being in the last third of the century: Italy and Germany are the obvious examples.[9]

A number of European countries adopted what might be called the British model, that is to say they allowed the ships of any nation to participate in their coastal trade. This free competition policy was adopted by Britain in 1853 with the repeal of the Navigation Laws. It was also enshrined in law in Norway by an 1869 Customs Law, and Belgium, as we have seen, had no definition of, let alone protection for, the coastal trade. In theory the Netherlands, under an 1850 edict, could restrict entry to the coasting trade, but in

---

[7] David H. PINKNEY, Cabotage, France's forgotten common carrier, in: French Historical Studies 16 (1989), pp. 471–7.

[8] See the chapter by Hans Christian Johansen below.

[9] See the chapters by Andrea Giuntini and Ortwin Pelc, below.

practice it never exercised this right and hence free competition was the practice. Denmark was in an intermediate position. Under laws of 1819 – 20, internal trade carried out by ships of thirty net registered tons or less was reserved to Danish registered ships. The state could grant reciprocity rights to the ships of other nations and in practice did to those of Great Britain, Belgium, and a number of the north German states.

There is no evidence suggesting that any subsidies were paid to coastal shipping lines by national governments in order to encourage a more frequent or higher class service than would otherwise be offered. It is conceivable that some earnt mail contracts, especially to islands where railway competition was not possible, but in theory this was a straightforward payment for services rendered, rather than a subsidy. Thus there seem to be only two broad models, as far as government and European coastal shipping are concerned, though with some minor variations. Either the trade was restricted to ships of the national flag or it was wide open to any competitor. The former was much more the norm. The latter was restricted to those countries with very small coastlines or which enjoyed a massive technological and competitive advantage.

Statistical sources

Given the nature of the enquiry – investigating the impact of coastal shipping on the European economies – some quantitative evidence would be very helpful, if not essential to a full understanding. Ideally, in order to make trans-European comparisons these statistical sources should measure similar activities in similar units. Unfortunately reality is not that simple. This section examines the sorts of statistics which would be preferred and the problems of constructing long-run time series comparable over time and between nations.

The first problem is geographical. Since we have accepted the most common definition of coastal trade as that within national borders, or internal trade, it seems this is clear enough. It is however, not so, as over the nearly two centuries from 1750 to 1914 national boundaries changed drastically for some countries and to some extent for all. At the most extreme, present day Finland, Poland or Ireland had no separate existence in this period but were part of much larger empires. Thus »internal trade« for Finnish ships meant the whole of the Czarist empire from 1809. Poland was in a similar position. After the partitions of the late eighteenth century and the confusion of the Napoleonic Wars it too was part of the Russian empire until the First World War and the Bolshevik revolution. At the other extreme, before the 1870s, neither Italy not Germany were unified nations but rather were a series of separate states, some of which were very small. It does not make much sense to insist on measuring the internal trade of some small duchies or tiny bishoprics but it may be impossible to find statistics on the coastal shipping of Italy or Germany as defined in 1900, for the pre 1870 period. Even countries such as Belgium, Denmark, Greece, the Netherlands and Norway experienced quite drastic boundary changes at various times within our period making it less likely that a consistent series of statistics would have been collected. The latter is borne out in that even in those countries which had minimal boundary changes, like Britain, Spain and Portugal, or where the change had little effect on shipping patterns, such as France's loss of Alsace-Lorraine, there was no guarantee that consistent statistics would be collected and survive over such a long period. Thus there are huge problems in creating time series of a consistent sort.

Even if boundary changes were not a problem, there are a number of other difficulties. At the simplest, did the government, if it collected any statistics, differentiate between various types of trade? One would wish the coastal trade to be separated from both overseas trade and inland navigation, by river or canal. In those countries which drew no real distinction between overseas and coastal voyages, it is quite conceivable that the statistics will not be collected separately. In others, given that small coasters could and did proceed many miles inland on navigable rivers, and even some canals, it is possible that the two types of navigation were not separated but conflated.

A further complication arises, where statistics were collected, as to the precise nature of the measurements. The most likely thing to be counted is the ships themselves, as the most visible items. This too poses some difficulties as, if only the number of ships is counted, it ignores differences in size, so ideally one wants numbers of ships and their tonnage. This gives a better idea of the amount of work performed. Two further complications occur. Firstly there are different tons.[10] In shipping there are three usual measures of tonnage, gross registered, net registered, and deadweight. The first two are rather artificial and used for calculating taxes or harbour dues, the latter is a measure of carrying capacity or burthen. Deadweight tonnage is the measure which will give the most accurate indication of the cargo carrying capacity of a ship, and the one, ideally, we wish to see calculated. In practice it is the least likely to be collected as fiscal purposes often drove statistical recording. This is not quite such a drawback, as Maywald has worked out the ratio between net registered tonnage and deadweight tonnage of ships, taking into account hull material

---

[10] A useful article on the intricacies of tonnage measurement is Yrjo KAUKIAINEN, Tons and tonnages: ship measurement and shipping statistics, c. 1870–1980, in: International Journal of Maritime History 7 (1995), pp. 29–56, and on the earlier period: Simon VILLE, The problem of tonnage measurement in the English shipping industry, 1780–1830, in: International Journal of Maritime History 1 (1989), pp. 65–83.

and date of build.[11] These allow us to convert one to the other. The second question is whether the statistics collected are simply those of the coastal fleet, ideally numbers and tonnage, or of the number and tonnage of ships entering or leaving ports in the coastal trade. The problem with the former is that it gives no idea of work performed as we do not know the number of voyages made in a year, or the routes served. Provided that it distinguishes between loaded ships and those in ballast, the latter statistic, of entrances and clearances, is superior since, it gives a good measure of the cargo carrying capacity of the fleet in any given period, taking into account multiple movements by ships.

Two further features need comment. Given that much of the former discussion is aimed at finding a proxy for the quantity of cargo carried in the coasting trade, the ideal statistic to discover would be an actual measurement of this: the quantity of cargo in tons carried in the coasting trade for a given time period, ideally broken down by type of cargo carried. In a truly ideal world this would also state the port of departure and destination so that the distance of the haul could be measured and an average haul length calculated, for in transport provision the ideal statistic is that of ton mileage (or ton-kilometres) to indicate the amount of work performed. Sadly it is rare that these statistics were collected and even rarer that they survived. Even the components, from which historians could calculate their aggregates are also *rara avis*, which, however, should not discourage us from attempting to reconstruct such series if the amount and quality of data allows for it.

The problem of compiling time series

Statistical sources represents only raw data from which time series can be compiled or reconstructed. The international scope of the Hamburg workshop made it possible to query participants on the state of the art on historical coastal shipping statistics in their respective countries. The results of this survey, covering the period from the mid-eighteenth century to the present, are presented in table 1 (see following page).

---

[11] K. MAYWALD, The construction costs and value of the British merchant fleet, 1850–1938, in: Scottish Journal of Political Economy 3 (1956), pp. 47–9.

Table 1: Survey on coastal shipping statistics

Country	National language term	separate entry?	Can time series be constructed? 18th	19th	20th	Aggregate level of series ports	regions	national	other	Do time series already exist?	Are they being constructed?	Main categories in official statistics	Reported by
Denmark	Kystfart	no	no	yes	yes	yes	yes	yes	no	no	no	number of ships tonnage and flag sail/steam	H. Ch. Johansen
Germany	Küsten-schiffahrt	no	perhaps	yes	yes	yes	partially	perhaps	yes	no	yes	number of ships tonnage and cargo sail/steam flag and destinations	A. Kunz D. Rabuzzi U. Albrecht O. Pelc
Belgium	Kustvaart cabotage	no	no	yes	yes	yes	no	no	yes	no	yes	number, tonnage and cargo of ships sail/steam origin/destination	G. Devos
Finland	Rannikkome-Renkulku	no	no	1880 –>	yes	yes	no	yes	no	no	no	number of ships net tonnage cargo	Y. Kaukiainen J. Ojala
Sweden	Inrikes sjofart	yes	no	1858 –>	yes	yes	yes	yes	no	no	yes	number of ships tonnage	0. Krantz
Great Britain (U.K.)	coastal or coastwise shipping (cabotage)	yes	yes	yes	yes	yes	yes	yes	no	yes	no	Number of ships tonnage crew details of cargo	J. Armstrong G. Jackson
France	cabotage	yes	perhaps	yes	yes	yes	?	yes	?	partially	yes	Number of ships tonnage cargo and crew origin/destination	P. Voss
Italy	cabotaggio	yes	no	1861 –>	yes	yes	yes	yes	?	no	yes	number of ships cargo sail/steam flag	A. Giuntini
Spain	cabotage	yes	no	1857–>	– >1927	yes	yes	yes	yes	yes	no	size of fleet tonnage and value of cargo origin and destination (until 1882)	A. Gómez-Mendoza

A first glance at the returns to questionnaires, which were sent out to participants in the workshop, seems to indicate that similar problems exist in the statistical history of coastal shipping in European countries. There is information on nine countries (Denmark, Germany, Belgium, Finland, Sweden, Great Britain, France, Italy and Spain). Of these four countries (Denmark, Germany, Belgium, and Finland) do not have coastal shipping as a separate entry in their historical national statistics, while five (Sweden, Great Britain, France, Italy, and Spain) do. In most cases time series can be compiled, even with respect to the first mentioned four countries. The possibility of reconstruction of such series increases the further one advances in time; it is best for the mid-nineteenth century up to and including the twentieth century, and worst for the eighteenth century, which is not surprising. Time series can apparently best be reconstructed at the level of the individual port, and in some countries problems seem to exist in compiling those at the regional and national levels. It is somewhat surprising that the fourth category »other«, which includes shipping firms, cartels associations, etc., only received three affirmative answers (Germany, Belgium and Spain), particularly since steamship companies played such a large role in the development of coastal trade. Many of these firms did not compile and publish statistical information on their performance, perhaps because they wished to keep commercial secrets from their rivals, or, if they did, they have not survived. Moving to the next column it becomes clear that there is a dearth of statistical series on coastal shipping, but it is reassuring that in five countries at least (Germany, Belgium, Sweden, France and Italy) efforts are currently being made to remedy the situation. These results indicate the problems of doing research on the coastal trade throughout Europe, and of making cross country comparisons, if even the basic statistics were not recorded and time series have not been compiled. This provides an opportunity for an enterprising scholar with a statistical bent.

Acknowledgements

The editors wish to thank the following without whom this volume would not have been possible: the Fritz Thyssen Stiftung, Cologne, for funding the original workshop; Giuliana Taborelli and colleagues for computer type setting in London, Christine Weil for computer type setting in Mainz; Natalie Klein and Annette Reichardt for compiling the index; John Williamson and Joachim Robert Moeschl for cartography.

Map 1: Europe in 1914
(Ports shown are those mentioned in the text)

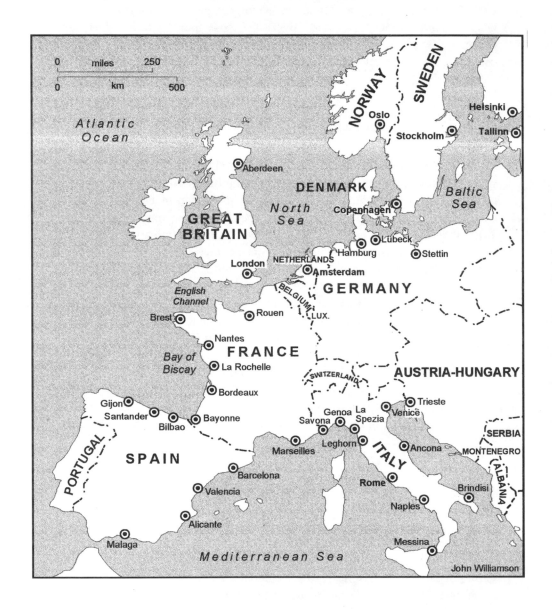

BRITISH COASTAL SHIPPING: A RESEARCH AGENDA FOR THE EUROPEAN PERSPECTIVE

JOHN ARMSTRONG

In the UK until recently the coastal trade was largely ignored when transport developments were discussed.[1] Over the last decade or so much more research has been published on this topic, and the broad outlines of the structure of the industry, the commodities carried, the routes worked and the role of the coaster in industrialisation are now known.[2] This paper will review that literature, in order to establish the broad parameters of the economics of the British coastal trade in the hope that it may suggest the sort of topics and angles which need to be researched on a European-wide basis.

An acceptable definition of what is meant by coastal trade is crucial, since there is no guarantee that the idea of coastal trade in one country will be the same as in the other twenty five or so European states. In this regard the United Kingdom has an advantage over its continental neighbours, because of its geographical make up. Britain is a series of islands and therefore it was completely separate from all other countries, so coastal trade was internal trade and this is a commonly used definition. For instance, the Customs Consolidation Act of 1876, section 140, stated that »all trade by sea from one part of the United Kingdom to any part thereof shall be deemed to be coasting trade«.[3] To go foreign meant venturing into deeper water and abandoning the coastline. This is the definition I have used in my work and the one most commonly used in British writing on this topic. This definition does not fit other European countries so well. They had common boundaries and thus, whereas in Britain sticking to the coast ensured the ship stayed in British waters, on the mainland of Europe it was very easy to go into foreign waters

---

[1] For example, standard texts on the development of British transport devoted a few pages to coastal shipping: H. J. DYOS/D. H. ALDCROFT, British Transport. An economic survey from the seventeenth century to the twentieth, Leicester 1969, pp. 45–6, 52, 208–210; T. C. BARKER/C. I. SAVAGE, An Economic History of Transport in Britain, London 1974, pp. 70–2.

[2] For a recent survey of the literature, see John ARMSTRONG (ed.), Coastal and Short Sea Shipping, Aldershot 1996.

[3] P. FORD/J. A. BOUND, Coastwise Shipping and the Small Ports, Oxford 1951, p. 48.

by following the coastline. However, internal trade could be one definition of coasting trade.

In Britain the distinction between coasting and foreign trade was reinforced in law by the question of certificates of competency for masters and mates. Under the Mercantile Marine Act of 1850 both officers had to obtain such a certificate, but only if the ship was foreign-going.[4] A new concept, »the home trade«, was introduced by the act. Masters of ships sailing in the home trade needed no qualifications until 1854 and thereafter only if their ships carried passengers.[5] Thus from 1854 the coastal liner trade had certified officers. In addition, from 1862 coastal steamships, along with foreign-going, had to have certified engineers.[6] However, sailing ships plying in the home trade, which did not carry passengers could be skippered by totally uncertificated men until the First World War.[7] In 1894 the limits of the home trade were defined to include voyages to the near-continent, between Brest in France and the mouth of the river Elbe in Germany.[8] Hence about half of both the French and German coastline and all of Belgium and the Netherlands were capable of being visited by sailing ships with uncertificated masters. It would be interesting to discover how far other European countries had similar distinctions in qualification and certification for masters and mates who were foreign-going compared to the coastal trade only.

Another common phrase which might be confused with coastal shipping is »short-sea shipping.« For instance, the British Shipping Federation for some years had a Short Sea Trades Committee and in the 1960s, both a Short Sea Liner Section and a Coastal and Short Sea Tramp Section.[9] This usage was to distinguish between deep water or blue sea voyages, such as across the Atlantic or to the Far East and those going to the Mediterranean or Baltic. The latter were within slightly more protected waters where there was insufficient space to allow waves to build up the long swells typical of deep water seas.[10] In this case, »short sea shipping« included the coastal trade but was more than it alone, extending to near continental and European voyages but excluding inter-continental journeys. Thus many ferry journeys from the United Kingdom to European destinations counted as short sea but not coastal. In main-

---

[4] Nicholas Cox, The records of the Registrar-General of Shipping and Seamen, in: Maritime History 2 (1972), pp. 179; Emrys Hughes/Aled Eames, Porthmadog Ships, Gwynedd 1975, pp. 77–8; Clifford Jeans, The first statutory qualifications for seafarers, in: Transport History 6 (1973), p. 255.

[5] Cox, The records, p. 179.

[6] Ibid., p. 180.

[7] Basil Greenhill, The Merchant Schooners, London 1988, p. 119.

[8] J. A. MacRae/C. V. Waine, The Steam Collier Fleet, Wolverhampton 1990, p. 30.

[9] L. H. Powell, The Shipping Federation, London 1950, p.73.

[10] Ian Dear/Peter Kemp, An A-Z of Sailing Terms, Oxford 1992, p. 168.

land European states it is conceivable that journeys could commence as coastal and then continue into short sea with no real distinction.

Another defining feature of coastal trade was that in many European countries it was reserved for the ships of nationals only, or at least ships which were registered in that country. In Britain the coastal trade had been protected under the Navigation Act of 1660[11], but was opened to foreign competition in 1853.[12] It was part of the general liberalisation of Britain's trade, at a time when British shipbuilders and shippers had technological and organisational competitive advantages over other nations. In practice the liberalisation had no effect before the First World War. The proportion of non-British ships plying in the coastal trade was tiny and British shipping made up the vast majority of clearances and entrances. This was quite different from many other European countries which retained protection of their coastal trade for their own ships and seamen. This restriction may have been beneficial in that it required inspection and enforcement and may therefore have generated records for the historian. Some nations, such as Greece, still reserve their cabotage for their own nationals, though that is to be phased out in the new century.[13]

It has sometimes been suggested that it is foolish to study the coastal trade as separate from the general history of shipping and maritime activity. Among the reasons put forward for this view are that changes in technology, whether on the ship or at the dockside affect all shipping irrespective of trades. Sailors did not differentiate between the trades, and of a more practical nature, that the ships did not distinguish between coastal and overseas destinations but went where there was a cargo to be carried at a remunerative freight rate. Thus it is a false dichotomy to separate coastal from overseas ships, as there was much crossover. All of these points can be disputed, but now is not the time or place. What matters here is that we are not solely interested in the *ships*, but the voyages they made. If we accept the definition of coastal trade as internal trade then all voyages between two internal ports are coastal and all between one internal and one foreign are foreign voyages. We can then study those voyages which we have designated as coastal, to determine their characteristics. It becomes a little more complex when we wish to investigate the ships themselves, but I will argue later that there are many ships which can be identified as almost entirely operating in the coastal trade and that as specialisation of shipping type increased over time this distinction became even sharper.

---

[11] Ronald HOPE, A New History of British Shipping, London 1990, p. 188.

[12] Adam W. KIRKALDY, British Shipping. Its History, Organisation and Importance, Newton Abbot 1970, p. 27.

[13] Marie LEKAKOV/E. TZANNATOS, Policy options for increasing the competitiveness of intra-Greek cargo coastal shipping, in: Third European Research Roundtable Conference on Shortsea Shipping, Delft 1996, pp. 471–85.

The main aim of this book is to examine the relationship between the coastal trade and economic development and it is to this that I now turn. I wish to argue that the coaster was crucial in supporting and encouraging the rapid industrialisation usually designated »the industrial revolution«; that it continued to be important in fostering economic growth throughout the long nineteenth century, despite the advent of the railway; and that the coaster had special advantages over the long haul and in carrying bulky low-value goods, but also played a part in moving high-value goods. The economic advantage of the coaster was based on large capacity and low unit operating costs compared to its rival modes of transport. Let us look firstly at the coaster's role in industrialisation. In Britain, as elsewhere, industrialisation accompanied urbanisation. The coaster played a crucial role in both movements. Urbanisation meant a large increase in the physical structure of towns. This required bricks or stone, timber, slates, sand, lime and plaster for building houses, factories and offices. Granite setts were needed for roadways, and as much traffic was horse-drawn huge amounts of hay, straw and oats and other grains were required, as each horse ate about twenty pounds of grain per day. The increased population of these towns and cities required food and drink, and the main fuel for heat, light and power was coal. Many of these commodities came long distances or from specific locations. Thus taking London alone, most of its coal came from the north east[14], a journey of about 300 miles, granite setts and kerbs came from Aberdeen[15], over 400 miles distant, Portland stone came from the south coast for public buildings and civic improvements such as The Embankment, slates came from north Wales[16], cheese from Cheshire[17], salmon and beef from northern Scotland.[18] Some products came more locally, grain from Kent and East Anglia[19], hay from west Middlesex, but one of the characteristics of British urban growth was the wide network of trade flows. Many of these commodities reached the cities which were on the sea or navigable rivers by coaster. It should be borne in mind that the last

[14] Raymond SMITH, Sea-Coal for London. History of the Coal Factors in the London Market, London 1961, pp. 15–22, and 276–96; Roger FINCH, Coals from Newcastle, The Story of the North East Coal Trade in the Days of Sail, Lavenham 1973.

[15] Clive H. LEE, Some aspects of the coastal shipping trade: the Aberdeen Steam Navigation Company, 1835–80, in: The Journal of Transport History, 2nd series, 3 (1975), p. 95, reprinted in John ARMSTRONG (ed.), Coastal and Short Sea Shipping, Aldershot, 1996, p. 91.

[16] Jean LINDSAY, A History of the North Wales Slate Industry, Newton Abbot 1974, pp. 188–94.

[17] Robin CRAIG, Some aspects of the trade and shipping of the River Dee in the eighteenth century, in: Transactions of the Historic Society of Lancashire and Cheshire114 (1963), pp. 99–128; Walter M. STERN, Cheese shipped coastwise to London towards the middle of the eighteenth century, in: Guildhall Miscellany, 4 (1973), pp. 207–21.

[18] See LEE, Some aspects, p. 95.

[19] Guildhall Record Office, London, Mss 1667/1–3.

qualification was no problem. Eight out of the top twelve of Britain's urban centres were either on the sea or a navigable river. The east coast coal fleet is well known as were the regular sailing packets from Aberdeen and Dundee. Cheshire cheese came by sea, as did Welsh slate and Aberdeen granite. Many of these were sent in large consignments and were of low intrinsic value. Many also demonstrated punctiform characteristics, that is needing to be moved from one location to one destination. In addition to the large variety of goods flowing into the towns and cities, there was also a need for a less pleasant outward flow. Night soil, horse droppings from stables and the roads[20], the ash from boilers and domestic hearths[21], broken glass, brick rubble, and numerous other waste or bye products had to be removed from urban areas if the death rate was not to rise to even worse proportions. Again much of this refuse was cleared from the cities by coastal ships. Thames barges brought wheat and barley from East Anglia and took back night soil or horse manure to fertilise the ground. Cullet was carried back to Newcastle for re-using, ashes were taken out to Kentish brick makers to be used in their trade and brick rubble often acted as ballast for coasters sailing light.

Industrial growth created similar strains in terms of requiring large amounts of bulky raw materials to be moved around the country. Coal was pre eminent as an industrial fuel and large amounts of salt, china clay, iron and copper ores, timber for pit props, pig iron, and alkalis also needed to be moved. These too required the transport services of the coaster, for they needed to move long distances and in large quantities. Such goods could not stand high unit costs or they were priced out of the market.

If it is accepted that urbanisation and industrialisation required the transport of large consignments of relatively lowly valued raw materials over long distances, perhaps we should now explain the dynamics of the coaster's competitive advantage. Essentially, before the railway, the only real competitor to coastal transport was land transport by packhorse, horse and cart or horse-drawn waggon. For the United Kingdom we can dismiss river and canal traffic as competitors to the coaster since sailing coasters could and did sail far up rivers and hence river trade was often an extension of coastal trade and even some canals were accessible to coastal ships and acted in the same way. Canals were rarely built parallel to the ocean, which might have provided competition for the coaster. Rather they were built from port or navigable river to an inland town or between two inland towns. In this sense canals did not compete for the same traffic as the coaster, but instead extended the all-water routes either by small coasters entering canals directly or by unloading over

---

[20] Hervey BENHAM, Down Tops'l, London 1951, pp. 139–41.

[21] Patricia E. MALCOLMSON, Getting a living in the slums of Victorian Kensington, in: London Journal, 1 (1975), p. 37.

John Armstrong

the side into barges or lighters which continued the journey. Thus canals, river transport and coasters were not competitors but complemented each other.

This leaves only horse-drawn road haulage as an alternative to the sailing coaster in the industrial revolution. Here again, there was relatively little real competition. Each mode had its economic strengths and weaknesses which determined in which routes and trades it was likely to thrive. Compare the capacities of the two modes. A horse-drawn waggon could carry up to four tons by the 1760s[22], a cart perhaps thirty hundredweight and a pack-horse a couple of hundredweight. The average coaster in the middle of the eighteenth century carried seventy tons[23], and there were some much larger, for instance in the east coast coal trade, where Ville believes them to have been about 300 ton burthen ships.[24] Thus whereas a consignment of thirty or fifty tons would have been easy for a single coaster, it would have required a string of waggons and a plethora of carts. The operating costs of horse-drawn road transport were also much greater per unit carried than was the case for the coaster. Each waggon needed a human conductor and, if it was carrying four tons, about six horses.[25] Thus to carry the previously cited fifty tons would have taken thirteen waggon drivers and about eighty horses. By comparison the crew of a coaster which could carry fifty tons would be four of five[26], so that the labour costs of a coaster were much lower per ton of cargo than those of horse-drawn road transport. Horses were also expensive to feed, consuming about twenty pounds of corn or grain a day as well as prodigious amounts of hay.[27] By comparison the wind came free and when it took a toll on sails, spars or other gear, it was part of the implicit contract with sailors that among their duties were to repair, paint, and generally maintain the fabric of the ship. A mariner who could not stitch a sail, scrape a spar, or caulk a seam was not worth hiring. Horses were not merely expensive to feed, they also contracted diseases and ailments which reduced their output, required them to rest, and incurred vets' bills, or in extreme cases killed them early. They were also expensive pieces of capital equipment. A mature carthorse in the late eighteenth century cost about £10, to give £60 for the full team. A broad

[22] John A. CHARTRES, Road transport and economic growth in the eighteenth century, in: ReFRESH 8 (1989), p. 7. Twenty hundred weight made one ton.

[23] T. S. WILLAN, The English Coasting Trade, 1600–1750, Manchester 1938, pp. 11–13.

[24] Simon P. VILLE, Total factor productivity in the English shipping industry: the northeast coal trade, 1700–1850, in: Economic History Review, 2nd series, 39 (1986), p. 360.

[25] Dorian GERHOLD, Packhorses and wheeled vehicles in England, 1550–1800, in: The Journal of Transport History, 3rd series, 14 (1993), p. 20.

[26] WILLAN, The English, pp. 16–17.

[27] GERHOLD, Packhorses, p. 16; John Tilling, Kings of the Highway, London 1957, p. 80.

wheeled waggon at the same time cost between £30 and £40[28], to give a total outlay of between £90 and £100 for the whole equipage, which carried about four tons. A coastal ship's initial cost has been calculated by Craig to have been about £5 to £6 per ton in the late eighteenth century.[29] Thus to build and outfit four tons of carrying space on a coaster might cost between £20 and £24, considerably less than the initial cost of a waggon and six horses. Although the coaster represented a larger initial outlay, for the minimum size was about thirty tons burthen, and the average about seventy to give capital costs of £150 to £420, capital costs per ton of capacity were lower than for road haulage. Thus freight costs per ton mile by sea were much lower than by land, perhaps a quarter or even a fifth of land rates.

In addition the coaster had particular advantages on long hauls. Such trades were quite normal, the east coast coal trade from the Newcastle region to London and the south coast being one example and Cheshire cheese from the north west to London being another. The explanation of the coaster's advantage in long hauls lies in many of its costs being terminal costs, that is incurred going into or leaving a port, and fixed irrespective of the length of the journey made. For example harbour or quay costs were usually charged per ton of ship. Unloading, where not carried out entirely by the crew, was a function of cargo size; pilotage was a fixed sum, the costs of taking on ballast, or discharging it lawfully were also incurred at the end or beginning of the voyage. These costs, fixed irrespective of the length of the journey, were obviously lowered per ton mile as the voyage length increased. By contrast, road transport's costs were much more proportional to the journey length as horse feed, and wage costs were incurred relative to length of haul and not a once and for all charge, each journey.

A further consideration which pointed up the cost advantage of the coaster was longevity. A waggon horse had a working life of only five or six years, then it was too feeble to continue in harness.[30] This meant continuing costs of replacement of capital and hence high depreciation costs – though not expressed as such contemporaneously. By comparison the waggon, as the coastal ship, was capable of lasting decades, subject to relatively minor repairs and maintenance. The objection to this raised by road haulage experts is that ships sunk whereas waggons did not. However waggons were occasionally wrecked due to overturning or running away on hills, and the rate of coaster wrecking is contentious and uncertain. The point is that whereas the coaster could be

[28] Gerard L. TURNBULL, Traffic and Transport: An Economic History of Pickfords, London 1979, pp. 17–18.

[29] Robin CRAIG, Capital formation in shipping, in: J. P. P. HIGGINS and Sidney POLLARD (eds.), Aspects of Capital Investment in Great Britain, 1750–1850, London 1971, pp. 143–4; WILLAN, The English, p. 39; Edward HUGHES, North Country Life in the Eighteenth Century. Volume II: Cumberland and Westmoreland, 1700–1830, Oxford 1965, p. 187.

[30] TILLING, Kings of, pp. 63 and 81.

depreciated at five per cent, assuming a twenty year life, for road transport, horses needed to be written off over five years, or at twenty per cent per annum, and they were the preponderant capital cost in that mode.

Nor should the coaster be dismissed as much slower than horse-drawn road transport. Chartres believed large, heavily laden waggons travelled around twenty miles per day.[31] They needed to stop at night to allow drivers time to rest and feed, and more importantly for the horses to do likewise. Not allowing the horse to rest, or requiring it to pull extra loads, or up steep inclines increased fodder consumption and reduced longevity, so pushing up costs. By comparison the coaster travelled twenty-four hours a day, once at sea and was capable of six or seven knots given a wind of appropriate strength and direction. Thus in a day it could manage a journey of 140 miles or so. For instance in 1687 the ketch *Edward and Jane* averaged just under 100 miles per day on its journey from London to Lancaster.[32] The coaster only needed to sail at one knot on average over the day to travel further than a road vehicle. Fast passages were achieved and even at average rates of progress a coastal voyage was quicker than a similar journey by road. The disadvantage of the coaster was its unpredictability. It could make fast passages, but it could also be locked into a harbour by lack of wind, or too much of a blow, or from the wrong direction. Similarly once at sea it was at the mercy of winds and tides and whereas the latter were predictable the former were not. By comparison road transport was less likely to be affected by weather and more able to predict times of arrival, as Gerhold has shown for Russell's the Exeter carriers.[33]

As a result of these different characteristics, the two modes catered for different routes and commodities. Low-value goods requiring long distance transport had to go by coaster. Land carriage of such products was only possible for a few miles as otherwise the good was priced out of its market. Similarly, wherever the point of origin and the ultimate destination were within a few miles of water and the haul was long, say over forty miles, the coaster was the first choice, because of its low cost, even when the commodity was more intrinsically valuable. Land carriage was used for long journeys when both origin and destination were well inland; for short journeys within towns, such as from quay to warehouse or factory; for long journeys when the good was very highly valued, such as bullion, specie, or spices, and not very voluminous. When the good was bulky, but low weight and high value, such

---

[31] CHARTRES, Road transport, p. 7.

[32] John D. MARSHALL (ed.), The Autobiography of William Stout of Lancaster, 1665–1752, Manchester 1967, p. 89.

[33] Dorian GERHOLD, Road Transport before the Railways: Russell's London Flying Waggons, Cambridge 1993.

as Dent's stockings[34] or the serge carried by Russell & Co.[35], it went by road. In addition, at certain times the coaster suffered because of external conditions. When Britain was at war with another maritime power its shipping was subject to predation by pirates, privateers, and enemy men of war. As a result insurance rates rose steeply and delivery times suffered as ships waited in port to make up a convoy. At this time high-value goods were likely to prefer the less vulnerable land route rather than the riskier, and now more expensive because of the increased insurance premiums, sea journey. This could be compounded where consignments were small size and the frequency of coastal services was low. As Turnbull has shown, where the product was high value, such as fine linen cloth, the consignments small, and the frequency of a coastal service low, it made more sense to send the parcels by road carrier, even though the price was several times higher than by sea.[36] This was compounded when war aggravated the coastal trade, and there were many years in the late-eighteenth century when Britain was at war with at least one maritime power. However, in general shippers did not have a real choice between modes, it was only for expensive low-weight goods that there was any possibility of long-distance road carriage. Even when war made coastal shipping riskier and more expensive the vast majority of low-value, high bulk goods could not travel by road.

Thus in the United Kingdom the coastal ship was crucial to industrialisation and urbanisation and it is difficult to imagine the »industrial revolution« taking place without it. The fact that Britain was particularly well endowed with a long coastline, ample navigable rivers, and very few urban centres more than ten miles from navigable water, may well have aided her in being the first to industrialise. For no other European country was so richly endowed. The extent to which this British model was similar to the mainland continental experience is more uncertain. Apparently Britain had an advantage in her abundance of coastline compared say, to France or Germany, but countries like Denmark, Norway or Italy in theory had extensive coasts and should have faced similar cost conditions and demands.

The early nineteenth century saw the application of steam power to marine navigation, with Henry Bell's *Comet* plying from Glasgow in 1812.[37] In theory this should have removed one of the coastal ship's weaknesses. By

---

[34] T. S. WILLAN, An Eighteenth Century Shopkeeper. Abraham Dent of Kirkby Stephen, Manchester 1970.

[35] GERHOLD, Road Transport.

[36] Gerard L. TURNBULL, Scotch linen, storms, wars and privateers: John Wilson & Son, Leeds linen merchants, 1754–1800, in: The Journal of Transport History, 3rd series, 3 (1982), pp. 47–69; reprinted in Dorian GERHOLD (ed.), Road Transport in the Horse-Drawn Era, Aldershot 1996, pp. 75–98.

[37] Brian D. OSBORNE, The Ingenious Mr Bell. A Life of Henry Bell (1767–1830) Pioneer of Steam Navigation, Argyll 1995.

allowing it to proceed at a steady pace irrespective of wind strengths or direction, it became more reliable and predictable, hence more able to compete with road transport. In practice the early steamboats required so much space for their engines and bunker fuel as to have limited range and restricted cargo capacity, so that they carried passengers, perishables, parcels and high-value, low-weight commodities. However, over time their efficiency improved, thanks to compounding and later triple expansion steam engines which, combined with more efficient boiler designs reduced the coal consumption drastically for any given power output. Thus by the 1850s they were in widespread use.

The role of the coastal ship in the second half of the nineteenth century was similar to that in the industrial revolution, but with added strengths and a more effective competition. The advent of steam gave birth to the coastal liner trade which ran to a scheduled time of departure and arrival.[38] It was fast, as the most modern ships were employed, reliable, as skippers were expected to adhere to posted times of departure and arrival, and convenient as small consignments were carried. It was also frequent, many services between major cities being twice weekly. Thus the coastal steam liner brought a new quality of service to coastal trade, and along with improvements in dockside facilities, a new reliability and rapidity. For coastal liners represented significant aggregations of capital and hence needed to be used intensively. They also were large ships which meant great quantities of cargo to be loaded and discharged. Time was also of the essence because they had a schedule to adhere to and so would not stand the lowly place in the pecking order to which most coasters were consigned. To obviate this many coastal liner companies bought or hired their own dedicated wharf so their vessels did not have to await a turn, and installed appropriate dockside equipment for loading and unloading.

However, if steam eliminated the main weaknesses of the sailing coaster it also brought a potent new competitor in the form of the railway. Initially this was no real threat to the coaster for the early lines tended to complement the coastal routes, running from coal field to port or from inland city to port city.[39] Indeed in two regards the early railway enhanced the coaster's trade by requiring large quantities of bulky material, such as sleepers, rails, ballast, chairs, and even locomotives, to be carried around the coast, and also by unlocking a flow of goods from the interior to the coast for onward transmission by coaster. These early railway lines were also generally short distance,

[38] John ARMSTRONG, Freight pricing policy in coastal liner companies before the First World War, in: The Journal of Transport History, 3rd series, 10 (1989), pp. 180–97; reprinted in ARMSTRONG, Coastal and, pp. 112–29.

[39] John ARMSTRONG, Management response in British coastal shipping companies to railway competition, in: The Northern Mariner 8 (1997), pp. 17–28.

thus competing more with horse traffic than sea-borne By the 1850s a national structure of long distance through railway lines was beginning to emerge, thanks to expansion, mergers, working agreements and the work of the Railway Clearing House.[40] However, even then the railway did not prevent the coaster from continuing to expand its service. The statistics collected by government of ships entering and clearing each port in the coastal trade, despite the occasional alteration in the basis on which the figures were collected, show a steady if unspectacular growth rate of about two per cent per annum on average from 1830 to the First World War.[41] Other evidence suggests a flourishing coastal trade until this date: the data on coal carried coastwise[42], the occasional glimpses of annual cargoes carried by a coastal company, the growth in the frequency and coverage of the coastal liner network.

How do we explain the continuing ability of the coaster to compete with the shining new technology of the railway, which some transport historians have portrayed as all-conquering in the nineteenth century? The answer might be sought in several features and it is interesting to consider how many of these were at work in other European countries. One feature already alluded to is that the coaster segmented its market to provide differing types of service to different customer needs. This varied from the cheap but unreliable sailing ship for low-value, non-deteriorating, bulky goods, via the steam tramp for large consignments of irregular despatch, and regular traders specialising in a shuttle service of one commodity, such as the east coast screw colliers[43], to the highly reliable coastal liner, carrying mixed manufactured goods in small consignments such as Bovril meat extract and Lever's soap[44] as well as passengers and livestock. In this way, different levels of service were offered at different price levels to cater for a range of trades.

In addition, just like the railway, technology in the coastal ship was not static.[45] There were dramatic improvements in the technology of engines and boilers, to give lower fuel consumption per unit of output and hence lower cost. The hulls were initially made of wood, then composite, and later all iron;

---

[40] Philip S. BAGWELL, The Railway Clearing House in the British Economy, 1842–1922, London 1968.

[41] Michael J. FREEMAN/Derek H. ALDCROFT (eds.), Transport in Victorian Britain, Manchester 1988, p. 172.

[42] Ibid., pp. 183–90.

[43] John ARMSTRONG, Late nineteenth-century freight rates revisited: some evidence from the British coastal coal trade, in: International Journal of Maritime History 6 (1994), pp. 45–81.

[44] ARMSTRONG, Freight pricing, p. 194.

[45] This is well dealt with by J. Graeme BRUCE, The contribution of cross-channel and coastal vessels to developments in marine practice, in: The Journal of Transport History, 1st series, 4 (1958), pp. 65–80; reprinted in ARMSTRONG, Coastal and, pp. 57–72.

by the late nineteenth century steel was being used. Metal hulls allowed larger ships without losing structural integrity and hence the average size of ships in the British coastal fleet increased. Overall coaster size rose from about 100 tons in mid-century to nearly 200 tons just before the First World War.[46] By then some of the steam colliers were capable of carrying cargoes of coal in excess of 1,500 tons.[47] In addition innovations such as water ballast cut costs and speeded up turnaround times, the use of propeller rather than paddles made for more slender lines and greater speed. The coasting trade acted as a nursery for overseas shipping in the sense that most of the technical innovations were pioneered on coastal routes, and only when imperfections had been ironed out did they then go on to be adopted in blue water trades.

In this way the coastal ship was continually being refined and improved, to provide lower operating costs, economies of scale, greater speed and more rapid turnarounds. Nor were such improvements confined to steamers. Sailing ships too were subject to technical change. The most obvious is the move away from square rigs to fore-and-aft which cut crew requirements drastically. In addition the use of winches, pulleys and roller reefing allowed more to be done on deck and to be carried out quicker.[48] The design of hatches and the use of winches also allowed quicker loading and unloading and the carriage of larger objects. Thus the coastal ship of the early-twentieth century was a far more efficient and productive instrument than its predecessor of mid-century.

Given the emphasis placed upon railway development in most textbooks of nineteenth-century transport[49], we need to explain why the coaster did not succumb to the railway. One important aspect of its success was that its rates for other than very short journeys were significantly lower than the appropriate rail rate. The coaster continued to have competitive advantage on long hauls, say over 100 miles, because its costs were peculiarly bunched at the terminal points of its voyages irrespective of distance travelled, whereas the railway's costs were much more proportional to distance travelled as it needed to own land, construct expensive civil engineering works, and guard, maintain and repair its property. In addition the railways were not always able to offer merchants the service they needed. Goods trains gave way to passenger trains often by sitting idle in a siding. Their braking equipment was normally antiquated and incompatible, so speeds were notoriously slow. Train load traffic was a largely alien concept, so much time was lost in assembling and

---

[46] FREEMAN/ALDCROFT, Transport in, p. 172.

[47] ARMSTRONG, Late nineteenth-century, pp. 70–1.

[48] GREENHILL, The Merchant, p. 80–1; Hervey BENHAM, Once Upon a Tide, London 1955, p. 47.

[49] For instance H. J. DYOS/D. H. ALDCROFT, British Transport. An Economic Survey from the Seventeenth Century to the Twentieth, Leicester 1969; T. C. BARKER/C. I. SAVAGE, An Economic History of Transport, London 1974.

disassembling trains and shunting. Waggons were not always readily available and remained small size. As a result many movers of goods preferred to use the coaster to the railway. An extreme example of this was the Wilson Line of Hull running fortnightly steamers between Hull and Liverpool, a distance of about 1000 miles when the land route was only one fifth of this, because the railway provision between the two cities was so slow, unpredictable and untraceable.[50] It would be interesting to know how far railways in other European countries were similarly unable to offer a sufficiently superior service to offset their higher costs.

There are many other aspects of the coastal trade which require investigation. The extent to which ships stuck to coastal trading or moved into near continental work; the nature of the coasters' crews. Was the coasting trade a nursery for seamen in that many started there and then moved to deep water work, or did sailors specialise in one or the other? Ownership is another important aspect. Who invested in coastal ships and why? Were the owners people who had a direct interest in the venture because they had goods to ship, or hoped for employment, or to sell goods or services to the shipping firm? Did ownership vary between sail and steam or tramp and liner? We think we know what were the main commodities carried in the United Kingdom, but how profitable were particular trades and indeed coastal ship ownership per se. A colleague recently remarked that as far as the coastal trade was concerned we were starting with a blank slate. I do not entirely agree, there is a little faint writing on the slate but there is still much to be explained. Hopefully this chapter has indicated some of the gaps in our knowledge of the British experience and hence where future research effort is needed. In addition it may suggest some worthwhile possibilities for investigation on a European-wide scale.

---

[50] See John ARMSTRONG/Julie STEVENSON, From Liverpool to Hull – by Sea? In: Mariner's Mirror 83 (1997), pp. 150–68.

Map 2: Northern European ports in 1914
(Ports shown are those mentioned in the text)

3

DANISH COASTAL SHIPPING c. 1750–1914

HANS CHRISTIAN JOHANSEN

Kystfart – *a vague concept*

The Danish word for coastal shipping is *kystfart* and this term is defined in the official Danish dictionary[1] as 'carrying trade between ports in the same country or within boundaries laid down in various regulations'. The first part of this definition is easy to understand, whereas the second part is due to the fact that the term is used with a different meaning in several acts on shipping. In the Danish Merchant Shipping Act of 1861 a *sætteskipper* (a home-trade master) is defined as a person who was allowed to command a ship in the coastal trade and was allowed to sail east of a line from Cape Lindesnæs (the southernmost tip of Norway) and Texel in the Netherlands and west of a line from Rügenwalde in Pomerania to Kalmar in southern Sweden. When the act was revised in 1916 this type of master was called a *kystskipper* (coastal master), but voyages in the same area were now called *udvidet kystfart* (extended coastal trade).

Even if we were to limit ourselves to the first part of the official definition – between ports in the same country – we would, however, run into difficulties when describing the development from 1750 to 1914 because the Danish realm changed borders several times during this period. In 1750 the Danish king ruled in Europe over Denmark, Norway, the Faroe Islands, Iceland, and in northern Germany over the duchies of Schleswig and Holstein (partly) and the county of Oldenburg. The latter county was exchanged in 1773 for the remaining areas in Holstein. Norway was ceded to Sweden in 1814, but as a modest compensation the duchy of Lauenburg became Danish. The German provinces were lost in 1864 and Iceland got a sort of home rule in 1874.

Voyages between ports in the same country in 1750 include both sailing in an open boat along the coast in sheltered waters between Elsinore and Copenhagen and also sailing with some of the larger ships of the merchant fleet on their way to northern Norway or Iceland in the rough waters of the north Atlantic, whereas the same definition in 1914 to a large extent would be limited to traffic between Copenhagen and the provincial ports in Denmark

---

[1] Ordbog over det danske Sprog, Copenhagen 1929, vol. XI, p. 1055.

proper, that is sailings across the Kattegat and through the Belts and the Sound.

In order to find a more manageable way of analysing Danish coastal shipping in this long period more pragmatic criteria have been used in this chapter. Four years have been selected – 1787, 1844, 1879 and 1910. For each of these years voyages between ports in Denmark proper have been included and where Danish ships used on these routes were also sailing in other waters, traffic between these ports and Denmark is included in the coastal trade. The result is that in 1787 the area covered is Denmark, the ports along the coasts of the Oslo fjord, Schleswig, Holstein, the German Baltic ports from Lübeck to Stettin, and also Hamburg and some smaller ports along the Elbe. During the nineteenth century the area gradually diminishes, and for 1910 it is only traffic between ports in Denmark proper and to and from nearby Swedish ports which is included.

Sources

The basic material on Danish shipping before 1914 was collected by the customs authorities and written down in the port books, but since they have survived for only a few years it is, on the whole, not possible from them to follow the routes used by the ships.[2] On various occasions the College of Customs did, however, use the material in the port books for statistics, mainly on international traffic. In 1826, 1834 and 1837 and from 1843 yearly such statistics were published in the official statistical series, although in the years until the early 1840s not in a very satisfactory way as far as coastal shipping is concerned.[3] On the other hand, from 1844 onwards they are very detailed and provide a good background for analyzing Danish coastal shipping.

For an earlier period it is necessary to use a combination of sources and the data for 1787 are therefore collected from several archival series. In Norway the situation concerning the eighteenth century is much better than in Denmark, since nearly all port books from the eighteenth century still exist and are available in the Norwegian national archives.[4] Danish traffic to and from southern Norway can consequently be followed from these port books. In Copenhagen all departing ships had to report to the *waterschout*, a naval officer who was responsible for controlling recruitment of crews and checking whether crew members were conscripted sailors in the navy. In his archives it is possible to find the names of all ships leaving the capital, the name of the

---

[2] Compare the list of surviving port books in A. Monrad MØLLER, Kongerigske toldregnskaber fra det 18. århundrede, in: Fortid og Nutid 26 (1975), pp. 86–103.

[3] Statistisk Tabelværk, ældste række, nr. 3 ff.

[4] Riksarkivet, Oslo, Tollregnskaper.

master, the size of the ship and its destination.[5] Other sources which can be
used are lists of ships passing the Sound (excluding those who sailed between
ports in Denmark and the Duchies)[6], ships passing the Great Belt[7], consular
lists from several German ports, especially Lübeck[8], and various other archival material.

These sources have been combined in a database with information about all
Danish, Norwegian, and Schleswig-Holsteinian ships in 1787 and about the
voyages which are mentioned in the sources used. The list is not complete, the
most obvious shortcomings being lack of information about most of the traffic
from one provincial port to another and from a provincial port to Hamburg and
vice versa. In this chapter some attempts will, however, be made to overcome
these problems by using sources from other years.

Previous research

In the eighteenth and early-nineteenth-century most of the coastal shipping between ports in Denmark proper was undertaken by ships belonging to the
provincial ports, whereas the merchant fleet of Copenhagen was dominated by
larger ships engaged in European and overseas trade. The provincial shipping
has been analyzed in two monographs by Anders Monrad Møller with detailed
information about the the size of each port's merchant fleet and their sailing
patterns and also data on the sailors and the shipowners.[9] The eighteenth-
century traffic between Denmark and Norway is explained in two articles by
Hans Chr. Johansen[10], and information about the shipping from individual
ports can be found in studies of local shipping communities and in the rich
literature of broader urban studies.

As demonstrated in a later section a single steamship company played a
dominating role in Danish traffic after 1870 and this company has been
studied in several jubilee publications, although some of them with a special
interest in the ships and the routes, whereas the economic background is less

---

[5] Rigsarkivet, Copenhagen, Søetatens arkiv, søindrull-eringen, Journal over udgående
skippere fra København.

[6] Rigsarkivet, Copenhagen, Øresundsregnskaber. »Duchies« refers to the duchies of
Schleswig, Holstein and Lunenburg.

[7] Rigsarkivet, Copenhagen, Admiralitetet, Indkomne sager, 1787, various numbers.

[8] Rigsarkivet, Copenhagen, Kommercekollegiet, journalsager, 1787–1788.

[9] A. Monrad MØLLER, Fra galeoth til galease, Esbjerg 1981 and idem, Jagt og skonnert,
Copenhagen 1988.

[10] Hans Chr. JOHANSEN, København-Norge, en handels- og skibsfartsakse i slutningen af
1700-tallet, in: Søfart Politik Identitet, tilegnet Ole Feldbæk, Helsingør 1996, pp. 295–303;
idem., Sejlads og handel mellem Norge og Danmark i 1700-tallet, in: I det lange løp,
Essays i økonomisk historie tilegnet Fritz Hodne, Bergen 1997, pp. 293–304.

well documented.[11] There are also some local studies of the shipping activities in this period, but most relevant publications deal mainly with shipping to European and overseas destinations. A comprehensive seven volume Danish maritime history has been written and was published from 1997 to 1999. Volumes three to five survey the importance of the coastal trade in the total activities of the Danish merchant fleet between 1700 and 1920.[12]

Late-eighteenth-century Danish coastal shipping

The database containing information about the voyages of Danish ships in 1787 has been used to get a first impression of how the merchant fleet was used in the late eighteenth century. As can be seen from table 1, it was mainly ships of less than thirty commercial lasts[13] that were sailing between Danish ports. As mentioned, the database has little information about voyages from one Danish provincial port to another, but studies for both earlier and later years in the century demonstrate that this traffic was of little importance.[14] Most of the domestic traffic was between Copenhagen and a provincial port and these voyages are included in the material used. Sources which could illustrate the traffic between Danish provincial ports and Schleswig-Holstein in 1787 are also missing, but in both 1733 and 1798 less than ten per cent of arrivals in the provincial ports came from the Duchies.[15]

It is evident from table 1 that ships from provincial ports were responsible for most of the domestic seaborne traffic, which means voyages to and from Copenhagen, and that the same type of ships although on average a little larger were sailing between Danish and Norwegian ports and that these two voyage patterns were the backbone of eighteenth century coastal shipping. In order to understand why this was the case, attention should be drawn to the natural resources and the economic conditions in the different regions belonging to the Danish monarchy. Denmark proper was at that time dominated by rural parishes – except for Copenhagen with close to 100,000 inhabitants. About eighty per cent of the population lived by agriculture and all the provincial towns were small, the largest being Odense with about 5,000 inhabitants. Although the productivity in agriculture was low compared to modern standards it was high enough in normal harvest years to provide not only for

[11] J. SCHOVELIN, Blade af den danske dampskibsfarts historie, Copenhagen 1891, and S. THORSØE [et al.], DFDS 1866–1991, Copenhagen 1991.

[12] Dansk Søfarts Historie, volume 3 was written by Ole FELDBÆK, Copenhagen 1997; volume 4 by Anders Monrad MØLLER, Copenhagen 1998; and volume 5 by Anders Monrad MØLLER, Henrik DETHLEVSEN, and Hans Chr. JOHANSEN, Copenhagen 1998.

[13] The last is equal to approx. 2.4 tons.

[14] See MØLLER, Fra galeoth til galease, p. 143 f.

[15] Ibid., p. 124.

the needs of the Danish population but also for a substantial export. Since Norway could not grow sufficient grain to supply its population there was a natural basis for large grain cargoes from Denmark to Norway every year. Danish grain had until 1788 special privileges when imported into southern Norway. In 1786 the harvest in Denmark was, however, below normal and this is the reason why there was some import both in Norway and Denmark of Baltic grain, mainly from Königsberg and Danzig. The number of Danish ships taking part in these Baltic trades shown in table 1 was consequently above average for the late eighteenth century.

On the other hand Denmark had little forest, and timber of good quality had to be imported. Here Norway was a natural supplier although in competition with timber from Pomerania and Sweden, but the Norwegian supplies were by far the most important. In the German provinces the situation was different. This was the most developed part of the monarchy. The two Duchies had a surplus of grain which was exported to other parts of Germany, and also in the coastal trade with Copenhagen and Norway. This pattern is similar to the exports from the Danish provinces, but since manufacturing was of a high standard in several towns there was little that could be bought in Copenhagen in return.

Table 1: Voyage patterns of Danish ships, 1787

a) provincial ships (number of ships)

Destinations

	Denmark	Duchies	Norway	Northern German ports	Other Baltic ports	Other European ports	Overseas
(lasts)							
5 – 9	104	2	47	24	3	5	0
10 – 19	71	2	158	13	37	10	–
20 – 29	40	3	39	2	11	7	–
30 – 39	11	–	14	1	7	5	–
40 – 49	–	–	2	–	1	8	–
50 – 99	–	–	–	–	1	7	–
100 – 199	–	–	–	–	–	1	–
Total	226	7	260	40	60	43	–

b)　Copenhagen ships

	Denmark	Duchies	Norway	Northern German ports	Other Baltic ports	Other European ports	Overseas
(lasts)							
5 – 9	9	–	–	–	–	1	–
10 – 19	6	1	3	4	1	8	–
20 – 29	6	3	4	5	10	6	–
30 – 39	5	11	6	–	9	22	–
40 – 49	–	1	2	–	4	39	1
50 – 99	3	1	2	1	4	44	27
100 – 199	–	–	1	–	1	25	53
200 –	–	–	–	–	–	–	13
Total	29	17	18	10	29	145	94

Note: Ships used on more than one route during 1787 are included in the group with the most distant destination. Ships which were laid up during 1787 are excluded. Dash indicates a zero value.

Source: The 1787 data base, Odense University.

The traffic resulting from these natural differences between the Danish provincial grain exporting ports and Norway was in 1787 undertaken by 1008 north going voyages and 1033 sailing south and about 60 per cent of the tonnage used was Danish. Besides rye and barley there was also meat, butter and cheese on board the ships and a few Danish towns had a local surplus production of handicrafts which found customers in Norway. Most ships sailing north called at the ports along the Oslo fjord with the largest populations and Christiania (Oslo) and Drammen were the most important. Drammen was at that time port city for the silver mining community of Kongsberg with about 8,000 inhabitants. Timber was loaded in the ports situated at the mouths of rivers, down which timber was floated from inland Norway to the coast. Some ships also loaded stoves and other ironware from local iron works, glass from Norwegian glassworks, and salt. The ships used were mainly galleasses with Danish masters and brigs by the Norwegians. The average size of the ships was about twenty seven lasts but with a range from small open boats to a few above fifty lasts.

A voyage from Denmark to Norway would normally take ten to fourteen days and since it could take a long time to find buyers and later to buy timber a Danish ship in this trade might need as much as two months from leaving a Danish port until the master was ready to weigh his anchor for a second journey. Because of rough weather in the early months of the year the ships stayed in port for three to four winter months and the sailing season would therefore most often only allow for four voyages to Norway.

As an example of the traffic in 1787 we can follow master Johan Nielsen Just of Nakskov, a port on the island of Lolland, sailing with the galleass *Catharina Juul* of twenty two lasts. In the data base he is recorded with the following information:

April 25: Passing the Great Belt from Nakskov to Christiania.
May 10: Arrived in Christiania from Nakskov with grain.
May 14: Left Christiania for Nakskov with timber.
June 27: Passing the Great Belt from Nakskov to Christiania.
July 9: Arrived in Christiania from Nakskov with grain.
July 12: Left Christiania for Nakskov with timber and iron.
July 27: Passing the Great Belt from Christiania to Nakskov.
August 26: Passing the Great Belt from Nakskov to Arendal.
September 9: Arrived in Arendal from Nakskov with grain.
September 15: Left Arendal for Nakskov with coal.
September 28: Passing the Great Belt from Arendal to Nakskov.
October 31: Passing the Great Belt from Nakskov to Christiania.
November 9: Arrived in Christiania from Nakskov with grain.
November 16: Left Christiania for Nakskov with timber and iron.
November 24: Passing the Great Belt from Christiania to Nakskov.

Here the master has no doubt made arrangements in advance with merchants in Christiania and Arendal which secured a rapid turnaround in Norway, but nonetheless he was able to complete only four return voyages. Maybe the merchant in Nakskov had difficulties in providing sufficient cargo so that the ship had to wait about a month in Nakskov before leaving for the next voyage to Norway, or perhaps the ship did not leave until new orders arrived from Norway.

The sailing pattern of Johan Nielsen Just is typical in so far as he always started in his home town and returned to it directly from the Norwegian destination. The only exceptions to this pattern were masters from some small shipping communities without a natural hinterland. Such masters from, for example, Dragør and Fanø often went in ballast from their home to a Danish port but then started the same type of return voyages as the other provincial skippers. The same was typical for masters from the community of Marstal on the island of Ærø which at that time belonged to the Duchy of Schleswig. The masters very often sailed from Danish ports.

The traffic to and from Copenhagen was of a different nature and included not only voyages to and from provincial ports but also to and from Norwegian and Schleswig-Holsteinian ports. Copenhagen was the great entrepôt for most of the cities of the monarchy. Ships from all over the world brought colonial goods, French wine, south European fruits, English or Scottish coal, Dutch tobacco etc. to the capital and although much was consumed by the citizens of Copenhagen part of it was loaded into smaller ships providing the Danish provinces, and to some extent also southern Norway and the Duchies with these commodities. On the other hand, many supplies were necessary to feed people in the capital. Grain, meat and domestic fruits were coming from provincial ports and Schleswig-Holstein, firewood from eastern Jutland and the Duchies, and timber and iron from Norway.

The size of this traffic out of the port of Copenhagen in 1787 is shown in table 2.

Table 2: Ships leaving Copenhagen in 1787 destined for Danish provincial ports, Norway and Schleswig-Holstein

		Destination		
		Danish Provinces	Norway	Schleswig-Holstein
(a)	Danish ships			
	Number of departures	1,354	41	97
	Tonnage (1000 kml)	24	2	3
	Average size (kml)	17	36	30
(b)	Norwegian ships			
	Number of departures	1	153	–
	Tonnage (1000 kml)	–	5	–
	Average size (kml)	45	30	–
(c)	Schleswig-Holsteinian ships			
	Number of departures	79	6	587
	Tonnage (1000 kml)	1	–	9
	Average size (kml)	10	17	15

Source: The 1787 database, Odense University.

The smaller ships engaged in the Copenhagen trade sailed in the same fixed pattern as between Norway and Danish provincial ports, but in the local traffic between the capital and nearby ports it was, of course, possible to undertake more voyages during a year, in some cases up to twelve return voyages are recorded. The smallest ships were sloops, whereas many of the larger ones were galleasses.

The traffic to Norway in table 2, however, includes more than purely coastal traffic. There is a limited number of very large ships among those found in the departure lists from Copenhagen. Some of them were Norwegian ships which had started the season with a timber cargo from Norway to western Europe. Here it was normally very difficult to find a return cargo to Norway, and most of these ships returned in ballast. Some might find a cargo for Copenhagen and they would then be recorded in Copenhagen when leaving this port for their home. Also some of the larger Danish ships called in Norway after having left Copenhagen and found a cargo there for western Europe. These non-coasters are the main reason why the average size of the ships on the route to Norway is larger than in other coastal traffic. In the traffic to and from the Duchies, Schleswig-Holsteinian ships dominated. Several small communities in this area had ships which specialized in this traffic, such as Marstal on Ærø, Burg on Fehmarn, and Kappeln on the Schlei.

Although eighteenth century legislation in many ways had tried to enhance Copenhagen as the entrepôt for the kingdom the provincial ports' old links to Germany persisted and some of the towns were supplied with foreign commodities from Lübeck and Hamburg using the same types of ships as those sailing to and from Copenhagen, so that these voyages also should be considered as part of the coastal trade. Lübeck was more important than Hamburg since the latter mainly served the west coast of Jutland where few Danish ports were situated. If we, however, include the Hamburg traffic of the total kingdom in the coastal trade then the outcome is quite different. We do not have lists of individual ships entering the port of Hamburg, but in 1788 the British consul in the Hanse city reported that the port in 1787 had been visited by 445 Danish ships plus '2,074 small craft from Holland, Bremen and Denmark'.[16] Most of the larger ships were from Altona, then a free city within the Danish realm, and the majority of the small crafts were probably from Holstein. Finally some of the smaller Danish ships also loaded cargoes of firewood in small ports along the coast of Mecklenburg and Pomerania.[17]

The coastal trade was in this way a very important link in keeping together the various parts of a large kingdom with a small population. Furthermore it was nearly the only way in which bulk cargoes could be transported since the road system was very bad and only used for passenger traffic and for transport of goods between a city and its closest hinterland. The Danish realm had, on the other hand, a shape which was very well fitted for sea transport. Nearly all towns were situated close to the sea and the inner parts of the kingdom were very sparsely populated, perhaps because of high transport costs which prevented these areas from taking part in a wider division of labour.

Mid-nineteenth century Danish coastal shipping

When Norway was ceded to Sweden in 1814 the special privileges for Danish ships in Norway and for Norwegian ships in Denmark were abolished and it was not until 1826 that normal conditions between the two countries were re-

[16] Public Record Office, London, Foreign Office 97/240.
[17] Aarge RASCH, Forbindelsen mellem København og de nordtyske Østersøbyer 1750–1807, in: Erhvervshistorisk Årbog (1963), pp. 74–92.

established. These problems reduced for some years the coastal traffic across the Skagerrak, but the economic advantages of the trade were so obvious that there was an increase again after 1826, but it was now Norwegian ships which dominated – perhaps because the Danish grain exporters found the Norwegian market less interesting when British demand for imported grain increased. Many ships could consequently only get a southbound timber cargo, but for the Norwegian ships this was probably less of a problem because they continued into the Baltic and found a cargo there for Norway or other places in western Europe.

For Danish ships it is evident from table 3 that coastal trade was now dominated by the provincial towns trading with each other, and with the capital and the Duchies, whereas Norway had lost its importance as a destination for Danish ships. It is only when Norwegian ships are included that the volume of the cargoes between Danish and Norwegian ports is almost as important as the trade between the capital and the Provinces. Some of the traffic with Norway had changed in character for Danish ships. The pattern with return voyages to and from a Danish port was no longer the rule. When the Danish ships called at Norwegian ports it was often part of a more complicated pattern which included sailing to other ports in western Europe or in the Baltic on the same voyage. Norway was gradually losing its role as part of the Danish coastal trade.

Voyages between the provincial ports were still to a large extent in ballast, but there was now also some traffic between regional centres and nearby smaller ports because many of these centres had established their own traffic with the large west European entrepôts and consequently no longer had to sail to Copenhagen in order to get colonial and south European goods.

The traffic to and from Copenhagen carried the same flows of commodities as in 1787, but there was now a larger concentration on trade with the eastern part of Denmark, while Jutland on the other hand had been more dependent upon trade with northern Germany. Firewood from Jutland which was still important had also got competition from coal imported from Britain. The diminishing importance of Copenhagen as a supplier for provincial towns is demonstrated by the fact that the flows to the capital were now more voluminous than the return freights, and many ships had to sail in ballast on their way back from the capital.

The progress in the provincial trade with Schleswig and Holstein was of a dual nature. Part of it was caused by imports from Hamburg via the Schleswig-Holstein canal and Kiel which in the statistics was reported as sales from Holstein. Another important factor were bricks and other tile products from the tileworks close to the Flensburg Fjord, a very favourable position for sea transport, and the demand for bricks was increasing in Denmark proper with the growth of the provincial towns. The Danish cargoes to the Duchies

Table 3: Coastal sailings to and from Danish ports, 1844
          (excluding steamships)

From	To Copenhagen	Provincial ports	Duchies	Norway	Hamburg and Lübeck
Copenhagen:					
No. of departures	–	2,807	597	115	13
Tonnage (1000 kml)	–	45	8	3	–
Average size (kml)	–	16	15	26	28
With cargo (%)	–	39	15	50	80
Cargo in Danish ships (%)	–	–	27	14	81
Provincial ports:					
No. of departures	2,725	5,005	3,105	2,114	93
Tonnage (1000 kml)	35	51	25	36	1
Average size (kml)	13	10	8	17	9
With cargo (%)	76	31	56	57	46
Cargo in Danish ships (%)	93	88	34	41	42
Duchies:					
No. of arrivals	732	3,003	–	...	...
Tonnage (1000 kml)	9	25	–	...	...
Average size (kml)	12	8	–	...	...
With cargo (%)	80	41	–	...	...
Cargo in Danish ships (%)	22	46	–	...	...
Norway:					
No. of arrivals	113	2,001	...	–	...
Tonnage (1000 kml)	3	32	...	–	...
Average size (kml)	28	16	...	–	...
With cargo (%)	89	93	...	–	...
Cargo in Danish ships (%)	18	25	...	...	...
Hamburg and Lübeck:					
No. of arrivals	12	178	...	...	–
Tonnage (1000 kml)	–	3	...	...	–
Average size (kml)	28	15	...	...	–
With cargo (%)	64	25	...	...	–
Cargo in Danish ships (%)	78	80	...	...	–

Note: *With cargo* is calculated as total freight in lasts (kml) as a percent of total tonnage in lasts. ... indicates these are not Danish coastal routes; a dash means no data is available.

Source: Statistisk Tabelværk, ældste række, hæfte 12.

were very mixed, but there were many ships sailing in ballast. The customs
barriers between Denmark proper and the Duchies had been removed in 1838,
and this caused an increase in the trade in agricultural and other domestic
products between areas close to the old customs barrier, and also to more
Danish exports passing Holstein on their way to Hamburg.

The figures in table 3 include only sailing vessels, which underwent little
change in size, whereas there were some changes in rigging. The smallest
ships were still mainly sloops, whereas schooners were growing in importance
among the middle-sized ships. The first steamers had also entered Danish
waters, but they were in 1844, responsible for only about ten per cent of
coastal freight transport, whereas they played a larger role in passenger
transport after the establishment of packet-boats from Copenhagen to Kiel and
of steam-ferries on the main domestic routes between the islands and to and
from Jutland.[18]

Water transport still dominated domestic traffic. Roads had been improved
by building a network of macademized highways in the eastern part of the
country and in the Duchies, but in most cases they had only local importance
for goods transport, since traffic remained slow and cumbersome and no faster
than sailing ships. Only in passenger traffic did they have an advantage when
the first stage coach routes came into operation. The first railway opened in
1844 from Altona to Kiel and was soon an efficient substitute for road traffic
between the two towns avoiding the long passage via the Skagerrak or the
expensive route through the Schleswig-Holstein canal.

Coastal shipping around 1879

Between 1857 and 1870 the trunk lines of the Danish railway system were
constructed which changed the cost pattern in domestic traffic. The influence
on coastal shipping was, however, smaller than in many other countries
because Denmark is a country of many islands and in the first decades of the
railway era there were no railway ferries. Cargoes going by rail from one part
of the country to another had in many cases, to be reloaded in the ferry ports
and this gave coastal shipping an advantage on many routes. The railways
were, therefore, at first serious competitors over short distances only, for
example between Copenhagen and port towns in the island of Sealand. They
had also great importance in opening up the interior of Jutland where
population density grew rapidly in these years.

The first railway ferry went into service on the Little Belt in 1872, but it was
not until the main route on the Great Belt got steam ferries in 1883 that the

---

[18] The structure of internal trade and shipping is described in A. F. BERGSØE, Den
danske Stats Statistik, Copenhagen 1847, vol. 2, pp. 479–504.

trunk lines were united into a single network so that reloading in the ports was avoided. Consequently, coastal shipping still dominated internal trade in 1879. Another technological factor which changed the situation for coastal shipping between the 1840s and 1879 was the use of steamers not only on domestic passenger routes but now in cargo traffic as well. Some of the first steamer routes which carried both passengers and cargo were Copenhagen-Sønder-borg-Flensborg and Copenhagen-Horsens-Randers, both in 1850, and from Korsør to Kiel and Århus in 1857.[19] Several others followed and in 1866 the largest of them merged in Det forenede Dampskibsselskab A/S (The United Steamship Company Ltd.) abbreviated to DFDS. The company over a decade built up a network of routes connecting Copenhagen with about fifty towns situated in all parts of Denmark, either by establishing new routes or taking over existing ones, and the activities included routes to Norway, into the Baltic, and to Britain. In coastal shipping most of these ships were from c. 80 to 200 net register tons. The older ones were paddle steamers, whereas most of those built in the years just before 1879 were screw ships.

As a background to Danish coastal traffic around 1879 it should be remembered that after the unfortunate war in 1864 Denmark lost Schleswig, Holstein and Lauenburg to Prussia and Austria, and that these Duchies soon became economically integrated into first the North German Customs Union and after 1871 into the German Empire.

How these changes had influenced Danish coastal shipping around 1879 is shown in table 4.

Table 4: Coastal sailings to and from Danish ports, 1879

From	To Copenhagen	Provincial ports	Duchies	Norway	Sweden	Hamburg and Lübeck
Copenhagen:						
No. of departures	–	6,234	186	165	5,831	278
Tonnage (1000 rt)	–	327	14	48	454	37
Average size (rt)	–	52	74	288	78	134
With cargo (%)	–	37	55	25	13	13
Cargo in steamers (%)	–	70	85	93	80	90
Cargo in Danish ships (%)	–	99	91	87	53	1

[19] In 1857 the railway line from Copenhagen to Korsør was opened and steamer routes from the port in the latter town were established in order to give rapid transport from the railway terminal to other parts of the monarchy.

	Copenhagen	Provincial ports	Duchies	Norway	Sweden	Hamburg and Lübeck
Provincial ports:						
No. of departures	6,703	12,088	3,204	1,887	2,798	232
Tonnage (1000 rt)	284	333	142	92	195	9
Average size (rt)	42	28	44	49	70	37
With cargo (%)	42	21	33	26	5	57
Cargo in steamers (%)	49	20	52	41	45	38
Cargo in Danish ships (%)	99	97	75	66	53	85
Duchies:						
No. of arrivals	254	3,186	–			
Tonnage (1000 rt)	15	161	–	...	...	...
Average size (rt)	60	51	–	...	...	...
With cargo (%)	67	21	–	...	...	...
Cargo in steamers (%)	62	41	–	...	...	...
Cargo in Danish ships (%)	74	85	–	...	...	...
Norway:						
No. of arrivals	220	1,568	...	–	...	...
Tonnage (1000 rt)	38	65	...	–	...	...
Average size (rt)	174	42	...	–	...	...
With cargo (%)	39	55	...	–	...	...
Cargo in steamers (%)	57	4	...	–	...	...
Cargo in Danish ships (%)	57	23	...			
Sweden:						
No. of arrivals	5,825	2,796	...	...	–	...
Tonnage (1000 rt)	410	148	...	...	–	...
Average size (rt)	70	53	...	...	–	...
With cargo (%)	31	59	... .	...	–	...
Cargo in steamers (%)	76	8	...	...	–	...
Cargo in Danish ships (%)	41	28	...	...	–	...
Hamburg and Lübeck:						
No. of arrivals	363	292	...	...	...	–
Tonnage (1000 rt)	45	12	...	...	...	–
Average size (rt)	124	39	...	...	...	–
With cargo (%)	29	61	...	...	...	–
Cargo in steamers (%)	69	48	...	...	...	–
Cargo in Danish ships (%)	6	70	...	...	...	–

Note: *With cargo* is calculated as total freight in register tons (rt) as a percentage of total tonnage in register tons.

Source: Statistisk Tabelværk, 4. rk. D,3.

Traffic between the provinces and Copenhagen, now measured in net register tons, was still important and had doubled since the 1840s, but the volume of goods from Copenhagen to the Provinces was three to four times larger than in 1844. Copenhagen had regained part of its earlier importance in Danish imports. The average size of the ships shows that it was not only the DFDS steamers which were active in this traffic. The steamers carried mostly mixed cargoes. The customer in the port of departure came to the port office of the company with his parcels and smaller quantities of commodities which were ordered by a merchant or a factory in the port of destination and used the liner routes with fixed timetables in order to be sure that the goods were delivered at the right time.

There was also a demand for bulk transport. Fertilizers, oil cake, metals, etc. were sent to Copenhagen and transshipped to the provinces and there was still a great need for transport of foodstuffs to the rapidly growing population in the capital. This was the basis for a fleet of small sailing ships, sloops and schooners, from several provincial towns and also from maritime centres such as Dragør, localities in the southern part of Funen, and Marstal[20] which sailed in domestic trade for a season that was extended each year.

The same small ships were engaged in traffic between the provincial ports, where the demand for transport was increasing because several provincial towns were growing. Table 4 shows that it was still difficult to get return cargoes in the provinces. Part of the traffic is therefore most likely a voyage in ballast from a small home port to a neighbouring provincial port with better possibilities of finding a cargo. Table 4 is also a clear indication of the decline of Danish connections with the former parts of the Danish monarchy. Bricks were still imported from Flensburg into provincial towns, but compared to the total amount transported in the coastal trade, Norway and the Duchies, as well as Hamburg and Lübeck, were now of little significance.

A new growth area was the trade with Sweden. Both Copenhagen and the provinces now bought most of their timber in Swedish ports, and to a much lesser degree in Norway, compared to twenty to thirty years earlier. It is, however, difficult to find out how much of this import should be classified as coastal trade, because the timber might come from Swedish ports in the Kattegat which definitely was coastal trade, but just as well from ports further away in the Baltic and even in the Gulf of Bothnia. The size of the ships and consular reports from west Swedish ports indicate that a substantial part of the import must have arrived from nearby. Most of this timber was transported in Swedish ships.

---

[20] Marstal and the rest of the island of Ærø was not lost in 1864 as were the rest of the Duchies, but became a part of the county of Svendborg and was thus totally integrated into Denmark proper.

Coastal shipping on the eve of World War I

In the period between 1870 and 1914 Denmark industrialised rapidly. Copenhagen grew from about 200,000 to about 600,000 inhabitants and became a significant importer of both raw materials for manufacturing and foodstuffs for the population. The port was extended and a free port added in 1894 which re-established part of the eighteenth-century entrepôt role in the Baltic trade and also made the capital the natural unloading place for many overseas products destined for producers in the provinces. At the same time the importance of steam in the merchant fleet grew. In 1897 the tonnage of steamers surpassed that of sailing vessels and on the eve of World War I steamers dominated Danish coastal shipping except for the small schooners which were used in local voyages between provincial ports. DFDS was still the dominant shipowner on domestic routes and on the two most important from Copenhagen to Århus and Ålborg new combined passenger and cargo steamers of about 800 net register ton (nrt) were introduced shortly before the outbreak of the war.

Table 5:   Coastal sailings to and from Danish ports, 1910

From	To Copenhagen	Provincial ports	Duchies	Norway	Sweden	Hamburg and Lübeck
Copenhagen:						
No. of departures	–	7,851	4	270	6,995	369
Tonnage (1000 rt)	–	696	1	156	883	79
Average size (rt)	–	89	369	576	126	15
With cargo (%)	–	51	14	27	13	17
Cargo in steamers (%)	–	87	94	99	79	81
Cargo in Danish ships (%)	–	98	...	...	...	...
Provincial ports:						
No. of departures	6,026	23,427	3,670	1,554	10,178	1,440
Tonnage (1000 rt)	807	913	325	280	1785	195
Average size (rt)	134	39	89	180	175	135
With cargo (%)	32	34	24	10	5	34
Cargo in steamers (%)	74	31	64	56	72	75
Cargo in Danish ships (%)	97	92	...	...	...	...

	Copenhagen	Provincial ports	Duchies	Norway	Sweden	Hamburg and Lübeck
Duchies:						
No. of arrivals	56	3,860	–	...	...	...
Tonnage (1000 rt)	4	316	–	...	...	...
Average size (rt)	72	82	–	...	...	...
With cargo (%)	54	8	–	...	...	...
Cargo in steamers (%)	9	21	–	...	...	...
Cargo in Danish ships (%)	50	...	–	...	...	...
Norway:						
No. of arrivals	254	948	...	–	...	...
Tonnage (1000 rt)	134	133	...	–	...	...
Average size (rt)	528	140	...	–	...	...
With cargo (%)	32	14	...	–	...	...
Cargo in steamers (%)	87	32	...	–	...	...
Cargo in Danish ships (%)	50	...	...	–	...	...
Sweden:						
No. of arrivals	6,273	8,983	...	...	–	...
Tonnage (1000 rt)	793	1612	...	...	–	...
Average size (rt)	126	179	...	...	–	...
With cargo (%)	22	26	...	...	–	...
Cargo in steamers (%)	62	73	...	...	–	...
Cargo in Danish ships (%)	48		...	...	–	...
Hamburg and Lübeck:						
No. of arrivals	669	1,992	...	...	...	–
Tonnage (1000 rt)	169	196	...	...	...	–
Average size (rt)	252	98	...	...	...	–
With cargo (%)	51	76	...	...	...	–
Cargo in steamers (%)	92	51	...	...	...	–
Cargo in Danish ships (%)	44	...	...	...	...	–

Note: *With cargo* is calculated as total freight in register tons as a percentage of total tonnage in register tons.

Source: Statistisk Tabelværk, 5 rk. D,27.

The figures in table 5 show the same picture as in table 4. Coastal traffic between Danish ports was still the most important part and voyages to and from Sweden came next, but the total volume of goods transported more than doubled over thirty years. The basic factors behind the traffic were thus unchanged, but it is most likely that a larger proportion of the trade with Sweden now was voyages to and from ports in northeasten Sweden. In this period the forestry industry in this part of Sweden grew very rapidly. It is, consequently, doubtful whether this traffic was still coastal voyages. The traffic between Copenhagen and the provincial ports confirms the position of the capital in domestic trade and as in 1879, with more goods shipped to the provinces than from them. It is, however, clear that the trade between the provincial ports was now growing rapidly and there are several reasons for that. Among new cargoes was cement. Danish cement works had been established between 1873 and 1896 and production grew rapidly after 1900. The works were situated close to the coast near Ålborg and Mariager. They built their own ports from where shipments to other parts of Denmark, and in the last years also a large export took place. These ports were among the busiest in Denmark in the 1910s. Bricks were still an important cargo and there was also an important trade in agricultural products.

Coastal shipping was experiencing increased competition from the railways, whereas the number of lorries was too small to be of any importance. In the last years before World War I the railways transported about five times as many metric tons of goods as domestic shipping, but the difference in transport performance was much smaller, because the distance goods were transported by rail was much shorter than those by ship, and in the interior of Jutland there was no competition between the two carriers. A different measure of the relative positions could be the domestic sea transport between the capital and ports in Jutland and Funen on the one hand and goods crossing the Great Belt in rail waggons on the other. In 1910 this comparison shows a slight preference for coastal shipping. There was probably little difference in transport time and for heavier commodities shipping was the cheaper form of transport.

One and a half centuries in perspective

The period from the late eighteenth century to 1914 was a period of intensive growth for Danish coastal shipping. There were setbacks, for example during the war years of 1807 – 14, and in years of economic crisis, such as 1857, the late 1870s and the first years of the twentieth century. For the period as a whole the volume of goods transported in inter-Danish trade multiplied more than tenfold and during the whole period was almost exclusively reserved to the national flag. For the period after 1844 the growth is demonstrated in figure 1. This development is a clear indication of economic growth and of an increasing division of labour between the capital and the provincial towns and also between different parts of the provinces, reflecting phases of industrialisation and a restructuring of agriculture which created a basis for the transport of bulky raw materials and for new agricultural products.

It was also a period of structural change in coastal shipping. New national borders necessitated new trade flows. The role of Copenhagen as the major centre for Danish trade and shipping fluctuated in intensity from the golden age of the late eighteenth century via stagnation or decline at the beginning of the nineteenth century to a new boom on the eve of World War I. Among the structural shifts was competition from a new carrier, the railways, although this competition in Denmark was less pronounced than in countries with a shorter coastline because of ready access to ports in most of the country and the extra costs of reloading and later shunting in ferry ports. The importance of the railways was more decisive in the inner parts of Jutland where new market places developed at railway junctions. Taken as a whole the development of coastal shipping is a mirror of total Danish economic history, reflecting ups and downs in the growth process.

Figure 1: Danish coastal trade, 1844–1913

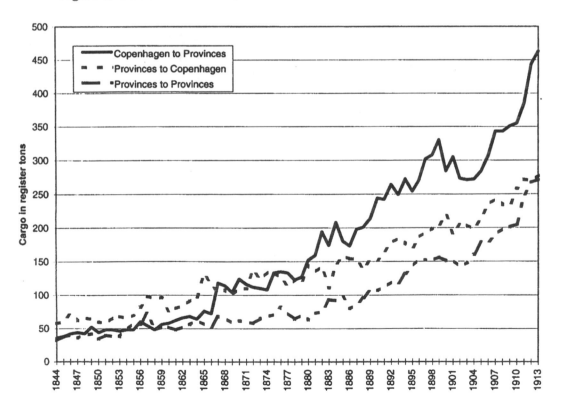

4

DOMESTIC SHIPPING IN SWEDISH HISTORICAL
NATIONAL ACCOUNTS

OLLE KRANTZ

Swedish industrialisation gained momentum in the mid-nineteenth century, and so did large-scale railway building.[1] The expansion of railway traffic had a great influence on domestic shipping[2], as did the expansion of automobile traffic in the twentieth century. This development was not confined to Sweden; similar processes occurred in all industrialising countries in that period, and they constituted essential elements of the overall economic performance. Thus, it is important not only to analyse individual countries but also to make comparisons and then it is essential to use the most reliable and valid instruments and variables as possible. In analysing *economic* performance, which is the economic historian's task, variables of economic relevance have to be employed. This may seem truistic, but, in fact, due to for example data shortage, other types of variables are often used. It is, for instance, commonplace to employ technical variables such as tons conveyed or ton-kilometres performed, which call for the data to be handled with utmost care.

What has been said about data problems may seem fairly obvious, but it is important to stress it since, in practice, these difficulties are often paid too little attention or are even totally ignored. Ton-kilometres, that is the physical transport performance, is affected by transport distance and quantity but not by the cost or price of the transport. To produce one ton-kilometre of sand is not the same as producing one ton-kilometre of gold and certainly not so if the sand transport is performed by rail and the gold transport by a security car. Thus, to get an economic measure it is important to consider the transport price, and this is done in common economic output measures. Such measures are used in national accounts in general and, hence, in historical national accounts (HNA). Since HNA, in principle, embrace all economic transactions in the society during the period in question, they can also provide a basis for

---

[1] See Olle KRANTZ, Swedish railway building in the nineteenth century in an international perspective, in: Umeå Papers in Economic History 6 (1992).

[2] I use the term domestic shipping, which includes coastal shipping and inland waterway traffic. The former dominated completely in Sweden, which is quite natural bearing in mind the very long coast line.

analyses of performance of the transport sector. Accordingly, HNA form an appropriate framework for economic historical analyses of different sectors and branches of the total economy. This is true especially when the accounts are detailed, which, unfortunately, is not always the case.

This paper shows how the transport sector and, in particular, domestic shipping are treated in the Swedish historical national accounts. The methods of construction of the series as well as the source materials are presented. After that, some series pertaining to the transport sector are briefly dealt with in a general economic development perspective, and some international comparisons are made.

Swedish Historical National Accounting

The first Swedish HNA were compiled by Lindahl/Dahlgren/Kock in a research project launched in the mid-1920s.[3] The series constructed in this project have formed the basis for historical national accounting in Sweden. The outcome of the next compilation – a crude one for 1861–1950 – was published in the early 1950s[4] and the third round was accomplished in the 1960s. It was inspired by Simon Kuznets' attempts to form an international network to create new series for as many countries as possible. The work on Sweden was carried out by Östen Johansson.[5] In the first half of the 1970s Krantz/Nilsson constructed Swedish historical national accounts, where constant price calculations were emphasised.[6] The intention was to raise some methodological questions, and to come to terms with the most severe inadequacies in the earlier works. This study formed the methodological starting point for an attempt to create more elaborate Swedish HNA in the project *Structural Changes in the Swedish Economy 1800–1980. Construction*

---

[3] Erik LINDAHL/Einar DAHLGREN/Karin KOCK, National Income of Sweden 1861–1930, vol. 1–2, Stockholm/London 1937. On the history of Swedish historical national accounts, see Jørgen Peter CHRISTENSEN [et al.], Nordic historical national accounts since the 1880s, in: Scandinavian Economic History Review 1 (1995). See also Olle KRANTZ, (ed.), Swedish Historical National Accounts – The state of the art, in: Nordiska Historiska Nationalräkenskaper, Workshop vid Olofsfors herrgård 27–28 maj 1994, Occasional Papers in Economic History – Umeå University, 1 (1994). The Lindahl-Dahlgren-Kock project is described in Benny CARLSSON, Bagge, Lindahl och nationalinkomsten. Om National Income of Sweden 1861–1930 [Bagge, Lindahl and National Income. On National Income of Sweden 1861–1930], in: Meddelande från Ekonomisk-historiska institutionen, Lunds universitet 27 (1982).

[4] Olof LINDAHL, Sveriges Nationalprodukt 1861–1951 [Swedish National Product 1861–1951], in: Meddelanden från Konjunkturinstitutet, Serie B:20, Stockholm 1956.

[5] Östen JOHANSSON, The Gross Domestic Product of Sweden and its Composition 1861–1955, Uppsala 1967.

[6] Olle KRANTZ, Carl-Axel Nilsson, Swedish National Product 1861–1970. New Aspects on Methods and Measurement, Lund 1975.

and Analysis of National Product Series. The intention was to calculate completely new series for the nineteenth century, and partly new, partly revised series for the twentieth century up to 1950. For the period after 1950 the project was to rely entirely on data from the contemporary NA estimated by *Statistics Sweden.* A further aim was to employ the new HNA series as a comprehensive and consistent quantitative basis for analyses of the long-run structural performance of the Swedish economy.

A division of labour was made so that Lennart Schön was responsible for commodity production, that is agriculture with ancillaries, manufacturing industry and handicrafts, and foreign trade, and Olle Krantz for service output, namely transport and communications, private and public services and construction. Some other scholars were also employed. The project was planned to be accomplished in the mid-80s, and to publish nine volumes containing the whole data collection down to the most detailed level both for the current values and for the material used for constant price calculations. The main series as well as an analysis of Swedish economic growth and structural change were planned to be published separately. These plans were, alas, not fulfilled, since all the work on the basic material was not completed as planned.[7]

The methodological issues concerning HNA are especially important for constant price estimates. A series for a certain item can vary considerably with different deflation techniques. It is important to be aware of the fact that there is no such thing as a 'true' series, that is one which is computed with an objectively perfect technique. Further, there is no computational method which could be called the best one in an objective sense. Instead, the deflation method – ideally – has to be chosen to fit the special purpose of the study. This means that the method can only be judged as more or less good, or bad, with reference to this purpose.

In the new Swedish HNA the solution of the deflation problem was adapted to the aim of making long-term analyses of economic growth and, in particu-

---

[7] Eight volumes have been published to date: Olle KRANTZ, Transporter och kommunikationer 1800–1980 [Transport and Communications 1800–1980], Lund 1986; Husligt arbete 1800–1980 [Domestic Work 1800–1980], Lund 1987; Offentlig verksamhet 1800–1980 [Public Services 1800–1980], Lund 1987; Privata tjänster 1800–1980 [Private Services 1800–1980], Lund 1991; Jonas LJUNGBERG, Deflatorer för industriproduktionen 1888–1955 [Deflators for Industrial Production 1888–1955], Lund 1988; Lars PETTERSSON, Byggnads- och anläggningsverksamheten 1800–1980 [Building and construction 1800–1980], Lund 1987; Lennart SCHÖN, Industri och hantverk 1800–1980 [Manufacturing Industry and Handicrafts 1800–1980], Lund 1988; and Jordbruk med binäringar 1800–1980 [Agriculture and Ancillaries], Lund 1995. One volume, Schön's on foreign trade, is still not published. Aggregated series for GDP, GDP per caput and output of the main sectors in current and constant prices are found in Olle KRANTZ, Swedish Historical National Accounts 1800–1990 – Aggregated Output Series (unpub. paper, 1995; slightly revised 1997).

lar, structural change. The whole time span is divided into sub-periods called deflation periods of about twenty years. Within each deflation period Paasche deflators are built up, and when deflating the current series with these deflators Laspeyre volume series are obtained where the first years in the period constitute the base period. Long series are then arrived at by linking the series for the deflation periods.

Domestic shipping

In the Swedish HNA transport and communications form one of seven sectors. Domestic shipping appears as a branch within the transport and communications sector, and the complete set of branches in this sector is as follows[8]:

Domestic shipping	Railways	Lorry traffic
International shipping	Transport with horses or oxen	Tramways
Posting services[9]	Foreign aviation	Domestic aviation
Stevedoring	Postal services	Tele communications
Timber-floating[10]	Taxi traffic	Bus traffic

Estimation of the performance of domestic shipping was made differently for different parts of the period. As mentioned above, the figures from 1950 onwards are taken from the official national accounts, which were re-weighted to fit the deflation scheme used for the entire HNA.

A general basis for the estimates are the official Swedish statistics published in SOS *Sjöfart* (Sweden's Official Statistics *Shipping*) from 1911 onwards and BiSOS *Inrikes sjöfart och handel* (Contributions to Sweden's Official Statistics *Domestic Shipping and trade*) for 1858–1910. Before 1858, data were published in *Commerce-Collegi Underdåniga Berättelse om Sveriges Inrikes Sjöfart* (*Respectful account of Sweden's domestic shipping by The Board of Commerce*) back to 1829. Prior to that, however, no usable official accounts were issued and instead other sources had to be utilised.

---

[8] The following account of calculation methods used in the transport and communication sector is based on KRANTZ, Transporter och Kommunikationer.

[9] This was a special form of passenger transport consisting of coach services provided as duties in kind by the peasantry.

[10] Most often in HNA, timber-floating is included in forestry, which is defined as a branch within agriculture. Here it is, however, considered as part of the transport and communication sector, which is logical since it is a question of transporting timber from one place to another. Furthermore, it is mostly managed by special actors, the so called floating associations, and not by the forest companies.

Domestic shipping was estimated separately in the Lindahl/Dahlgren/Kock work for the whole period in question. This computation depended heavily – and quite understandably – on the Swedish official statistics, but the resulting figures were shown by Thorburn[11] to be a great underestimate for his investigation years, 1873, 1893 and 1913. The differences between Thorburn's figures for total income (million SEK) in domestic shipping and Lindahl/Dahlgren/Kock's were as follows:

Year	Thorburn Total: (a)	of which: sailing ships (b)	LDK Total: (c)	of which: sailing ships (d)	a/c	b/d
1873	15.6	3.4	4.5	1.4	3.5	2.4
1893	18.5	2.7	11.8	2.4	1.6	1.1
1913	32.1	2.3	23.2	1.8	1.4	1.3

1933 and 1949 were also investigated by Thorburn, and for these years he divided total domestic shipping into passenger and goods traffic. A comparison between his figures and the official statistics shows great differences:

Year	Thorburn passenger traffic (a)	goods traffic (b)	Official statistics passenger traffic (c)	goods traffic (d)	a/c	b/d	(a+b)/(c+d)
1933	9.2	33.2	6.4	27.1	1.4	1.2	1.3
1949	14.3	71.0	9.9	55.8	1.5	1.3	1.4

Thus, for all years it can be concluded that the figures in the official statistics are too low. In an estimate of this branch in GDP these discrepancies should be taken into consideration, and this forms a starting point for the construction of new series for domestic shipping

When production data is not directly available and estimates of series in monetary terms in current as well as constant prices have to be made, it is advantageous to use ton-kilometres, and income (price) per ton-kilometre for freight transport and passenger-kilometres and income (price) per passenger-kilometre. Data for as many categories as possible should be used in an ordinary index calculation. Ton-kilometre series are sensitive both to distance and weight and so is income per ton-kilometre, which, in addition, also takes

---

[11] Thomas THORBURN, Sveriges inrikes sjöfart 1818–1949 [Sweden's Inland Navigation 1818–1949], Uddevalla 1958.

into account the character of the goods conveyed. Therefore, the latter could also form freight index series, and the same is true for passenger traffic. Data of this kind, however does not exist for most of the period and, hence, next-best solutions had to be chosen. The principal procedure was to use the quantity in tons and the number of passengers departing and arriving in ships at all Swedish ports as a measure of the transport performance and then combine this with some kind of freight indices. This should if possible be constructed separately for sailing ships and steamers, which, however, due to data shortage was very difficult.

When the series for transport performance and freight rates or passenger costs were multiplied a series indicating the development in current prices was arrived at. Thereafter the current value series were linked to Thorburn's data for the benchmark years chosen (1850, 1873, 1893, 1913 and 1949). This meant that the new series had to be calibrated to coincide with the benchmark data. After this, index series based on the freight rates could also be used as deflators for domestic shipping.

Due to the character of the source material, estimates were made for sub-periods, which are shown below.

1913–1980: Up to 1950 gross income figures for domestic shipping were taken from the official shipping statistics, and they were then adjusted to fit Thorburn's figures. The deflator, taken from a study of Swedish freight transport is based on estimated ton and ton-kilometre figures and income per ton-kilometre for a large number of goods.[12] From 1950 onwards the series for domestic shipping was estimated on the basis of the contemporary national accounts compiled by *Statistics Sweden*.[13] These series were adapted to the earlier by linking in the year 1950, which simply means an adaptation of levels.

1873–1913: Thorburn estimated a freight index for sailing ships for this period using average freight costs per ton for loaded sailing ships in traffic between Sweden and Denmark. His opinion was that these figures give a good representation also of domestic freight rates, and he argued this convincingly. Often the same ships were used in domestic shipping and in traffic to and from Denmark. There was also a state of almost perfect competition which made the differences between domestic and Swedish-Danish freight rates very small or non-existent. Even if there were some differences of an institutional character, such as harbour dues, Thorburn concluded that the freight index

---

[12] Olle KRANTZ, Studier i Svensk godstransportutveckling med särskild hänsyn till lastbilismens expansion efter 1920 [Studies in Swedish Freight Transport Performance, Especially the Expansion of Lorry Transportation after 1920], Lund 1972, Appendix B.

[13] Statistiska Meddelanden [Statistical Reports] N, various issues.

built on the Denmark trade could be used as a measure of the freight rate changes in domestic navigation.[14] This seems to be a sensible judgement.

Another important question is whether this freight index series can be used for steamships in domestic navigation as well. There are no other series for Sweden which provide possibilities for comparison, and therefore freight developments in international shipping may serve as guidance. I made a comparison with data from Hansen's Danish estimates where a series from Isserlis was used[15], and there are similarities as well as differences between these series. The foreign trade series falls more up to the early nineties and there are greater fluctuations. These differences could be caused by greater sensitivity to short term changes of a business cycle character in international than in regional and domestic shipping. Another argument in favour of Thorburn's series as an indicator also of freight rate changes for steamships is that, as mentioned above, there was practically unrestricted competition in the freight market which had an equalling influence on the price *changes* for sailing ships and steamers. Therefore I conclude that Thorburn's freight index is applicable to the entire Swedish domestic shipping in this period. This means that it is used together with the quantity series based on data on incoming and outgoing quantities in tons.

1850–1873: For 1870–73 the same procedure was used as for the period from 1873 onwards. Before 1870 data on incoming and outgoing quantities in tons were not available. Instead figures showing incoming and outgoing ships in domestic navigation were used as an indicator of the transport quantity performance. Unfortunately, a freight index pertaining to domestic shipping to use with this quantity series to form data in current prices could not be constructed since appropriate data could not be found. Therefore, the freight index used in the estimates of the freight performance in Swedish international shipping was applied. This series was constructed by using freight figures published in a Swedish newspaper, *Göteborgs Handels- och Sjöfartstidning, (Gothenburg's Trade and Shipping Gazette)*. They refer to freights between Gothenburg on the one hand and Hull, London and Antwerp on the other.[16] This is foreign shipping, but at least the index has to do with Swedish ships on not-too-long voyages. To use this index could, however, be a source of some error.

Before 1850: Back to 1838 the number of incoming and outgoing ships could be used and before that, back to 1829, data on loading capacity[17] of the

---

[14] THORBURN, Sveriges inrikes sjöfart, p. 377.

[15] Svend-Aage HANSEN, Økonomisk vækst i Danmark [Economic Growth in Denmark], vol. 2, Köpenhamn 1972, p. 312. Isserlis series is published in Journal of the Royal Statistical Society (1938), p. 122.

[16] KRANTZ, Transporter och kommunikationer, pp. 14 ff.

[17] In Swedish it is named *Lästetalet*.

ships utilised in domestic shipping were accepted. These data are shaky but with some corrections, partly made by Thorburn, they were judged to be usable. However, before 1829 no such data are available and therefore the number of ships in domestic navigation to and from Malmö harbour was used. These figures, which were found in an unpublished report are far from perfect, but it can be assumed that the main trends are shown, even if there are margins of error.

For 1819–1850 a special freight index series was constructed. The data used were taken from the so called *Magasinskontoret*, that is the storehouse or the warehouse office. All over the country there were storehouses owned by the central or local government where grain was stored to be used in case of crop failure or famine. Grain was shipped between some of these storehouses and the costs of these shipments were officially registered. By using these figures and the distances between the ports it was possible to arrive at a freight index series for this period. Before 1819 it was impossible to construct such a series and, instead, a freight index for international shipping constructed by North was used.[18]

The production figures in domestic shipping thus calculated for the whole period 1800–1980 are gross values, and an estimate of deduction items had to be made in order to arrive at value added series. However, up to 1950 it was impossible to make good annual estimates and, therefore, as in the Lindahl/Dahlgren/Kock project, an assumption or, rather, a guesstimate was made as to the relative magnitude of the deduction items. For the period after 1950 figures from Statistics Sweden were used here as well. As mentioned above, deflation is of central importance in national accounting. For domestic shipping, as described above, freight indices were employed in the estimate of the current value series. These indices were also used as deflators.

The performance of Swedish domestic shipping

The series for domestic shipping form, as mentioned above, part of the broad sector transport and communication in the HNA. The performance of this sector and of domestic shipping will now be analysed within the framework of the growth of the entire Swedish economy.

The first impression when looking at the performance of GDP or GDP per caput in Sweden from the early nineteenth to the mid twentieth century is that there was a smooth acceleration. However, Swedish development was not free from variations in the growth rate. There were short-term oscillations and also fluctuations of a long-term character. The former are not discussed here, but

[18] Douglas C. NORTH, The role of transportation in the economic development of north America, in: Les Grandes Voies Maritimes dans le Monde, XV⁰ – XIX⁰ Siècles, Paris 1965.

the latter are of interest since they indicate a periodicity in Swedish growth, and this pattern has a clear connection to the industrialisation process. This process is essential to the long-term changes in the transport and communications sector. The pattern, which is visible in a large number of key economic variables, has a clear resemblance to the so-called Kuznets cycles or long swings, meaning that there are periods of fifteen to twenty five years with different characteristics. One such period is constituted by the decades around 1900. Then the industrial breakthrough took place in Sweden.[19] The growth rates of each period are shown in table 1. This is, however, an approximation since in reality, the periods constituting the pattern are not exactly twenty years in length. They are used here only as a convenient way to show long-run changes.

Table 1: Annual percentage change in GDP per caput and in GDP, for some sectors, and domestic shipping during sub-periods, 1801–1955, constant prices

	GDP per caput	GDP	Agri-culture	Manu-facturing	Trans-port	Domestic shipping
1801/05 – 1851/55	0.4	1.2	1.1	1.6	1.0	4.5
1851/55 – 1871/75	1.8	2.7	1.0	4.0	4.3	4.4
1871/75 – 1891/95	1.1	1.7	1.0	3.9	3.3	2.8
1891/95 – 1911/15	2.5	3.3	1.5	5.8	4.9	1.8
1911/15 – 1931/35	1.9	2.4	1.2	3.1	2.8	2.4
1931/35 – 1951/55	2.9	3.6	0.1	5.0	5.0	4.0

Source: Olle Krantz, Swedish Historical National Accounts 1800–1990 – Aggregated Output Series (unpub. paper, 1995; slightly revised 1997).

The GDP performance alternates between periods of slower and periods of faster growth. This is true for manufacturing as well. Thus the stage is set for transport which shows the same pattern. The growth figures for domestic shipping, on the other hand, show a downward tendency to around 1910, then an acceleration is evident even if the figures are lower than for the entire transport and communications sector.

That domestic shipping in the first half of the nineteenth century showed a high rate of growth might appear enigmatic at first sight since this rate is

[19] See Olle KRANTZ, Notes on output levels and industrialisation in Denmark, Finland and Sweden 1870–1940, in: Olle KRANTZ (ed.), Cross-Country Comparisons of Industrialisation in Small Countries 1870–1940, Occasional Papers in Economic History – Umeå University 2 (1995).

considerably higher than the rates of the other variables. It is, however, easier to understand when looking at the sectoral distribution of total production as well as the share of domestic shipping in total transport. These figures are shown in table 2.

Table 2: Sectoral distribution of total production and the share of domestic shipping in total transport, 1811–1960 (per cent)

	Agri-culture	Manu-facturing industry	Building and con-struction	Private services	Public services	Transport and communi-cations	Domestic shipping in total transport
1811/20	44	13	7	22	7	7	6
1841/50	45	15	7	21	6	6	9
1871/80	42	18	10	18	6	6	9
1891/1900	35	25	8	18	6	8	7
1911/20	30	30	5	21	5	9	5
1931/40	19	34	8	22	8	9	3
1951/60	15	37	8	22	10	8	2

Source: See table 1.

The share of transport remained unchanged for most of the nineteenth century. In the first half of the century the share of domestic shipping of the transport sector grew by 50 per cent. Even if general economic growth was sluggish in this period it was not completely non-existent. Instead there was a slow modernisation, and the means of transport that expanded most were those that offered the cheapest transport. In this period cheap transport meant domestic shipping, so that it was preferred by the transport user wherever possible, and the possibilities increased, among other things, as a result of canal building. This changed, however, in the latter part of the century, when railways were built. The consequence was that domestic shipping declined relatively, and in absolute figures there was a gradually slower growth. In the twentieth century these tendencies were accentuated when motor transport of goods and passengers radically changed the transport situation.[20]

The growth of a number of transport variables in relation to total GDP is shown in table 3. As indicated previously in table 2, total transport grew

---

[20] The mechanisms are shown in a model of the distribution of transport between different modes which is developed in KRANTZ, Studier i svensk godstransportutveckling. It is presented briefly in Olle KRANTZ, Inland navigation and economic growth in Sweden in the nineteenth century, in: Andreas KUNZ and John ARMSTRONG (eds.), Inland Navigation and Economic Development in Nineteenth-Century Europe, Mainz 1995, pp. 100 ff.

relatively up to the 1890s which to a great extent had to do with the expansion of the railways. The latter increased relative to GDP also in the period following 1890, but less so than before. Since the two categories of shipping slowed down too, the total effect was that the relative transport growth slowed down. This is true also in the period up to the 1930s. The slight increase in transport relative to GDP in the last period was a result of the expansion of motor traffic.

Table 3: The growth of some transport variables in relation to GDP growth

	TT/GDP	DS/GDP	FS/GDP	RT/GDP
1801/05 – 1851/55	0.8	3.8	1.5	..
1851/55 – 1871/75	1.6	1.6	1.9	(7.8)
1871/75 – 1891/95	1.9	1.6	1.6	3.7
1891/95 – 1911/15	1.5	0.5	1.4	2.0
1911/15 – 1931/35	1.2	1.0	1.8	0.5
1931/35 – 1951/55	1.4	1.1	0.9	1.7

Note: TT = Total transport, DS = Domestic shipping, FS = Foreign shipping, RT = Railway transport.

Source: Krantz, Swedish Historical National Accounts 1800–1990, and Krantz, Transporter och Kommunikationer.

The choice of periods in table 2 does not perfectly reflect the impact of Swedish railway building in the second half of the nineteenth century. A swift railway expansion started in the 1850s, and the increase in the value added by railways was influenced both by a general traffic increase and an extension of the railway network. This was particularly true up to the 1880s. There was also great expansion in the railway network in the 1890s, but it was not of the same importance in increasing value added as in the 1870s. This is partly for simple arithmetical reasons. Even though the absolute increase was big, the percentage change was slower due to the earlier expansion. There was another reason too. Railway building in the 1890s was to a large extent concentrated in Norrland, that is the northern part of Sweden which is very sparsely populated. There, the traffic intensity, that is traffic per kilometre of railroad, was lower than in the southern part of the country. Furthermore, when comparing domestic shipping and railways, the sometimes large short-term fluctuations due to business cycles as well as political events have to be considered. To make this comparison more distinct, the ratio series between domestic shipping and railway traffic in Sweden is shown in diagram 1 as well.

In the first part of the period railway traffic grew very fast relative to domestic shipping, but already in the late 1860s there was a slowdown. From the
late 1880s there was a steady decrease up to the eve of the First World War,
and thereafter the ratio was stable. Thus the period of adjustment of domestic

Diagram 1: Sweden: domestic shipping – railways: value added ratio,
             1860–1914, constant prices

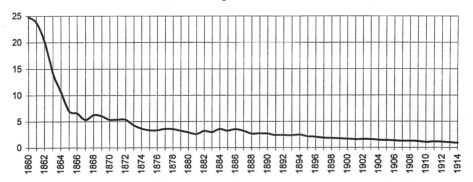

shipping to the new competitor was to a large extent located in the span from
the 1870s to the 1910s. Then, outside our research period, another adjustment
period came when motor traffic expanded. The adjustment in the nineteenth

Diagram 2: Sweden: domestic shipping – railways: value added ratio,
             1860–1914, constant prices, log scale

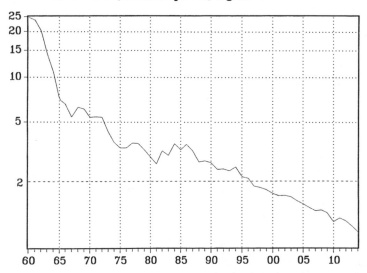

century meant, among other things, that there was a concentration on bulk goods to a much higher extent than before. These changes are more clearly demonstrated when a log-curve is used as in diagram 2. Now a pattern for the pre-war period can be traced: 1860–1868, 1868–1875, 1875–1888, 1888–1912. Thus, the slowdown went on at shorter intervals in the early part of the railway era than later.

Some international comparisons

The overall pattern of transport growth shown above can be compared with developments in other countries, and here some comparisons are made with Finland and Denmark. When trying to make comparisons between different countries' historical national accounts difficulties arise such as definitional problems, varying degrees of coverage, differences in how detailed the accounts are, different deflation methods, etc. Hence, it is necessary to be very cautious. At the same time, however, such comparisons are important to understand the processes of economic change and development.

In the case of Denmark a series exists for total transport and communications, and three sub-branches are specified, foreign shipping, total inland transport, and telecommunications. Inland transport is the total of railways, domestic shipping, tramways and part of horse-drawn transport.[21] Thus, it is not possible on the basis of these data to study domestic shipping separately and only the total transport series is used for Denmark in the comparison below.

In the Finnish historical national accounts total transport is divided in the following sub-branches up to 1913:[22]

Railways	Canal services
Tramways	Harbours
Horse transport	Stevedoring
Ocean and coastal transport	Postal services
Inland water transport (canals and lakes)	Telegraph and telephone services
Pilot and lighthouse services	

---

[21] HANSEN, Økonomisk vækst i Danmark, table 3–4.

[22] Matti T. PELTONEN, Liikene Suomessa 1860–1913 [Transport and Communication in Finland], Helsinki 1983, and Riitta HJERPPE, The Finnish Economy 1860–1985. Growth and Structural Change, Helsinki 1989. Peltonen's period is 1860–1913. The period 1900–1965 is dealt with in Seppo LEPPÄNEN, Liikene Suomessa 1900–1965 [Transport and Communication in Finland 1900–1965], Helsinki 1973. His branch division differs from Peltonen's since he uses only one category for water transport. The change in Leppänen's series between 1913 and 1914 has been used here for both series of Finnish shipping.

The categories are similar to the Swedish but there is an exception. One part of domestic shipping, coastal transport, forms part of ocean shipping, that is foreign shipping, while another part of domestic shipping, inland navigation, is shown separately. Unfortunately, this means that the ability to compare domestic shipping is restricted.

Total transport in relation to GDP in constant prices is shown in diagram 3. The Swedish curve has a steeper rise over the period 1860–1914 than those of the other two countries. Since the growth of total GDP volume was the same in all three countries, 2.6 per cent per year, differences in transport growth cannot be effects of differences in the overall economic performance.

Diagram 3: Value added in total transport in relation to GDP in Denmark, Finland, and Sweden, 1860–1914, constant prices, 1913 = 1

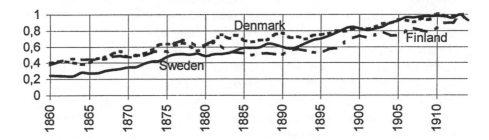

Thus, Swedish development was more transport intensive than the Danish and the Finnish – provided of course that the figures used here are reliable and comparable. The difference may be due to industrialisation being spread over a larger area in Sweden than in the other two countries; Sweden is among the biggest countries in Europe with Finland a bit smaller while Denmark had an area only one tenth of Sweden's. However, this explanation is not entirely convincing since Finland in that case would have had higher transport growth than Denmark, which was not the case. The similarities of the curves are instead greater between Sweden and Denmark than between those countries and Finland. Up to the middle or the latter part of the 1870s there is in all three countries a higher relative transport increase than during the rest of the period. However, while the curves of Sweden and Denmark show a rise even after the 1870s, Finland first exhibited stagnation or even decrease by the mid-1890s when new growth began. It is possible that the differences have to do not only with the spread of industrialisation but also with the development levels. In the latter half of the nineteenth century, of the three countries compared here,

Denmark had the highest income level per capita and Sweden the second highest while the lowest was found in Finland.[23] This could have caused the somewhat lower rate of transport change in Finland than in the other two countries.

Railway transport had a great influence on the curves just discussed. As in Sweden the extension of the railway network and the traffic expansion led to adjustment processes for the older means of transport, namely domestic shipping. However, as mentioned, there is no series for total domestic shipping in Finland, but two shipping series are available, that is inland shipping, which comprises canal and lake traffic, and sea shipping which comprises coastal and foreign shipping. These series in relation to railways are shown in diagram 4. The curves show the same profile as the Swedish one, which means that they start with a steep fall and proceed with a slower decrease. The details of the performance are more easily seen when using a log scale as in diagram 5.

Diagram 4: Finland: value added by sea (solid line) and inland navigation (dotted line) in relation to railways, 1860–1914, constant prices, 1913 = 1

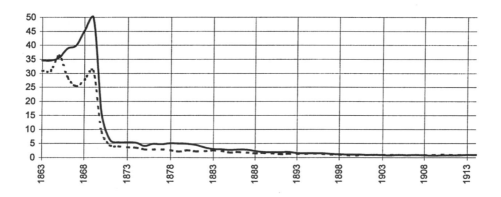

There is, however, not the same distinct periodisation as in the Swedish case. Instead, after the spectacular decrease for the inland navigation/railway ratio in the beginning there is a slow and steady downward tendency until the late 1890s, and after that there is practically no long-term change. For the sea

[23] Olle KRANTZ, Notes on Output Levels.

shipping/railway ratio the 1870s stand out as a period of slow growth, but thereafter the tendency is roughly the same as for the other curve.

Diagram 5: Value added in sea and inland navigation in relation to railways in Finland, 1860–1914, constant prices, index: 1913 = 1, log scale

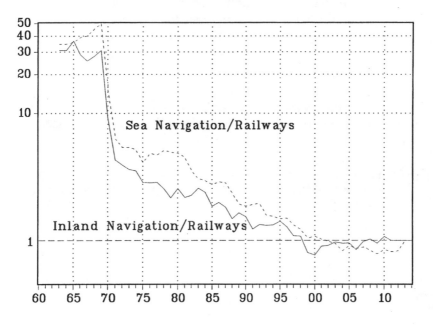

A plea for uniform data

Within the production boundaries chosen for historical national accounts they comprise, in principle all transactions in the society in a certain period, usually one year. The production boundaries are usually defined as embracing the market economy and public services, but they could be extended to other areas as well. Because of these properties HNA provide an excellent framework for analyses of economic growth and structural change in a long-run perspective including the performances of sectors and branches.

There can, however, be problems with data availability particularly when a small branch is the centre of interest, as is evident in this paper. It is quite natural that when constructing HNA all industries cannot be given the same emphasis and that most of the attention is paid to the larger industries and branches. There are also great differences in this respect. In the case of Sweden, for instance, data for domestic shipping exists and can be analysed. For many other countries data are not as detailed, which restricts the options for comparisons. It would be a good thing if data for the economic performance of domestic shipping were internationally comparable. The possibilities for this would be great if series were constructed employing the methods used in the framework of historical national accounts, which could be done even if the main aim were not to construct such accounts. Transport historians could make an important contribution, and the possibilities for comparative research could be greatly increased.

5

FINNISH COASTAL SHIPPING, 1750–1850

JARI OJALA

The long coastline (c. 4,600 km) of Finland provides a good basis for coastal shipping. During the Middle Ages the Hanseatic League dominated Finnish foreign trade and shipping, and during the sixteenth and seventeenth centuries Finnish exports were mainly carried in ships from Holland or Sweden. Finnish vessels dominated the local coastal trade. Finnish foreign trade and shipping began to grow after the mid-eighteenth century, when several Finnish towns obtained foreign trade rights.[1] Coastal shipping preserved its position, especially in the rural areas of Finland. Under the Swedish Navigation Act of 1726, coastal shipping was forbidden to foreign hulls, therefore, coastal shipping remained in domestic hands.

No monograph on the history of Finnish coastal shipping exists. Still, some studies touch on the topic. Older research is basically divided between studies of shipping in urban areas and those of rural districts. In urban histories or in the shipping histories of single ports coastal shipping is usually ignored, simply because of the lack of source material.[2] A wide variety of studies about shipping in rural areas contain basic information on coastal shipping, because rural shipowners were not allowed to engage in foreign shipping before the mid-nineteenth century.[3] Some general studies attempt to summarise the importance of coastal shipping.[4]

[1] Yrjö KAUKIAINEN, A History of Finnish Shipping, London/New York 1993, p. 3. Jari OJALA, Tuhannen purjelaivan kaupunki. Kokkolan purjemerenkulun historia, Jyväskylä 1996, pp. 63–89.

[2] The statistics of coastal shipping are included in the shipping histories of ports such as Turku (Åbo in Swedish), Pori (Björneborg) and Kokkola ([Gamla] Karleby): Aimo WUORINEN, Turku kauppakaupunkina Ruotsin vallan loppukautena, vols. 1–2, Helsinki 1959, 1966. Carl-Erik OLIN, Åbo sjöfarts historia I. Intill branden 1827, Åbo 1927. Arne ENGSTRÖM, Åbo sjöfarts historia II:1. Segelsjöfarten 1827–1856, Åbo 1930; Oscar NIKULA, Åbo sjöfarts historia II:2. Segelsjöfarten 1856–1926, Åbo 1930. L. I. KAUKAMAA, Porin puutavarakaupasta ja metsänkäytöstä kaupungin kauppapiirissä »suuren laivanvarustustoimen« aikana 1809–1856, Helsinki 1941.

[3] For studies of Finnish rural shipping see especially: Yrjö KAUKIAINEN, Suomen talonpoikaispurjehdus 1800-luvun alkupuoliskolla (1810–1858), Helsinki 1970. Jan-Erik BÖRMAN, Åboländsk bygdeseglation 1850–1920. Farkoster, redare, resor och ekonomi, Helsingfors 1979, pp. 12–16. David PAPP, Åländsk allmogeseglation. Med särskild hänsyn till sjöfarten på Stockholm. Sjöfarten i Lemlands socken 1800–1940, Lund 1977, pp. 11–12.

Finnish coastal shipping can be understood as shipping: a) inside the Baltic area (the broader view); b) between the ports of Finland or between Finland and the mother country (either Sweden c. 1200–1809 or Russia 1809–1917); c) shipping between coastal towns and villages within Finland. Definitions b) and c) are closest to the traditional view of coastal shipping, namely, domestic traffic between the ports of one country (*cabotage*). Because of the nature of the sources and the administrative regulations, coastal shipping, is in this paper defined as shipping inside the northern Baltic area, including Stockholm, Tallinn and St Petersburg. It would, therefore, be congruent with the term »short sea shipping«.

There were differences in coastal shipping in the various geographical areas of Finland. Coastal shipping in small vessels was much more common in south-western and southern areas of Finland: ships carried firewood and food supplies to the big towns such as Stockholm and St Petersburg, and even iron ore from Sweden to Finnish ironworks. On the north-west coast, the Ostrobothnia area, coastal ships took tar to Stockholm. During the nineteenth century coastal shipping played a fairly minor role in the Ostrobothnia area compared to southern Finland, because the large scale tar trade to Stockholm ceased as a consequence of Finland's annexation by Russia. Domestic coastal shipping, between Finnish ports, was insignificant compared to coastal shipping between Finland and the mother country (either Sweden or Russia), or direct foreign shipping. This was partly related to the fact that in Finland there were no fast growing urban centres which needed supplies provided by the coasters.

In the case of Finland all long distance shipping was a privilege of the citizens of towns until the mid-nineteenth century. Peasants, on the other hand, were allowed to engage in coastal trade with small ships. As Yrjö Kaukiainen and Eino Jutikkala have shown, peasant shipping was quite large scale enterprise at least from the late eighteenth century on. Coastal shipping also played an important role in the economies of the Finnish merchants. Especially during the seventeenth and eighteenth centuries, when most of the Finnish towns did not have foreign trade rights (staple rights), most of the shipping was in fact short sea shipping, either between Finnish ports or between Finnish and Swedish ports, basically between home town and the capital, Stockholm.

Eino JUTIKKALA, Suomen talonpoikaispurjehtijat ja heidän aluksensa Ruotsin-ajan lopussa, in: Historiallinen aikakauskirja 48 (1950), pp. 85-94. Georg KÅHRE/Karl KÅHRE, Den Åländska segelsjöfartens historia. Förkortad upplaga av Georg Kåhres historik utgiven 1942 med försättning till segelsjöfartens slutskede 1949, compiled by Karl Kåhre, Marienhamn 1988.

  4 See especially: KAUKIAINEN, History of Finnish Shipping; Aulis J. ALANEN, Der Außenhandel und die Schiffahrt Finnlands im 18. Jahrhundert, Helsinki 1957; Staffan HÖGBERG, Utrikeshandel och sjöfart på 1700-talet. Stapelvaror i svensk export och import 1738–1808, Lund 1969.

The lack of primary sources makes it difficult to study Finnish coastal shipping. Although we have some figures on coastal shipping in the urban areas, we have almost none on rural coastal shipping. The smallest coastal ships are not included in any statistics. These ships mainly carried sawn timber from the rural areas to the ports to be loaded into ocean sailing vessels. Even rowboats were used to carry these cargoes. In some private shipowners' account books these kinds of vessels are also mentioned.[5]

The coastal vessels were in many cases not used in pure *cabotage*, instead, they were infrequently used as well during the winter in the foreign trade. The frozen sea made it impossible to continue shipping during wintertime. Usually coasters were employed as long as possible; in many cases the ships were frozen, for instance, in the harbour of St Petersburg, and the crew members had to travel to their home towns by land. The roads were not a real threat to coastal shipping even during the winters before the railway age, because the small volumes of cargoes could be carried by coasters during the sailing period. For the masters, mates and seamen the short sailing period was, of course, a real problem, because they were out of work for the whole winter. Rural coastal shipping was therefore usually only a part-time occupation for the local farmers. In towns, the crews of the coastal ships was usually older, married seamen, while the younger bachelors enrolled on the ocean going vessels.[6]

II

Finland was a part of Sweden up to 1809. From this period we have only sporadic data on the coastal shipping of Finnish towns. Peasant shipping or shipping in rural districts is entirely missing from the data.[7] During the Swedish era shipping statistics consist of only the vessels engaged in foreign trade. Therefore coastal ships, also those which sailed between Finland and Sweden, are not included in the statistics. The customs account books, which included the numbers in domestic shipping, were destroyed, since the Royal Swedish Navy used the old folios for wrapping cartouches.[8]

[5] OJALA, Tuhannen purjelaivan kaupunki, pp. 123–4.

[6] Yrjö KAUKIAINEN, Sailing into Twilight. Finnish Shipping in an Age of Transport Revolution 1860–1914, Helsinki 1991, p. 113; OJALA, Tuhannen purjelaivan kaupunki, pp. 227–8.

[7] Not all rural ships were owned by peasants; some ships were also owned by the local nobility, civil servants or even by priests. Eino JUTIKKALA, Suomen talonpoik-aispurjeh-tijat, p. 93; OJALA, Tuhannen purjelaivan kaupunki, p. 185; Jan-Erik BÖRMAN, Åboländsk bygdeseglation, pp. 75–85.

[8] Staffan HÖGBERG, Utrikeshandel och sjöfart på 1700-talet, pp. 9–13; KAUKIAINEN, History of Finnish Shipping, p. 45.

Peasants were given the right to carry out maritime trade with all domestic seaports in 1765. This shipping was especially important for Stockholm, because the Swedish and Finnish peasants supplied food and firewood to the capital. Peasant ships were allowed to carry their own produce to market, but not export cargoes or the products of other people for reward. These ships usually made four to six voyages during the sailing season, therefore the actual number of ship movements and the tonnage were quite low.[9] Customs accounts from Stockholm show that peasant shipping from Finland to the capital was quite a large enterprise.[10] This was, of course, related to ongoing urbanisation: these vessels carried bulky goods to the growing capital.

The earliest useful statistical information on Finnish coastal shipping dates to 1747. For this year we have the number and tonnage of ships in the Finnish and Swedish towns engaged in foreign and domestic shipping. According to table 1, in 1747 about 67 per cent of the Finnish tonnage was engaged in domestic, namely coastal, shipping.[11] Furthermore, in 1747 only twelve Finnish-owned ships passed through the Sound either to the west or returning to the east. Because at least some of those vessels were the same ships, which passed the Sound in early summer and came back in autumn, the actual number of long distance ships was probably below ten.[12] Ships engaged in foreign shipping were carrying cargoes inside the Baltic area.[13] In the mid-eighteenth century about 80 to 90 per cent of Finnish shipping was more or less short sea shipping, either between Finland and Sweden or inside the Baltic area. Furthermore, if we had the number of rural ships, the share of coastal ships would rise even more, because the peasant shipowners were not allowed to carry cargoes outside the Baltic, in practise, outside the northern Baltic region.[14]

---

[9] Aimo WUORINEN, Turku kauppakaupunkina, vol. 1, pp. 84, 394–5. KAUKIAINEN, Suomen talonpoikaispurjehdus, pp. 24–5, 52. KAUKIAINEN, History of Finnish Shipping, pp. 37, 50–2. PAPP, Åländsk allmogeseglation, pp. 134–60.

[10] Aimo WUORINEN, Turku kauppakaupunkina, vol. 1, p. 414; ALANEN, Der Außenhandel und die Schiffahrt Finnlands; KAUKIAINEN, Suomen talonpoikaispurjehdus, p. 16; KAUKIAINEN, History of Finnish Shipping, p. 14.

[11] In the whole of Sweden (including Finland) the share of the tonnage in domestic shipping was much lower: only 34 per cent of the tonnage was engaged in domestic shipping. The share of Finnish ships of the total Swedish tonnage was only 15 per cent. Daniel ALMQVIST, Tillståndet i Sveriges städer 1747, in: Historisk Tidskrift, Stockholm 1949, pp. 379–80. KAUKIAINEN, History of Finnish Shipping, pp. 44–9.

[12] Jan-Erik BÖRMAN, Genom Öresund. Öresundstullen-skepps-farten på Finland 1500–1800, Helsingfors 1981, pp. 209–86. N. E. BANG/K. KORST, Tabeller over skibsfart og varetransport gennem Øresund 1661–1783 og gennem Storebælt 1701–1748. Første del: Tabeller over Skibsfarten, Copenhagen 1930, p. 247.

[13] The fact that the ships engaged in foreign trade were actually smaller (approximately 37 lästs) than the ships in domestic trade (c. 44 lästs) indicates, that most of them were used on relatively short routes, basically between the Finnish and Russian ports.

[14] KAUKIAINEN, History of Finnish Shipping, pp. 17–58; OJALA, Tuhannen purjelaivan kaupunki, pp. 63–76.

Table 1: Finnish ships engaged in domestic and foreign trade in 1747

	Number of ships	Tonnage of ships, in *lästs*	Share of number (%)	Share of tonnage(%)
Domestic shipping	108	4,762	63	67
Foreign shipping	63	2,359	37	33
Total	171	7,121	100	100

Source: Daniel Almqvist, »Tillståndet i Sveriges städer 1747«, *Historisk Tidskrift*, vol. XII (Stockholm, 1949), pp. 369–82. One Finnish *läst* equals 1.85 net register tons.

A substantial number of Finnish towns earned the right to conduct their own foreign trade and shipping during the late eighteenth century. This initiated foreign shipping in Finland. Coastal shipping remained an important part of shipping in the new »staple« towns.[15] There were, however, differences between different towns. For example in Kokkola, which achieved foreign trade rights in 1765, in the early 1770s there were far more ships engaged in domestic than in foreign shipping. This was because the ships carried tar to the Stockholm traders, who merchanted it to Great Britain. It was not until the late eighteenth century that more tar from Kokkola was taken abroad than to the capital. At least in the cases of the trading houses Donner and Kyntzell from Kokkola, the Baltic ports accounted for over 50 per cent of the voyages made at the turn of the eighteenth and nineteenth centuries, as seen in table 2. Although these figures include the long distance ships that carried freight to the Baltic area, most of the ships were carrying cargoes only within the northern Baltic, especially from their home port to Stockholm.[16] Furthermore, in Turku (Åbo in Swedish) about 73 per cent of the ships, and a little over 50 per cent of the tonnage was engaged in coastal shipping in 1766–99.[17]

In the year 1800 the total capacity of urban ships was about 20,000 *lästs*.[18] The tonnage of rural ships was about 9,000 *lästs*.[19] Therefore, the whole ton-

[15] KAUKIAINEN, History of Finnish Shipping, p. 49.

[16] OJALA, Tuhannen purjelaivan kaupunki, pp. 172–80; Aulis J. ALANEN, Pohjanlahden vapaasta purjehduksesta 1766–1808, in: Historiallinen Arkisto 53 (1950), p. 96. KAUKIAINEN, History of Finnish Shipping, p. 36. Staffan HÖGBERG, Utrikeshandel och sjöfart på 1700-talet, pp. 9–33, 121, 162–3; ALANEN, Der Außenhandel und die Schiffahrt Finnlands, p. 134.

[17] Aimo WUORINEN, Turku kauppakaupunkina, vol. 1, pp. 408–409, 412, 414–415.

[18] Jari OJALA, Rikkauden lähteellä. Kokkolan kauppamerenkulku isostavihasta ensimmäiseen maailmansotaan (n. 1721–1914), Unpublished licentiate thesis, University of Jyväskylä, 1996, p. 255.

[19] According to Jutikkala, in the southern and south-west parts of Finland the average size of peasant ships was below 20 *lästs*, but in the northern parts of Finland over 30 *lästs*.

nage in Finland was about 29,000 *lästs*.[20] Furthermore, if the capacity of the urban ships engaged in coastal shipping was about 50 per cent (about 10,000 *lästs*), as in the cases of Kokkola and Turku[21], then the total tonnage of ships used in the Baltic in 1800 was about 19,000 *lästs*; thus, about 66 per cent of the total tonnage was used in coastal shipping. This figure is perhaps a little too high, because the urban coastal ships were smaller than the long distance ships. On the other hand, in some southern towns there were only a couple of ships – if any at all – in long distance trade, as their ships were mainly used in the coastal trade. The share of coastal tonnage is probably somewhere between 60 and 70 per cent of the whole merchant fleet at the end of the eighteenth and beginning of the nineteenth century.

Table 2: Ports in the Baltic area and outside the Baltic visited by vessels of the trading houses Donner, 1793–1863, and Kyntzell, 1810–1851

	Baltic ports	Outside Baltic	Total	Share of Baltic ports (%)
1793–99	10	6	16	63
1800–09	25	20	45	56
1810–19	37	41	78	47
1820–29	47	45	92	51
1830–39	26	95	121	21
1840–49	29	123	152	19
1850–59	4	20	24	17
1860–63	1	14	15	7
Total	179	364	543	33

Sources: Finnish National Archives, Archives of trading house Donner, Shipping Accounts 1793–1863. K.H. Renlund Museum, Kokkola. Archives of trading house Donner, Shipping Accounts 1802–1854. Finnish National Archives, Archives of E. E. Kaila, the Archives of commercial counsellor Anders Kyntzell 1810–1851.

Eino JUTIKKALA, Suomen talonpoikaispurjehtijat, pp. 89, 91–93. KAUKIAINEN, Suomen talonpoikaispurjehdus, Appendix, Table I. KAUKIANEN, History of Finnish Shipping, p. 52. In the Åland islands the capacity of the vessels used in coastal shipping between Åland and Stockholm was about 30–40 *lästs*; the smallest vessels carried only about 3–5 *lästs* at the turn of the eighteenth century: PAPP, Åländsk allmogeseglation, pp. 46–56.

[20] Compare KAUKIAINEN, History of Finnish Shipping, p. 52; see also KAUKIAINEN, Suomen talonpoikaispurjehdus, p. 237.

[21] In Pori (Sw. Björneborg), in south-west Finland, in 1808 about 43 per cent of the tonnage was engaged in coastal shipping. During the nineteenth century the absolute tonnage used in the Baltic area rose but so did the long distance shipping. In the early 1840s about 42 per cent of the ships in Pori were engaged in coastal shipping in the Baltic: L. I. KAUKAMAA, Porin puutavarakaupasta, pp. 40–1, 67–8.

After Finland was annexed by imperial Russia in 1809, the urban ship lists include the coastal ships from 1815 on. This can be deduced from the fact that more ships stayed during the winter in their home port than under Swedish rule. In the ship lists no separation is made between ships that were engaged in coastal shipping and those that sailed beyond Elsinore (Helsingør in Danish) in the Sound.[22]

Although we have quite good data sets on ships from Finnish towns during the early part of the nineteenth century, the data on the rural or peasant ships is more sporadic. From the 1840s we have annual lists of peasant shipping. After Finland was ceded to Russia, the export trade to Russia by sea was duty free; therefore, there is no data on the small coastal ships that carried cargoes to Russia, especially to the capital St Petersburg, which was a fast growing city. Furthermore, shipping inside Finland was not registered at all.[23]

In 1830 all coastal towns were allowed to trade abroad using their own vessels, and even the peasant vessels were allowed to trade their products within the entire Baltic. Peasants carried not only agricultural products or firewood but sawn goods as well. Furthermore, these cargoes were taken not only to St Petersburg, Tallinn or Stockholm but also to the northern German ports and Copenhagen. The peasant fleet saw enormous growth during the early part of the nineteenth century: in 1853 it was about 60 per cent larger than in 1810.[24] The growth of St Petersburg especially accelerated this trade.

The share of the Baltic area as a destination for, for example, Kokkola's sailing fleet was about 47 per cent of tonnage in 1815–19, as seen in table 3.[25] After that the share diminished to 20 per cent in the 1830s and then slowly grew up to the late 1880s. In the late nineteenth century there were no more deep sea sailing vessels in Kokkola; therefore the share of the tonnage engaged in coastal shipping rose to 100 per cent.

---

[22] Some authors have called coastal ships those, which were, according to the ship lists, »at home« at the end of the year. This kind of calculation leads to false conclusions, because these home-based ships included several ships that sailed beyond the Baltic in the summer yet returned before winter. There were also large ocean going vessels which were under repair during the whole winter. See for example: Heimer BJÖRKQVIST, Handelsflottan och dess betydelse för sysselsättningen i de svensk-österbottniska städerna åren 1815–1858, in: Österbotten 1970, Vasa 1970, pp. 227–9.

[23] KAUKIAINEN, Suomen talonpoikaispurjehdus, pp. 34, 37, 42–4.

[24] KAUKIAINEN, History of Finnish Shipping, pp. 52, 60–4, 74. KAUKIAINEN, Suomen talonpoikaispurjehdus, pp. 53–104, 144–6.

[25] Table 3 has limitations also. The numbers are collected from the annual hiring lists. Large deep sea sailing vessels did not visit home ports nor hire men every year. Ships could be on voyages for several years. Furthermore, men were hired to the small coastal ships usually several times during the sailing season. Therefore, the share of the coastal ships tends to be overestimated. At the same time the share of the ships of 50 *lästs* or below was only about 10–15 per cent of Kokkola's fleet.

Table 3:   Tonnage leaving Kokkola harbour for the Baltic area and
            outside the Baltic, 1815–1910, in *lästs*

Year	Baltic	Outside Baltic	Total	Share of Baltic (%)	Number of Cases
1815–19	7,197	7,990	15,187	47	198
1820–29	9,136	22,993	32,129	28	499
1830–39	6,903	27,037	33,940	20	444
1840–49	6,620	22,811	29,431	22	328
1850–59	4,760	11,436	16,196	29	227
1860–69	3,137	11,291	14,428	22	173
1870–79	2,515	6,865	9,380	27	96
1880–89	1,551	2,842	4,394	35	36
1890–89	273	–	273	100	13
1900–10	272	–	272	100	11
Total	42,364	113,266	155,630	27	2,025

Sources: Vaasa Provincial Archives, Vaasa, Archives of the Kokkola Seamen's House, Hiring lists 1815–1914.

The tonnage figures for coastal shipping in 1842 and 1850 for Finland as a whole are given in table 4. A basic assumption is made that ships of 50 *lästs* or less were used in coastal and the larger ones in long distance shipping.[26] For these years we also have accurate data on rural shipping. Thus, these numbers are quite close to the actual tonnage-share figures of coastal (inside the Baltic) and long distance shipping.

As we can see from table 4, the share of the tonnage engaged in coastal shipping was about 40 per cent in 1842, and this remained almost the same in 1850. Although the tonnage and number of urban ships engaged in coastal shipping diminished, the number and especially the tonnage of rural ships grew. In table 2 the first Finnish seagoing steam vessels are also included as

---

[26] This is, of course, quite a rough division. There were also ships below 50 *lästs* engaged in long distance shipping, and many ships over 50 *lästs* were used only in the Baltic. This can be detected, for example, from the fact that many ships over 50 *lästs* were clinker built, from which we may assume that they were not used in long distance shipping. There were also administrative regulations concerning this: rural ships were not allowed to be over 50 *lästs*, and there were several customs reductions for ships over 50 *lästs*. Carl Gustaf WOLFF, Finlands Skepps-kalender 1842 & 1850, Wasa 1842 & 1850; OJALA, Tuhannen purjelaivan kaupunki, pp. 65, 121. PAPP, Åländsk allmogeseglation, p. 58. KAUKIAINEN, Suomen talonpoikaispurjehdus, p. 54.

coastal ships. The first steam-powered vessels appeared on coastal routes in Finland during the 1830s.[27]

Table 4: Finnish coastal ships in rural districts and towns, 1842 and 1850

	1842		1850	
	Number	*Lästs*	Number	*Lästs*
Rural ships	831	20,100	888	23,950
Town ships, coastal[28]	164	5,151	142	4,399
Total, coastal	995	25,251	1,030	28,349
Town ships, long distance[29]	286	41,737	328	47,152
Total ships	1,281	66,988	1,358	75,501
Coastal share of total (%)	77.7	37.7	75.9	37.5

Sources: Yrjö Kaukiainen, *Suomen talonpoikaispurjehdus*, Appendix, Table I. Carl Gustaf Wolff, *Finlands Skepps-kalender 1842 & 1850* (Wasa, 1842 & 1850).

III

Finnish shipping was fundamentally coastal shipping before the middle of the eighteenth century. After Finnish shipowners started to engage in foreign trade and shipping as well, share of coastal ships diminished gradually. In the middle of the nineteenth century the share of the tonnage in coastal shipping was about 40 per cent, whereas a century before it had been about 90 per cent. The tonnage share of coastal shipping is somewhat smaller, if we interpret coastal shipping as shipping only on the Finnish coast or between Finland and the motherland, either Sweden or Russia. In that case, the share of coastal vessels in the middle of the eighteenth century was about two-thirds, and it diminished to about one-third by the middle of the nineteenth century. The volume of ships engaged in coastal shipping inside the Baltic also diminished, if we look at shipping in the urban areas only. Peasant shipping, however, continued to play an important role in coastal shipping and the share of peasant shipping grew during the nineteenth century.

The absolute gains of coastal shipping were quite low compared to deep sea shipping. For the merchants coastal shipping was a means of supporting other

[27] Erkki RIIMALA, Höyrylaivan tulo Pohjolaan and Suomen ensimmäiset höyrylaivat, in: Erkki RIIMALA (ed.), Navis Fennica. Suomen merenkulun historia, vol. 2, Porvoo 1994, pp. 28–40. KAUKIAINEN, History of Finnish Shipping, p. 66.

[28] Only ships with a capacity of 50 *lästs* or below.

[29] Ships with a capacity of over 50 *lästs*.

lines of business such as retail trade. Furthermore, short sea shipping was possible only during the summer, which diminished the profits. According to some account books from Raahe, Finland, the average rate of return on coastal vessels was actually quite high: during the years 1818 to 1904 the average rate of return on some of the local coasters was about 15 per cent, as seen in table 5. This is partly due to some extraordinarily high profits; usually the rate of return was about ten per cent. The profitability of the coasters varied quite sharply in line with market fluctuations. After Finland was annexed to Russia shipping and trade were in crisis. This can be seen from the Raahe coasters' low profits. During the 1820s coasters were mainly used in the trade between Stockholm and Finland, because at the time the trade between Finland and Sweden remained domestic trade. It was not until the 1830s and 1840s that the trade between Finland and Sweden was legally classified as foreign trade and custom tariffs rose. This, of course, diminished the coastal trade gradually and also the coasters' returns. During the 1830s and 1840s coasters were mainly used in short distance trades, for example in collecting timber cargoes from rural harbours which large ocean-going vessels could not enter. High profits during the 1850s can be explained by the Crimean War: ocean-going vessels were either sold or captured by British naval forces and therefore all the trade was carried in small coasters, which operated mainly between Stockholm and their home town. High profits during the 1880s can only be explained by the small number of cases (only two tiny ships). Competition from railways made coastal shipping unprofitable during the early twentieth century. This was shown by the diminishing trade and shipping of Raahe at the time. Although the absolute profits of coasters were quite low, capital, operating and voyage costs were small as well. The crew members were hired only for the season and the number of seamen was low: in many cases, there was only one seaman besides the master on board.[30] There were, however, differences between the earnings of individual ships: a low-valued coaster could earn almost its building value during the sailing season. A large and expensive ocean going vessel, which was sometimes used in coastal trade, operated quite unprofitably on short routes because of the low-valued freights and the high expenses of the large vessel. Therefore, there are huge differences in the rates of return during different decades in table 5, simply because of the low number of cases.[31]

[30] OJALA, Tuhannen purjelaivan kaupunki, p. 240.

[31] See Table 5. Number of cases is 63. These accounts are collected from the archives of trading house Sovelius, which includes also the accounts of trading house Franzén and Lang. They include only the ships sailing in the northern Baltic region, including Stockholm, Tallin and St Petersburg; namely, the »real« coastal shipping. The annual net results are compared to the current ship value; this value is taken either from the account books or from the probate inventories. Rate of return is calculated by using the methods introduced in Yrjö KAUKIAINEN, Sailing into Twilight, pp. 220–277 and Jari OJALA, Productivity and

Table 5: Rate of return of Raahe coastal vessels in 1818–1904
(ten year averages, per cent)

Years	Rate of return (%)	Number of Cases
1810–19	6.79	1
1820–29	27.43	11
1830–39	4.90	19
1840–49	19.89	13
1850–59	49.21	3
1860–69	–	–
1870–79	5.60	1
1880–89	62.58	2
1890–99	9.16	8
1900–10	–10.88	5
Average	15.20	63

Sources: Oulu Provincial Archives, Oulu. Archives of Trading House Sovelius, Shipping Accounts.

In the rural areas coastal shipping was especially important for the local economy, and for the urban merchants coastal shipping offered opportunities for extra income as well. Before the mid-nineteenth century, coastal shipping was basically a part-time occupation both in the rural areas and for the urban shipowners. Only afterwards did some specialised steamship companies open liner routes on the Finnish coast. The peasants' coastal shipping was basically a source for extra income, and for the urban traders it was meant to support retail and foreign trade.[32] One should not underestimate the large urban centres' importance for Finnish coastal shipping. Stockholm and St Petersburg later also Tallinn and Helsinki were growing rapidly during this period offering good opportunities for Finnish coasters in carrying firewood, food supplies

Profitability of Shipping by Sail in the Long-run. The Case of Finland, ca. 1750–1914, paper presented at The Third World Congress of Cliometrics, Munich Germany 10–13 July, 1997, pp. 356–8.

[32] Basil GREENHILL, Aspects of late nineteenth century rural shipowning in south-western Britain, in: Keith MATTHEWS/Gerald PANTING (eds.), Ships and Shipbuilding in the North Atlantic Region, St John's 1978, p. 159; OJALA, Tuhannen purjelaivan kaupunki, p. 142; Eino JUTIKKALA, Suomen talonpoikaispurjehtijat, pp. 85–94. In the Åland islands about 20 per cent of all farms owned shares in peasant ships in the early part of the nineteenth century. Coastal shipping was mainly a part-time occupation for the rural ship-owners, but its importance for employment was great: KAUKIAINEN, Suomen talonpoikaispurjehdus, pp. 236–8.

and building materials to the cities. The volume and number of ships engaged in coastal shipping rose throughout the period from the mid-eighteenth century to the mid-nineteenth century. At the same time Finnish long distance shipping grew even more rapidly; therefore, the share of coastal tonnage diminished.

6

THE MODERNIZATION OF FINNISH COASTAL SHIPPING AND RAILWAY COMPETITION c. 1830–1913

YRJÖ KAUKIAINEN

In the Finnish context, a fairly natural domain for coastal shipping consisted of the waters of the Gulfs of Finland and Bothnia as well as of the northern Baltic, roughly north of 59 degrees, or the latitude of Stockholm. In navigational sense, of course, one could claim that an even wider definition might be relevant. Long trips could be made across the Baltic without losing visual contact with the coastline. In practice, however, such small Finnish tonnage as can be termed »coastal« only very seldom sailed beyond Stockholm or the northwestern tip of the Estonian coast. Thus, in this article, coastal shipping is understood to be almost synonymous with the term *cabotage* (that is, coastal traffic between ports of one country, domestic traffic), with the addition of the most proximate coasts of Sweden, Russia and Estonia.[1]

Finland was a country with fairly small regional variances in economic structure, at least as far as coastal districts were concerned. Although commerce was the sole privilege of towns until the 1850s, there were no really large urban centres which attracted primary products or labour from large rural areas. Just as the classic law of comparative advantage predicts, the main part of the commerce of coastal towns (whether in terms of bulk or value) consisted of trade with foreign places, involving more or less extended direct shipping. Accordingly, the demand for domestic coastwise maritime transport between Finnish urban sites was fairly small until the middle of the nineteenth century. There was some transport of iron manufactures from south Finnish ironworks, of limestone from the few localities where it was to be found, and of firewood and fish plus certain other food products from archipelagoes to larger towns. Only when we look at shipping crossing over to Sweden, Estonia and northwest Russia do we find maritime transport on a larger scale. Above

---

[1] Before 1808, Sweden was domestic trade for Finnish sailors, and even after that, the eastern coast of Sweden was a special case which in many respects was regarded as comparable with domestic ports. After 1808 Russian and Estonian ports became domestic for Finns. This definition is also compatible with certain legal practices; thus, for example, until the First World War, any Finnish citizen of good reputation could act as master on coastal vessels plying these waters, while those on longer trades, e.g. over the Baltic, were required to engage masters with higher qualifications and formal examinations.

all, there was a massive trade in firewood to Stockholm and St Petersburg and return loads of iron ore from the Stockholm archipelago (Utö) to Finnish south-coast ironworks, mainly carried on by coastal peasant vessels. Traditionally, there was also the all-important shipping of tar from Ostrobothnia to Stockholm, which mainly took place on urban-owned tonnage. When Finland was ceded to Russia in 1809, tar shipments to Stockholm diminished rapidly and, more gradually, even ore imports declined after the 1840s. On the other hand, grain imports from St Petersburg started to grow as did the export of certain manufactures to Estonia and northwest Russia.[2]

Before the era of steam, there was only occasional coastwise passenger traffic. Most passengers travelled on dry land as long as they could and only when crossing over to Sweden were compelled to use seaborne transport. This took place either in small »packets« between Turku and Stockholm or in small boats along the old mail route across the Turku and Aaland archipelagoes and the Aaland Sea between Eckerö and Grisslehamn. Reading of the experiences of some eighteenth-century travellers on narrow Finnish dirt roads it is not difficult to imagine that there may have been a latent demand for a more comfortable way of moving.[3] Such a new system of transport was created when the first steamships started to ply these northern waters. As practically everywhere else, the new technology was initially applied for the carrying of passengers and, therefore, it did not so much compete with the existing coastal trade (with the exception of »packets«, of course) as with horse and cart. Thus, steamships, by offering a totally new standard of service, created new demand rather than penetrating the existing, fairly primitive market.

Not surprisingly, the development was initiated by a Swedish company, headed by the well-known engine-builder Samuel Owen, which started sailing between Stockholm and Turku in October 1821. The traffic was carried on for only a few years. The company would have liked to have continued the line to Helsinki but this was not possible because the Swedish Navigation Act of 1726, which was still valid in Finland, explicitly forbade cabotage by foreign vessels. This gave domestic entrepreneurs a definite upper hand, but it was only in 1836 that a Turku-based company, *Åbo Ångfartygsaktiebolaget*, started anew the traffic to Stockholm and, in the following year, with another ship to Helsinki, Tallinn and St Petersburg. In 1838, two more steamers entered coastal traffic, one sailing between Turku and Oulu and the other, which was mainly intended to carry cargo, on coastal routes between the Russian capital and Turku and Ostrobothnian towns. Even local traffic by

[2] See e.g. Yrjö KAUKIAINEN, A History of Finnish Shipping, London/New York 1993, pp. 45–52, 59–62, 74–76.

[3] See e.g. William COXE, Travels into Poland, Russia, Sweden and Denmark, London 1784; E. D. CLARKE, Travels in various countries of Europe Asia and Africa. Part the third, Scandinavia, vol. II, London 1824; John CARR, A Northern Summer, London 1805.

small steam vessels was started around a few coastal towns. Demand, however, was still limited and although a few attempts were made to extend regular services, the traffic based on Stockholm, St Petersburg and Bothnian towns provided profitable employment for only three larger steamers.[4]

Fairly rapid growth was experienced between the Crimean War and the late 1870s. Immediately after the war, a company with state subventions ordered from England four iron-hulled steamers of 200 tons or more.[5] New steamer companies were also formed in Helsinki, Turku and the Bothnian towns and, by 1865, the total number of steamships of over 100 net tons had risen to eleven. A second rapid investment boom was experienced between 1871 and 1876, when ten more fairly large (200–300 ton) passenger steamers were added to the fleet. Some of these replaced older vessels but there was also a number of new enterprises; thus, in the late 1870s, the number of steamers of over 100 tons amounted to more than thirty. In one sense, however, this represented the apex of development. Very few ships were added to the coastal fleet from then to 1913.[6]

Unfortunately, Finnish shipping statistics make it very difficult to specify the share of coastal traffic for either transport output or tonnage involved and this refers, in particular, to that part of the trade which did not cross the national boundaries. Until 1891, data for vessels entered and cleared in domestic traffic were published, but separate figures for steam and sail can only be found from 1883 onwards. Because the primary data of maritime traffic was compiled by customs officials, and there was no customs dues to be paid in domestic traffic, the data cannot be regarded as very reliable. Neither is it systematic in coverage – in particular no distinction was made between ships in the pure domestic trade and those ultimately aiming at Russian or Swedish ports. After 1891, a new statistical class, combining domestic and foreign traffic (»Cabotage mixte«) was created, but it means that earlier series are not comparable with the new one. It was only in 1894 that statistics on liner traffic were published (see table 1), but this was a one-off case and was never repeated.

[4] A fairly detailed account of early steamship traffic can be found in Ernst LINDBERG, Ångbåtssjöfart i Åbo 1836–1928, Åbo Sjöfarts historia, vol. 3, Åbo 1928, p. 4–98.

[5] LINDBERG, Ångbåtssjöfart, pp. 140–53.

[6] For the development of tonnage, see Yrjö KAUKIAINEN, Sailing into Twilight, Jyväskylä 1991, appendix I. Most of the ships built in the 1870s sailed until the First World War because they were fairly modern and practical ships with all-iron hulls and compound machines. Their typical overall lengths varied between 51 and 56 metres, beams 5 and 8 metres and net tonnages between 200 and 300. For more data on these ships, see Matti PIETIKÄINEN/Bengt SJÖSTRÖM (eds.), The Ships of our First Century. The Effoa Fleet 1883–1983, Keuruu 1983, pp. 15–21.

Table 1: Regular foreign-going coastal lines in Finland, 1894

Line	Ships		Return voyages	
	Number	Tonnage	Number	Aggregate tons
St Petersburg-Wiborg-Saimaa	6	671	112	12,547
St Petersburg-Helsinki-Oulu	4	1,253	37	11,660
St Petersburg-Helsinki	2*	371	53	9,797
St Petersburg-Helsinki-Pori-Sundsvall	1	204	14	2,856
Tallinn-Hanko-Pori	1	128	16	2,048
Stockholm-Turku-St Petersburg	1	243	15	3,645
Stockholm-Turku	1	125	23	2,875
Stockholm-Turku-Pori	1	180	28	5,040
Stockholm-Pori-Vaasa	1	254	25	6,350
Total	18	3,429	323	56,818

Source: Finnish Official Statistics, ser. I, Foreign Trade and Shipping, 1894, table 10.
The Stockholm-Hanko line, which ran through the northern Baltic and was a special wintertime connection, is not included.

* The same ships also sailed between Tallinn and Helsinki

Although the sources leave much to be desired, one thing can clearly be seen: the development of coastal services increased the volume of domestic shipping quite substantially. In 1867/68, the total amount of entrances and clearances in domestic traffic amounted to no more than 110,000 net tons a year; in the middle of the 1880s, corresponding figures already exceeded 350,000. The same story is told by the fact that in the 1880s sailing vessels – which represent the »traditional« coastal trade – only accounted for some 10–5 per cent of total domestic traffic. Although much of the growth shown in the statistics resulted from the fact that steamships on regular lines were recorded several times during a long coastal voyage, it still seems accurate to say that the »new« element of coastal shipping had clearly outpaced the old one.[7]

Until the late 1870s, the mainstay of steam shipping consisted of passenger services and imports from Russia. Practically all Finnish steam tonnage was occupied on either coastal or Baltic traffic.[8] Fortunately, there are insurance

[7] Finnish Official Shipping Statistics, 1856–1914. On the quality of the data, see KAUKIAINEN, Sailing into Twilight, pp. 129–31.

[8] KAUKIAINEN, Sailing into Twilight, pp. 181–6.

data[9] which include the majority of steamships over 100 tons and which also indicate the trade in which the vessels were sailing. For around 1875, such data (plus some additional literary information)[10] exist for twenty steamers (which means that data is missing for less than ten) of over 100 tons and all except two of them were sailing in more or less regular traffic. Of these eighteen, six traded to Lübeck or other destinations across the Baltic, four were engaged on lines between Stockholm and St Petersburg, another four between St Petersburg and Ostrobothnia, and two between St Petersburg and Helsinki. Around 1885, the corresponding group amounted to twenty-two (excluding four ships sailing regularly outside the Baltic; thus, data was missing for six ships). Of these, only two were sailing to Lübeck, one between Vaasa and Sundsvall (Sweden), three between Stockholm and St Petersburg, five between Helsinki and/or Turku and St Petersburg, five (or four) between St Petersburg and Ostrobothnia, one between Turku and Stockholm and three on the Finnish southern coast, thereof one between Turku and Aaland islands. Coastal traffic dominated over Baltic lines. Non-domestic destinations, however, were essential for these coastal lines and, all told, St Petersburg seems to have been more important than Stockholm. This probably resulted from the fact that connections with the Russian capital were needed not only by passengers but equally by those who imported grain, hemp or sail cloth from Russia. In any case, the lines covered the Finnish coasts quite well, extending right to the northern extremes of the Gulf of Bothnia (Tornio and Oulu). Steamers running on these routes normally visited many towns, thus maintaining a fairly good and frequent connection, much like railway lines. As the ships did not normally sail at night, travelling was not very fast: a return voyage between Oulu and St Petersburg normally required a fortnight.[11] Although this was not necessarily a great improvement in speed compared with overland travel, it certainly was in terms of comfort.

At the same time as coastal steamer lines had established themselves a new revolution in travelling, the building of railways, was starting in earnest. The first railway between Helsinki and Hämeenlinna was no alternative to coastal lines, but the line to St Petersburg which was opened in 1870 was already a very potent competitor. Compared with two days on a ship, the train travelled this distance in a fraction of time, twelve hours.[12] This new railway soon attracted a high share of the transport of manufactured goods between south-

[9] Registers of the Finnish Mutual Maritime Insurance Association, Maritime archives, Åbo Akademi.

[10] LINDBERG, Ångbåtssjöfart.

[11] Ibid., p. 150.

[12] Suomen valtionrautatiet 1862–1912, vol. 2, Helsinki 1916, p. 587.

ern Finland and northwest Russia.[13] Yet the new services seemed to have amazingly little impact on long coastal routes – the number of ships sailing to St Petersburg via Finland's south coast actually increased between 1875 and 1885. Obviously the railway was an option only for those living in Helsinki and east of it so that the long coastal lines still retained most of their natural »hinterland«. Even the fact that a number of ships (at least four around 1885) sailed via Tallinn may have helped their competitive position, although even Tallinn got a railway to St Petersburg in 1870.

After 1870, the emphasis in railway construction was in the eastern interior. Therefore, the real competition with coastal lines started only in the late 1880s, when the northwestern trunk line was extended to Ostrobothnia. It reached Vaasa at the end of 1882, Kokkola three years later and, finally, Oulu in October 1886. Later, branch lines were constructed to Pietarsaari (1887) and Raahe (1900) and the trunk line was continued to Tornio in 1903. Southward, Pori was connected to the network in 1899 and a direct connection between Helsinki and Turku was opened in 1903 (since 1876, however, there had been a much longer indirect connection branching from the Hämeenlinna-Tampere railway).[14]

The Bothnian railway offered an attractive opportunity for passengers. It reduced the travelling time between Helsinki and Oulu to about twenty-four hours as compared with five days on coastal steamers. Thus, it was a formidable competitor for steamer lines and it took over a good proportion of the market almost immediately. In a few years after 1886, annual steamship departures from Oulu to Russian destinations, fell from over seventy to just a few and although there was obviously some recovery in the early 1890s, this was followed by a continuous, albeit more gradual, decline (see table 2). A corresponding decline can also be seen in other Ostrobothnian ports.[15] At first, the number of trips was reduced rather than the number of ships, but already by 1895 there were two steamers less on Bothnian lines than ten years earlier, that is, a drop from six to four, and, after the turn of the century, only one or two ships were sailing on these routes.[16] As can be seen from table 2, the figures for domestic departures show a sudden jump around 1890. This is difficult to explain and as it can be seen in almost all ports, may have resulted from a change in the statistical conventions. If this were so, there was soon a return to previous practices. It is difficult to believe that steam liners attracted more passengers from purely domestic traffic.

[13] Erkki PIHKALA, Suomen ulkomaankauppa/Finland's Foreign Trade, 1860–1917, Helsinki 1969, appendix tables 8 and 9.

[14] Suomen valtionrautatiet, p. 34–144.

[15] Finnish Official Statistics, ser. I (Foreign Trade and Shipping) and IB (Shipping).

[16] Data files compiled for my study: Sailing into Twilight (for more details see appendices III:1 and III:3A).

Table 2: Departures by loaded steamships with coastal destinations from selected Finnish ports, 1883–1913

Oulu

To:	1883		1886		1890		1894	
	No.	Tons	No.	Tons	No.	Tons	No.	Tons
Finnish ports	18	5,474	28	8,821	50	16,245	18	6,375
Russian ports	36	12,351	75	12,601	3	891	27	9,092
Swedish ports	8	1,432	10	3,236	3	553	3	790
To:	1898		1902		1906		1910	
Finnish ports	10	4,107	14	6,419	10	5,148	21	12,178
Russian ports	24	8,774	23	8,239	13	3,741	14	4,563
Swedish ports	19	4,169	–	–	1	324	7	168

Vaasa

To:	1883		1886		1890		1894	
Finnish ports	78	18,969	75	22,854	122	36,618	77	26,583
Russian ports	40	13,377	46	14,595	11	3,378	33	10,412
Swedish ports	92	20,968	90	18,911	71	13,955	59	12,518
To:	1898		1902		1906		1910	
Finnish ports	89	34,148	60	24,547	55	23,106	75	35,495
Russian ports	26	9,264	23	8,337	8	2,583	14	4,171
Swedish ports	75	14,187	50	9,750	98	15,790	84	15,553

Turku

To:	1883		1886		1890		1894	
Finnish ports	73	22,233	125	36,857	199	67,902	141	50,258
Russian ports	135	40,265	150	43,435	101	32,405	144	48,101
Swedish ports	92	25,856	93	29,438	92	28,229	172	49,940
To:	1898		1902		1906		1910	
Finnish ports	120	61,871	94	48,785	95	53,725	140	79,897
Russian ports	114	43,590	7	2,706	8	2,609	12	6,286
Swedish ports	135	54,892	178	74,003	138	56,544	261	38,534

Mariehamn

To:	1883		1886		1890		1894	
Finnish ports	5	1,199	17	4,055	58	11,977	58	9,873
Russian ports	–	–	–	–	–	–	43	14,300
Swedish ports	20	4,580	20	4,364	57	11,757	99	23,721

Mariehamn

To:	1898		1902		1906		1910	
	No.	Tons	No.	Tons	No.	Tons	No.	Tons
Finnish ports	63	21,105	79	33,282	75	31,264	120	77,402
Russian ports	34	13,815	3	968	12	4,140	17	7,985
Swedish ports	81	29,563	65	27,316	109	45,494	93	48,709

Helsinki

To:	1883		1886		1890		1894	
Finnish ports	105	17,703	140	29,383	239	73,216	95	36,139
Russian ports	147	42,815	185	48,846	194	54,519	266	74,165
Swedish ports	80	23,467	104	35,348	41	15,579	134	45,271

To:	1898		1902		1906		1910	
Finnish ports	125	59,805	106	47,204	116	54,219	162	90,121
Russian ports	222	85,644	154	52,577	164	66,048	146	66,393
Swedish ports	117	55,318	95	40,255	100	42,371	117	59,508

Viipuri

To:	1883		1886		1890		1894	
Finnish ports	18	1,584	27	2,352	209	34,471	118	19,666
Russian ports	54	8,294	53	5,887	55	6,840	123	26,405
Swedish ports	5	860	–	–	–	–	–	–

To:	1898		1902		1906		1910	
Finnish ports	58	13,363	24	8,770	35	6,192	44	14,799
Russian ports	99	24,404	43	5,499	68	9,536	80	8,483
Swedish ports	5	670	2	541	–	–	–	–

Source: Finnish Official Shipping Statistics, ser. I, foreign trade and shipping, 1883–1902; ibid., ser I B, shipping, 1903–1910.

On a longer run, however, owners of coastal steamers were not too badly hit. Traffic between St Petersburg and Stockholm and, in particular, between Turku and Stockholm was increasing. To no small degree this was the result of emigration which was growing both from Finland and northwestern Russia. This demand is clearly reflected in the shipping statistics. For example, the annual number of steamer departures from Turku for Stockholm increased from some ninety to over 150 between the mid-1880s and mid-1890s (see table 2). In this first phase, companies moved tonnage from Bothnian lines to Stockholm-St Petersburg or Turku-Stockholm lines, and the growth of shipping space may have occasionally exceeded actual demand. In the next phase, however, older tonnage was replaced with bigger and newly-built ships, in particular on the Turku line, and the number of departures fell at first while aggregate tonnage increased substantially. Just before the First World War even departures started to increase anew and, in terms of tonnage, the traffic grew more than five times larger than it had been in the mid-1880s.[17]

The growth of the Stockholm lines more than compensated for the fading of Bothnian traffic. Yet, these changes resulted in a transformation of coastwise shipping. The long lines between St Petersburg and Stockholm had, by virtue of calling at many intermediate Finnish ports, been important in linking domestic ports together. Now, as the ships visited only a few major ports, they lost this function and became mediators of longer range connections only. Thus, a kind of natural division of labour was established between railways and shipping.

The transformation, however, had one by-effect which actually led to an increase in coastal connections. As very few regular lines calling at most of the coastal towns remained, the connections of southwestern Finland, and particularly those in the archipelago, suffered. Therefore, a number of new short and middle range lines were established between Hanko and Uusikaupunki as well as between the mainland and Aaland Islands. They not only compensated for the disappearance of longer coastal lines but even improved short-distance services over the former levels. According to newspaper announcements, the number of local archipelago liners in the vicinity of Turku increased from six in 1885 to ten in 1895 and thirteen in 1905.[18] Similar increases in local traffic also took place around Helsinki and certain other larger coastal towns. Unfortunately, there are no statistics which reveal the actual number of such small passenger and cargo vessels. It is, however, indicative that the number of small steamers below 100 net tons increased at a good rate from the 1870s onwards. Although this category included steam barges which were used for carrying sawn wood to loading ports, it seems quite possible that the number of »genuine« small coasters increased from something like ten vessels in 1875 to at least fifty in the early 1910s.[19] Shipping statistics also suggest a substantial increase in »pure« domestic traffic: between 1894 and 1913, for example, the number of registered entrances, excluding inland shipping, grew from 6,900 net tons to 45,800. Yet, compared with »cabotage mixte«, which was mainly concerned with the long, foreign bound coastal lines, these were modest figures: at best only two per cent of the latter.[20]

[17] LINDBERG, Ångbåtssjöfart, pp. 243–76; Br. SUVIRANTA, Suomen Höyrylaiva Osakeyhtiö 1883–1958, Helsinki 1958, pp. 45–6.

[18] Yrjö KAUKIAINEN, The Transition from Sail to Steam in Finnish Shipping, in: The Scandinavian Economic History Review 28 (1980), p. 175.

[19] KAUKIAINEN, Sailing into Twilight, appendix I.

[20] Finnish Official Statistics, ser. I and IB. Figures for domestic shipping also include shipping by sailing vessels, but their proportion can only be determined overall (in 1894, about 18 % and in 1913, about 52 % of entrances) but not excluding inland traffic. The

In summary, it can be concluded that in Finland, with no massive domestic coastal traffic like the British coal trade, the modernization of coastal shipping started with passenger and goods traffic on steamers. Thus, it competed with existing land transport rather than shipping by sail. This very fact, however, made it sensitive to the development of railways and, therefore, the great reduction of north-bound (Bothnian) coastal lines was not unexpected. On the other hand, long coastal lines bound for St Petersburg and/or Stockholm managed to retain a good share of the market, at least as long as emigrant traffic via Sweden was lively. Services between Finland and Sweden, in particular, increased after the turn of the century.

Table 3: The development of »coastal« tonnage, 1865–1913 (sailing vessels of 20–100 net tons, steamships of 20–200 net tons, excluding inland districts)

| | Sailing vessels | | steamships | | | |
| | 20–100 | | 20–100 | | 100–200 | |
	No.	Net tons	No.	Net tons	No.	Net tons
1865	730	29,059	10	555	6	836
1875	671	29,031	16	847	11	2,125
1885	631	26,338	38	1,790	10	1,567
1895	694	29,722	59	2,748	15	2,102
1905	881	37,962	74	3,271	22	2,995
1913	912	40,474	04	4,541	22	3,201

Source: Yrjö Kaukiainen, *Sailing into Twilight* (Jyväskylä, 1991), appendix table I.

Traditional coastal traffic by sailing vessels fared quite differently. »Peasant« shipping to Sweden with firewood, fish and other farm produce diminished substantially during the 1820s, 1830s and 1840s; this, however, had nothing to do with the development of new steamer lines but was a direct consequence of the gradually increasing customs barrier between Finland and Sweden. Even later, Swedish exports remained fairly stagnant but they were still able to support a substantial fleet of small sailing vessels on the Aaland Islands and the southwestern Finnish coasts. On the other hand, firewood exports to St Petersburg grew almost continuously, as did the trade with stone and a few other building materials. From the 1880s onwards, in particular, the tonnage of sailing coasters increased substantially (see table 3). Thus, the development of »modern« and »traditional« coastal shipping were quite independent phenomena, in fact, it seems clear that these sectors depended on

great increase of steamers' overall percentage suggest in any case that they even increased in short-distance coastal traffic.

different, and separated, markets. While steamers carried passengers and premium rate general cargo, traditional small sailing vessels were loaded with cheap primary products, which could never have generated enough income on more expensive tonnage. Thus, while the separation of markets was unusually clear cut, it was more or less parallel with the overall division of labour between steam and sail.

Map 3: Western European ports in 1914
        (Ports shown are those mentioned in the text)

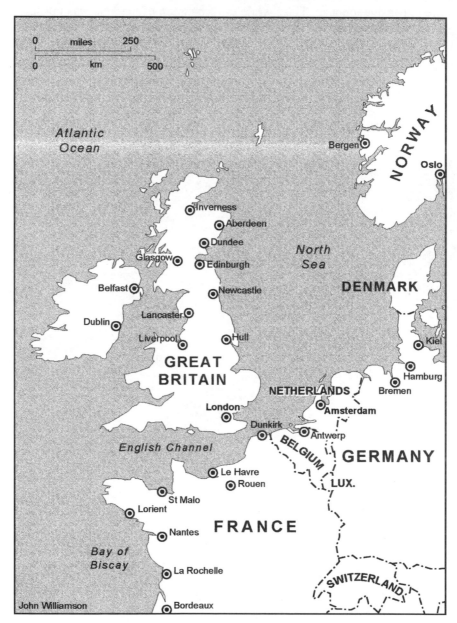

7

FROM COASTER TO STEAMER: COASTAL TRADE AND THE BIRTH OF STEAM SHIPPING IN SCOTLAND

GORDON JACKSON

Relative to its land area, Scotland has one of the longest coastlines in Europe. It also has one of the most difficult terrains and on the west very many islands, both inhibiting long-distance land communications. Roads outside the Central Belt from Glasgow to Edinburgh were minimal until well into the eighteenth century, and most of the rivers were navigable by large vessels for short distances only. Several of them supported ports adjacent to good agricultural land, especially Inverness, Aberdeen, Montrose and the small ports of the south west, but in truth the developing Scottish economy between 1750 and 1850 was not a heartland looking outwards so much as a periphery consisting of ports and coastal regions looking inwards when necessary, but more interested generally in trading among themselves. All the large towns were river- or sea-ports.

Most smaller ports on the open coast had grown up to service their immediate hinterlands, and were only part-time commercial traders. It is worth emphasising, because often forgotten, that fishing played important direct and indirect roles in their coastal trade. Ports commonly augmented agricultural poverty with the produce of simple fishing by line or trap, working from their own harbours or from satellite fishing villages which were either a subsidiary part of the ports themselves or neighbouring hamlets in the crofter-fishing tradition. Either way, because surplus fish caught in isolated areas was almost always entered into trade from commercial ports, and was often caught for this purpose rather than for subsistence, the creation of fishing villages by landowners eager to raise their income or care for their crofters added to coastal transactions. In fact most of the small ports were concerned chiefly in shipping herring or salmon and importing salt and staves. Montrose, for instance, received herring and cured cod and salmon from Johnshaven, Usan and Ferryden, for shipment to the industrial towns and London, and iced salmon and live lobsters from the 1780s[1]; Cellardyke sent pickled cod to

---

[1] Bruce WALKER, The salmon industry, p. 198, and David G. ADAMS, Sea fishing before 1800, in: Gordon JACKSON/S. G. E. LYTHE (eds.), The Port of Montrose, Tayport 1993, p. 230.

London and Liverpool and barrelled smoked haddock to Glasgow, Liverpool and on to Manchester; St Monans sent cured fish to London and fresh fish to Edinburgh.[2] Newhaven and Fisherrow, close by Edinburgh, thrived on serving the capital's market, while Peterhead shipped mostly to the Forth and to London. By far the most important development was the subsidized capitalist herring fishery encouraged in the second half of the eighteenth century by a mercantilist State to earn foreign exchange in the Baltic. The fishing villages created in response, especially Tobermory (Mull), Lochbay (Skye) and Ullapool (on the north west coast), became more or less out-stations for the merchants of Glasgow, though some shipped directly to West India merchants in London.[3] On the east coast the Forth ports were dominant in the »commercial« herring trade, and merchants there were active along the coast. Indeed, by the 1780s the Northumberland Fishing Company was also trading on the north east coast.[4] Only in the most expensive sort of fishing, for delivery fresh to the urban markets, were the boats likely to be based in important ports such as Greenock, but Coull has pointed out that as fishing became more commercial in the nineteenth century it tended to concentrate in fewer ports where coastal or foreign trade could be more easily organized.[5]

There were other aspects of the inter-relationship between the commercial ports and the seaside villages. The »Silver Darlings« also provided an important reservoir of men to cover seasonal fluctuations in coastal, and sometimes foreign-going, shipping. More directly, fishing boats, including heavy rowing-boats, were used to carry Fife coal to ports such as Montrose and Dundee[6], while on the west coast the smaller island and highland boats brought dairy produce and fish to exchange for manufactures, coal and luxuries in the major centres. On the other hand, colliers occasionally went fishing.[7] Finally, a direct and not-inconsiderable contribution to coastal traffic was made by peasants, principally on the west coast, who gathered kelp, an important source of alkali used in the manufacture of soap and glass. It was sold chiefly by landowners acting through agents in Glasgow, Liverpool, Newcastle and Hull, where shipping, insurance and sales were arranged.[8]

What has been said so far relates chiefly to the open coastline. Fortunately there were three large estuaries, the Tay, Forth and Clyde, penetrating deep

---

[2] P. SMITH, The Lammas Drave and the Winter Herrin': a history of the Herring Fishing from East Fife, Edinburgh 1985, p. 15.

[3] M. GRAY, The Highland Economy, 1750–1850, Edinburgh 1957, pp. 107–20.

[4] J. R. COULL, The Sea Fisheries of Scotland, Edinburgh 1996, pp. 33–49, 84–6.

[5] Ibid., p. 90.

[6] ADAMS, in Port of Montrose, ch. 10, p. 138.

[7] E. GRAHAM, The Shipping Trade of Ayrshire, 1689–1791 (= Ayrshire Monographs No. 8), Ayr 1991, p. 15.

[8] GRAY, Highland Economy, p. 129.

into the country, nurturing their more promising regional economies. Their major ports were the foci of the country's agricultural and industrial development, engrossing almost the entire foreign trade during the period of industrialisation. They could reach, by coasters, sloops, carriers' carts or rowing boats, much of the most fertile and mineral-bearing land. In the mid-eighteenth century Dundee, near the mouth of the Tay, succeeded the up-river port of Perth as the gateway for Perthshire as well as the lands both north and south of the river, and was fast developing as a linen town. Leith, on the Forth, was both the port for the capital, Edinburgh, and a major outlet for minerals and agricultural goods from the eastern part of the Central Belt of Scotland. The west of the country was served through the Clyde, dominated by Glasgow as a great transatlantic trading port developing into an industrial giant, and also having many minor ports shipping agricultural produce or Ayrshire coal. Technically Glasgow's trade went through its down-river satellites at Port Glasgow and Greenock, and some of its shipping was serviced by places such as Ayr, so its foreign trade inevitably included a coastal, or at least an estuarial, component.[9] Almost all the small ports obtained imports and sent exports via these hubs, or traded with each other; it is impossible to separate the beneficial effects of foreign trade from the admittedly dependent, but still dynamic, coastal trade. Indeed, coastal traffic was dominant, by volume if not by value, in most Scottish ports, and to this must be added the very important trade with Ireland, which was counted as foreign until the 1820s and as coastal thereafter. So far as most places were concerned it was not a matter of choice whether they were supplied by the coastal trade. When, in the middle of the eighteenth century, one of Scotland's greatest magnates, the Duke of Argyll, was building his castle and planned town at Inveraray, on Loch Fyne, it was almost impossible to attract cargoes of timber directly from Scandinavia or Russia, and not particularly easy to secure shipments from, or via, merchants in Leith or Glasgow.[10]

On shortbread tins the Scots burn peat; in real life most burned coal, and, as in England, this was a major component of coastal trade. It supported a good deal of the Clyde shipping servicing the strong Scottish-Irish link, and though places such as Glasgow had their own coal, the ability to ship it along both coasts encouraged or initiated iron works and forges, salt pans, maltkilns and limekilns. In Montrose, for instance, the abolition of duty on shipments of Scottish coal in 1793 initiated the manufacture of salt, bricks and tiles, and the

---

[9] Ayrshire vessels, for instance, were involved in Glasgow's tobacco trade, at least until the 1770s, and one of the leading nineteenth century shipowning families, the Allans, came from Saltcoates; GRAHAM, The Shipping Trade, pp. 22, 35.

[10] I. G. LINDSAY/M. COSH, Inveraray and the Dukes of Argyll, Edinburgh 1973, pp. 106–19. Some of this problem may have originated from the difficulty with which the duke raised ready money from his 8,000 square miles (including some water!) of Argyll.

burning of lime.[11] There were more direct consequences of the coal trade. It required the creation of a mass of wagonways and several major canals[12], and it was the coastal collier which first demanded port facilities at such places as Ayr, Troon, Ardrossan, Alloa and Methil. In Ayrshire, where shipowners in the eighteenth century were said to regulate shipments in their own interest, two coal owners spent around £100,000 each on developing their ports of Troon and Ardrossan.[13] Shipping figures are scanty, but east coast ports imported annually 150,000 tons of Scottish and 120,000 of English coal in 1810–15, and the trend was rising.[14] By 1840 Ayrshire was shipping some 345,000 tons of coal, chiefly to Ireland.[15]

Added to these trades were others which, while not special to Scotland, were more noticeable there than in England. The west coast highlands and islands depended for anything other than barest self-sufficiency on trade with Glasgow which rose as a great warehousing emporium for this external hinterland as much as for America. Some places were not even self-sufficient. Kilmartin, a few miles north of Crinan, could feed itself for only seven months in the year. »This country, and all the West Coast,« it was said of Gairloch, »are supplied in the Summer with meal, by vessels that come from the different ports at a distance; such as Caithness, Murray, Peterhead, Banff, Aberdeen, Greenock, etc.«[16] Indeed, imports of grain or meal were essential for the survival of large sections of the highland and islands population, certainly after c.1750.[17] The potato offered a more nutritious alternative and enabled population to grow from the 1820s, but the Scottish equivalent of the Irish Famine of the 1840s was more easily relieved because it occurred in the maritime regions of the west where the traditionally strong coastal trading network had been revolutionized by coastal steamers. In the words of T. M. Devine, »It was modern technology in the form of steam propulsion for ships which helped to save the people of the region from the full horrors of a pre-industrial subsistence crisis«.[18]

Shipping on the west coast was not all one-way traffic. In normal times men from Argyll brought oats, butter and rough woollens, while hams and eggs

---

[11] ADAMS, in Port of Montrose, ch. 10, p. 138.

[12] B. DUCKHAM, A History of the Scottish Coal Industry, 1700–1815, Newton Abbot 1970, pp. 217, 222–34.

[13] Ibid., pp. 93, 74.

[14] Ibid., p. 233. In fact most Scottish coal went to Edinburgh, and most of the English went to Inverness, Aberdeen, Montrose and Dundee, partly by usage as Scottish coal was taxed north of the Tay until 1793; ibid., pp. 230, 367.

[15] C. A. WHATLEY, »The finest place for a lasting colliery«: coal mining enterprise in Ayrshire, 1600–1849, in: Ayrshire Collections, vol. 14, no. 2 (1983), pp. 58–61.

[16] Old Statistical Account of Scotland, quoted in GRAY, Highland Economy, p. 43.

[17] GRAY, pp. 42–4.

[18] T. M. DEVINE, The Great Highland Famine, Edinburgh 1988, p. 114.

came from Ireland. Medium-sized boats of *c.* 20–50 tons, sometimes those used to carry kelp, ferried black cattle over from the western isles to begin their long walk to the trysting place at Falkirk and then down to England. Easdale and Luing, on the other hand, sent slates for the intense urbanization of the west of Scotland. It was to facilitate this western coastal trade and encourage development through extending the Glasgow network that the Crinan Ship Canal was cut through the Kintyre Peninsula at the turn of the century. Moreover, within the Clyde itself there was much general traffic, bringing goods to Glasgow or taking them to the ports along the coast to the English border.

On the other side of the country there was also extensive traffic on the Tay between Dundee and Perth, an important social and agricultural centre. More seriously, the agricultural revolution along the banks of the Tay itself owed everything to the coastal trade. One place, it was said, had »a sort of harbour ... Lime from Sunderland is frequently landed at it ... Grain too is shipped from it ... and of late years large quantities of potatoes for the London market.«[19] In the opposite direction the Dundee, Perth & London Shipping Company was so eager to capture the grocery trade of its hinterland that it offered to pay the Dundee shore dues of any groceries imported coastwise for towns in the counties of Forfar and Fife.[20] Coasters were also active wherever there was progress within the confines of the Firth of Forth. The agricultural development there aimed not least at feeding Edinburgh (and supplying its breweries), while Lothian and Fife coal fuelled the hearths and industries of the whole coast and probably employed more shipping space than any other commodity.

Finally, there was the longer-distance trade with England, already alluded to. On the east coast the Edinburgh elite demanded metropolitan luxuries, and English coal, lime and beer was needed further north. A large amount of Dundee's linen was exported via English ports. By the end of the century the old export staples of linen, food and stone were augmented by the industrial products of Carron, manufacturers of the carronade, which found their way to Carron Wharf on the Thames and the naval and military depôts. On the west coast there was also a trade in heavy industrial products, again encouraged by the access to fuel, in this case charcoal. From the 1720s English-based iron companies shipped iron ore north to furnaces established at Corpach, Bonawe and Furnace, and then shipped the pig iron down to Bristol and Lancashire, though their success was not great because of the distances involved. When

---

[19] Longforgan parish (1838), New Statistical Account of Forfarshire, Edinburgh 1845, p. 418. See also G. JACKSON, Trade and Shipping of Dundee, 1780–1850, Dundee 1991, chapters 1 and 4.

[20] Dundee Regional Archives, GD/DPL/1/1, Sederunt Book, 5 March 1829.

statistics become available, in 1846, 250,000 tons of iron was being shipped south along the coast each year.[21]

There was less West of Scotland interest in London sea trade, distance imposing a comparative disadvantage in all but East Indian imports (which were a London monopoly until 1813), but Glasgow was a leading player in the industrial revolution, with a deep interest in cotton textiles and the metal industries. The circumstances of transatlantic trade had, from the early eighteenth century, required the movement of sugar, tobacco, cotton and other goods between Glasgow and Liverpool, usually northwards, but in the opening up of Canada it was Glasgow in the lead in the timber trade and in the production of ships which were to be of great significance after 1815. In the cotton industry itself there was considerable inter-connection, and by the 1830s Glasgow and Manchester were often seen as twin pillars of the industry.[22]

Various aspects of the growth and importance of coastal trade are best discussed in terms of tonnage of coasters entering and leaving Scottish ports, see table 1. In the mid-eighteenth century trade was small by English standards and concentrated heavily on the east coast, though Bo'ness was the eastern gateway for Glasgow. By the end of the American Revolutionary War traffic had risen by about a third, chiefly because of a growth in the old distribution trades, the rapid rise of coal shipment and the exchange of manufactures for grain. Growth continued very strongly, reaching 466,000 tons inward and 431,000 outwards in 1791.[23] During the classic Industrial Revolution period from c.1780 to 1840 the movement of agricultural produce was very important for feeding the rising industrial regions in both Scotland and England but it was also significant after the Napoleonic War that coastal shipping began to open up and encourage growth in the Scottish periphery, especially around the turn of the century.[24] The somewhat slower growth in sail tonnage by 1841 is notable, but by then there was the important addition of the steam trade. The domination of Glasgow, Leith, Dundee and Aberdeen is also very clear.

The major port cities were likely to benefit from economic advance within their expanding regions and by inter-port transactions, but actually a good deal of the increase came from the English connection. It is not meaningful to talk of a purely Scottish coastal maritime economy in this period, but it is important to note that Scotland was isolated from England in terms of cheap

[21] R. H. CAMPBELL, Scotland since 1707, Oxford 1971, p. 127.

[22] The comparisons are made in G. WHITE, Glasgow and Manchester considered with reference to their means of growth, Glasgow 1847.

[23] PRO, Customs 17/12.

[24] PRO, T36/13/9, Vessels entering and clearing coastwise at specified ports, Scotland, 1788–1805.

Table 1: Tonnage of coasters inwards and outwards
at leading Scottish ports, 1764–1850 ('000 tons)

	1764 sail		1784 sail		1841				1850			
					sail		steam		sail		steam	
	In	Out	In	Out	In	Out	In	Out	In	Out	In	Out
Aberdeen	20	18	34	16	137	85	49	51	142	75	112	148
Alloa	4	16	22	57	14	60	8	0	8	27	0	0
Ayr	0	1	1	1	13	66	5	3	9	61	36	36
Banff	0	0	0	0	32	26	0	0	40	25	0	0
Campbeltown	2	6	6	7	15	6	18	17	23	4	9	10
Dumfries	0	0	2	3	54	30	62	28	35	14	53	52
Bo'ness	62	79	48	91	14	81	0	0	5	50	0	0
Dundee	16	7	22	10	134	60	33	31	152	46	30	29
Inverness	7	4	5	7	49	50	15	17	61	47	41	45
Irvine	0	0	3	2	11	133	4	1	8	178	68	72
Kirkcaldy	1	7	4	7	39	64	0	0	50	67	0	0
Kirkwall	0	0	2	3	13	14	0	0	9	7	19	19
Leith	27	9	44	19	150	113	131	139	85	68	191	191
Lerwick	1	3	1	1	7	8	7	7	9	9	10	10
Montrose	13	4	31	7	71	28	14	13	38	17	5	4
Perth	10	4	25	11	31	37	0	0	27	20	0	0
Wick	0	0	0	0	23	28	9	9	29	20	28	25
»Glasgow«	6	6	30	18	259	224	288	235	181	221	321	320
All ports	185	178	307	289	1,120	1,158	646	553	1,043	1,028	984	1,019

Sources: PRO, T36/13/7, »Account of . . . vessels entered and cleared out . . . to 5 Jan
1785«; British Parliamentary Paper 1842 (15), XXXIX, p. 625; BPP 1851 (92) LII, p. 201.

Notes: (1) »Glasgow« includes Glasgow, Port Glasgow and Greenock.
(2) Irish trade was counted as foreign in the eighteenth century. If Irish trade had
been counted as coastal, the figures for the Ayrshire ports would be c.10,000
in 1764 and c.19,000 in 1784.

inland transport; there were no canals, or even decent roads connecting the
two, though Glasgow Corporation, for instance, frequently contributed to the
building or upkeep of roads and bridges to the south for light goods and mail
purposes. With industrialization proceeding all over Britain, and the English
and Scottish economies interlocking, serious trade demanded regular long-
distance coastal shipping. Before the end of the eighteenth century traffic
along the east coast was sufficient for regularity to enter the route between
Aberdeen, Dundee and Edinburgh, followed by »lines« established by the
Aberdeen & Hull, Aberdeen, Leith & Clyde, Aberdeen & London, Dundee &

Hull and Dundee, Perth & London Shipping Companies.[25] Their employment of fast, time-tabled smacks encouraged agriculture and industry in places such as Dundee, with its heavy reliance on exporting through Glasgow and London, and such companies as Carron, with its agency in Glasgow, its London wharf and, for greater efficiency, its own shipping which in 1797 made up over half the coasters leaving Grangemouth, the new port at the end of the Forth & Clyde Canal.[26] By 1820 there were twenty three vessels linking Glasgow via the Forth & Clyde Canal with Aberdeen, Dundee, Montrose, Falkirk, Grangemouth, Leith, Newcastle, Hull and London, and another twenty two linking Greenock with Leith and London.[27] The Dundee & Hull Shipping Company was in 1829 advertising its weekly service linked to Manchester, all places on the Rochdale and Huddersfield canals, »and by river vessels to all inland places communicating with the rivers Humber and Trent«.[28]

Equally important was the growth of passenger traffic, for business and pleasure, which directly assisted enterprise through movement of commercial travellers. »Parties come from Glasgow [by sea]«, it was said of Aberdeen in 1839, »to sell goods all over the North of Scotland«.[29] There was also some benefit through the subsidy obtained by the relatively high rates for passengers compared with goods, especially on the long runs from Aberdeen, Dundee and Leith to Hull and London.

On the west, coastal liners were introduced to the Irish trade, not least by the Post Office via the new packet station at Portpatrick, but the chief of them linked Glasgow and, via the Forth & Clyde Canal, Leith, Dundee and Aberdeen to the international marketing skills of Liverpool and the industrial region of Lancashire. It is difficult to exaggerate this connection; in 1847 coastal shipping entering Glasgow from Liverpool equalled 75 per cent of that from the whole of Scotland and more than that from Ireland.[30] The Glasgow & Liverpool Shipping Company was chiefly a Glasgow affair, but the Clyde & Liverpool Shipping Company had shareholders in Liverpool, Manchester, Rochdale, Huddersfield and Leeds.[31] These and other companies fell increas-

---

[25] JACKSON, Trade and Shipping of Dundee, chapter 4, is a discussion of the role of DP&L in the growth of Dundee's economy in this period. The Scottish companies shared many characteristics with those of London, Liverpool and Hull.

[26] H. HAMILTON, An Economic History of Scotland in the Eighteenth Century, Oxford 1963, p. 214.

[27] Gordon JACKSON, New Horizons in Trade, in: T. M. DEVINE/Gordon JACKSON (eds.), Glasgow, vol. I: Beginnings to 1812, Manchester, 1995, pp. 230–1.

[28] Dundee Advertiser, 14 May 1829.

[29] Anon., Aberdeen Harbour: Evidence and proceedings in the Committee of the House of Commons in regard to the Aberdeen Harbour Bill, Aberdeen 1839, p. 212.

[30] Glasgow City Archives, Clyde Navigation Trust, T-CN 6/1. See also Gordon JACKSON/Charles MUNN, Trade commerce and finance, in: W. H. FRASER/Irene MAVER (eds.), Glasgow, vol. II: 1830–1912, Manchester 1996, pp. 52–96.

[31] Glasgow City Archives, Glasgow Shipping Registers, 3/1822–6/1822.

ingly under the control of shipping agents. They were, in effect, modern shipping businesses at a time when most foreign-going shipping was still owned by individuals or single ship companies in the transition stage between merchanting and shipowning.[32]

Coastal lines were crucial for the development of the general coastal trade, as opposed to bulk goods such as coal and slates carried by tramps. As manufacturing expanded in the major centres there was a bottleneck constricting the flow at the port on the seaward side. The most important and far reaching aspect of the modernization of coastal shipping was therefore the rapid adoption of steam power. As the leading coastal lines took up the technical challenge their output, in terms of ton/miles, made a notable contribution to the economy. In simple tonnage terms the relatively small number of steamers were by 1841 accounting for about a third of total traffic, and almost half by 1850. They played little part in the coal trade, as is obvious from table 1, but had a tremendous impact on traffic of an industrial nature, especially of cottons, linens and metal goods, and, more surprisingly, greatly encouraged the trade in live cattle and sides of beef, potatoes, beer (which the Scots imported from Newcastle), and such things as furniture and groceries. The fresh salmon and lobster industry, of great importance to the east coast fisheries, was greatly enhanced by fast coastal steamers, which also, incidentally, facilitated the better deployment of foreign-going vessels by moving masters and crews rapidly between ports while leaving their vessels in the hands of less qualified coast crews. Steamers also carried part cargoes between ports and speeded up the receipt and despatch of imports and exports, with consequent reductions in inventory costs.

The river steamers not only carried trade, they created it, and their contribution is seen at its simplest in the proportion of additional active tonnage seen in table 1 and its relationship to the number of steamers in service. They also diminished the pressure of huge flocks of sailing coasters that were jamming the major ports and brought a new organization to the port industry. In comparative terms, in 1841 20,023 entrances were made by sailing coasters at Scottish ports, accumulating 1,119,564 tons (registered); 2,946 steamers accumulated 645,707 tons. By the middle of the century the tonnages were almost equal though steamers made up only a quarter of the vessels.[33]

The importance of coastal traffic in facilitating regional specialization and economic growth, by moving raw materials and foodstuffs, imports, exports and re-exports, was undeniably increasing after 1815. There was, however, another, equally important aspect of the relationship between coastal trade and

[32] In the deployment of shipping coastal owners were in fact moving towards modern shipowning; many Aberdeen vessels, for instance, went coasting in winter and to the Baltic in summer. Anon., Aberdeen Harbour, p. 188.

[33] Parliamentary Papers, 1843 (216) lii, 383 and 1843 (207) lii, 396.

economic growth. The new steam coasters which enabled traffic to grow so strongly were at the van of the technological revolution in transport and providing the experimental phase for steam power at sea. Although there had been earlier experiments with steam propulsion, the commercial steamship grew out of the technological infrastructure of Glasgow, where the cotton industry encouraged the manufacture of machines and steam engines to work them; James Watt was not the only Glaswegian who knew how to make and maintain a steam engine! There were 242 engines in Glasgow factories in 1825.[34] Not surprisingly, in 1812 one had been put into the experimental *Comet*, a tourist attraction to carry visitors from Glasgow to a health spa down river. Its success was not lost on those who shipped goods around the Clyde estuary.[35]

The most notable contribution of coastal transport to the development of Scotland's steamship-building industry was to nurture the experimental stage when engines were being perfected, and the transitional stage between river and sea when they were increased in power, stability and reliability. Several engineers turned to marine engine building, but it was the Napier family, especially Robert, who forged ahead, experimenting, sometimes to the consternation of his customers, with ever greater engines, constructed on solid engine beds, which enabled hull size to increase, with the resultant power and strength allowing the move from river to coast. This development took about twenty years, during which time Glasgow coastal steamers increased in size from 28 tons to over 500 gross, though the Scottish share should not be exaggerated. The early lead was soon reduced and by the late 1830s Scotland owned only a fifth of the British total, though she was building around a third.[36] However, building the steamers was only the start of a complex web of inter-related problems to be solved. The coastal trade also acted as the proving ground for steamship organisation and, moreover, stimulated a revolution in port facilities beginning in the 1830s.

Firstly, because they were expensive, there had to be a new system of ownership. Coastal steamers, even more than the sailing liners, introduced capitalist company ownership to the shipping industry. The smaller Clyde river traders were devoted to very specific routes and initially owned by large single-ship companies of three hundred or more people with a specific interest in carrying groceries, bread, wine or legal services to outlying places.[37] It was simply an extension of inland transport; indeed, owners objected to registering

---

[34] J. CLELAND, Historical Account of the Steam Engine, Glasgow 1825, pp. 38–45. Another 68 drove ships.

[35] Brian D OSBORNE, The Ingenious Mr Bell, Glendaruel 1995.

[36] Account of Number and Tonnage of Steamers Built and Registered, 1814–36, Parliamentary Papers 1837–8 (137) xlvii, 60.

[37] SRO, CE 59/1/5, Customs letter books, 23 Jun 1819.

them because »they never go to open sea«.[38] There were twenty four steamers
listed in 1820, 53 in 1825 and 73 by 1840[39], but already by 1819 the *Robert
Bruce* went on the Liverpool run, and this, like the long runs down the east
coast to Hull and London, demanded a new order of capital, since a steam line
required three vessels and at least one spare boiler. The Dundee, Perth and
London Shipping Company, for instance was capitalised at £38,045 on its
formation in 1826 when it owned thirteen smacks and ten sloops, and this was
raised to £50,000 in 1830. When the first two steamers were acquired in 1832
for £36,000, capital was raised by a further £31,750, though there was a
continual reliance on heavy borrowings, sometimes to pay dividends.[40] These
companies were organised by agents who had been involved in the earlier
sailing lines, and already included names that would become well known in
the shipping world. Both the City of Glasgow Steam Packet Company and the
Clyde Steam Navigation Company had a Donaldson and MacConnell in
Glasgow and two McIvers in Liverpool; Glasgow and Liverpool Steam Ship
Company had a Martin and two Burns in Glasgow and a Martin in Liverpool.
It was this incestuous combination of agents in the Irish, Liverpool and
Canadian sail trades which put together its combined experience in 1840 as
the Glasgow Proprietary of the British and North American Royal Mail Steam
Packet Company, more usually known as Cunard, of which the trustees were
George Burns, David McIver, James Donaldson and James Brown.[41] For
many years their impressive vessels pounded the route from Glasgow to
Liverpool.

Running a steam line was nothing like running a sailing line. Companies
needed the latest technology and speeds, and this, when the technology was
still experimental, required great skills in negotiating with engineers and shipbuilders. This was a problem on the Clyde, which had little experience
building sailing ships (all the big ones were imported from Canada where they
were built by Glasgow firms such as Pollok & Gilmour and Kidstones); the
hulls built for Napier by John Wood were so poor that eventually he brought
in a London shipbuilder to supervise construction. The superb records of the
Dundee, Perth & London Shipping Company (DP&L) show that their
Steamship Committee kept up a barrage of complaints and inspections which
tell us a great deal about how early steamers were built.[42] Capital costs were

[38] SRO, CE 59/1/5, Scottish Board of Customs, letter books, collector to board, 205,
Glasgow, 23 June 1819.

[39] Glasgow Directories, passim. (Some of these were tugs and »luggage boats«).

[40] See JACKSON, Trade and Shipping of Dundee, pp. 54–6.

[41] Glasgow City Archives, Glasgow Shipping Registers, 36/1840 *Unicorn*, 51/40
Britannia, 58/40 *Acadia*, 66/40 *Caledonia* and 92/40 *Columbia*.

[42] See G. JACKSON, Operational problems of the transfer to steam: Dundee, Perth &
London Shipping Company, 1820–1845, in: T. C. SMOUT (ed.), Scotland and the Sea,
Edinburgh 1992, pp. 154–81.

such that constant employment and maximum cargo were essential, and far worse than mechanical troubles, though these were common, were incursions by rivals. Sailing vessels sought to undercut steamers for low-value cargoes, and DP&L even competed with their own sailing smacks which continued in service to keep the others at bay. Pricing was difficult and subject to constant adjustment as other coastal lines sought to increase their routes or market share or, more seriously, one of the larger London – or Dublin – companies invaded another's hopefully natural monopoly. It was discovered that competition was ruinous to shipowners, who through price wars, takeovers and amalgamations eventually learned how to run shipping lines at a profit. Most obviously, there was safety in size, enabling a wealthy company to run at a loss, as DP&L did on occasions. A further problem was maximizing income through balancing different types of cargo, and it was soon realized in all the estuaries that people paid best. Steamers homed-in on Leith when George IV visited Edinburgh, and William Harriston, the »Steamboat Poet« contrasted the horror of road transport to the comfort of steamers »As through the yielding waves they ply . . . To reach their goal, then, turn and fly«; and a wag in the crowd shouted »Sir, you perhaps could plan a steam balloon, To make a pleasure voyage to the moon«.[43] The cream of profits came from passengers on top of cargo, and they were enticed by the most luxurious cabins or saloons; so coastal liners became floating hotels. »It is believed that the splendour of the saloons of these steam ships,« it was said of the Glasgow & Liverpool Steamship Company's *Manchester, Eagle* and *Unicorn*, in 1835, »are not equalled by those of any vessels afloat.«[44] DP&L might have disputed this claim. They saw their chief stewards as crucial to their operations, and paid them accordingly. Napier had a whole package deal involving advice of suitable library books – all big ones – and cutlery – all Berlin metal – so designed because comfortable passengers might still disembark with anything small or valuable. On excursions, steamers had bands and refreshments, and enjoyment was such that on the Clyde the Sabbatarians tried to stop them on Sundays in 1859.[45]

There was a further part to Napier's package. How did one drive a steamship? Few people knew, and they had to be taught, commonly on those Glasgow-Liverpool steamers in which Napier had an interest. Steamers still were dangerous, and DP&L at least discovered that the major problem was that their senior sailing masters who took over the steamers were frequently, or permanently, drunk when they rammed piers or thought they were off the Humber when they were actually off the Wash. It took a long time to train

[43] W. HARRISTON, The King's Arrival, Glasgow 1823.

[44] J. CLELAND, A Few Statistical Facts . . ., Glasgow 1836, p. 13.

[45] Glasgow City Archives, T-CN3/120, Memorial of ... Glasgow Working Men's Protection Society, 5 July 1859.

masters who would eventually move out with the larger steamers into oceanic trades. It was not even easy to train the office clerks and secure the necessary technical infrastructure. The training of managers and determining hierarchies of command were also serious problems solved by coastal lines ready for their adoption by foreign-going lines which were often controlled by the shipowners or agents who had cut their teeth on the coast.

There were other problems caused by steamers that were not automatically the responsibility of the owners. River ports could accommodate them by building a wooden or – more usual in Scotland – a stone pier, but large ports could not cope with their constant movement and rapid turnaround demands on harbour space and facilities. By the 1830s, in Glasgow, two or three steamers were arriving every half-hour and turning round in an hour or so. They did not blend easily with the old tubs dozing at the quays for weeks on end. They clogged up Glasgow harbour, which was occasionally »jammed in from side to side, so that vessels could neither get up nor down«[46], and very suddenly the berthing of vessels became an exact science and timetabled operations entered dock working as much as on the railways, and perhaps with more difficulty. Glasgow's steamship harbour had to be constructed in a hurry for coastal steamers, and in Dundee the newly planned docks had to be altered to cater for DP&L's steamers. The details of extended or altered facilities round the coast are endless, and must be added to the influences on the construction side of the economy, particularly since steam coasters' impact was felt only shortly after the completion of the first round of dock building during the Napoleonic war. In London, for instance, DP&L steamers were too large to enter the docks, and only three wharves were large enough to service them, so the developmental stage in the servicing of steamers on the Thames was stimulated by DP&L's contract with Mrs Hoare's Wharf.

The contribution of coastal trade to the Scottish economy was therefore twofold. It stimulated activity by offering greater services for regional specialization and also linked Scotland with the industrial regions of Lancashire and Yorkshire and the great London entrepôt. More so than in England, the Scottish coastal trade was the inspiration for the initial development of steam shipping. This in turn encouraged the technical and business perfection of the vast Clyde shipbuilding industry which was linked, not least, to the servicing of the very large steam-powered coastal trade that developed in the second half of the nineteenth century and a world class steam fleet second only to that of Liverpool.

[46] Glasgow City Archives, T-CN/11/1, Evidence of ... harbour master, Clyde Navigation Bill, 1840.

Acknowledgements

I am grateful to the British Economic and Social Research Council for supporting a research programme on which this paper is based.

8

LIGHT AND SHADE IN SPANISH COASTAL SHIPPING IN THE SECOND HALF OF THE NINETEENTH CENTURY

ANTONIO GÓMEZ-MENDOZA

Spain's coastal trade in modern times has hardly attracted the attention of scholars. With less than half a dozen works published, one might feel tempted to infer that this lack of curiosity has been motivated by the absence of primary sources. However, such a hasty conclusion would be far from the truth. Spain's coastal trade statistics rank among the finest in Europe. Detailed information is provided on tonnage shipped, both ingoing and outgoing for each of 140 ports, and on the nature of the trade in eighty commodity categories. The shipping aspects are also considered: numbers of ships, registered tonnage, size of crew as well as the nationality are given, all this for a long period of time running from 1857 until 1920.[1]

Why, then, has coastal trade attracted so little attention from economic historians of modern Spain? Coastal trade has been seen in the literature as a relatively minor mode of transport on three grounds. First, Spanish coastal shipping was fairly small by international standards. In that regard, tonnage shipped coastwise amounted to 55 per cent of the Italian in the 1880s.[2] Second, coastal trade was also small at a domestic level. Freight moved by coasters amounted to 12 per cent of the tonnage carried by railways over the period 1860–1920. It was therefore concluded that coastal shipping was unable to oppose competition from the railway.[3] Third, coastal trade was hampered by the backwardness of port infrastructure. Around the middle decades of the nineteenth century, docking in many ports of the country was quite risky. Moreover, the lack of lanterns and lighthouses impeded mooring after sunset. In most ports, the water depth was too shallow for the larger ships which were forced to drop anchor offshore. As a result, the cost of loading and unloading was pushed up.[4]

---

[1] Estadística del Comercio de Cabotaje en España, 1855–1913.

[2] Esperanza FRAX, Puertos y Comercio de Cabotaje en España, 1857–1934, Madrid 1981, p. 39.

[3] Esperanza FRAX/María J. MATILLA, Transporte, comercio y comunicaciones, in: Miguel ARTOLA (ed.), Enciclopedia de Historia de España, vol. 1, Madrid 1988, p. 220.

[4] Ibid., p. 219.

While some features of Spain's coastal trade can be readily accepted, there are other traits which invite reflection. Coastal trade moved a relatively small volume of freight when compared to other countries. For example, the 2.95 million tons of cargo shipped between the ports of Spain in 1910 accounted for less than 4 per cent of the tonnage carried in the United Kingdom.[5] On the other hand, aggregate tonnage shipped by Spanish coasters increased at a rate of 2.9 per cent *per annum* over the period 1860–1920. This rate was twice the Italian over the same period of time. As a result, coastal trade in both countries was almost on an equal footing by 1920. Moreover, coastal trade was spatially concentrated on a small number of ports. Indeed, eight harbours contributed more than half of the tonnage shipped coastwise. Adding the next seventeen harbours to the count increases this to 80 per cent.[6] This implies that traffic was minimal for the remaining 115 Spanish harbours. Concentration on a small number of ports is further enhanced when value data are substituted for volume. Barcelona represented nearly 23 per cent of Spain's coastal trade when measured in value terms. The eighteen busiest ports bring this percentage up to 85 per cent.[7]

Nonetheless, coasters were certainly less dynamic than railways. Their economic impact was also relatively modest when compared to road carriers, although they were far more innovative. Before the advent of the internal combustion engine, the technology of road transport was virtually stagnant with regard to vehicles, motive power or highway construction. On the contrary, coastal shipping shared all the major breakthroughs in maritime transport, such as the introduction of steam power and iron hulls or improvements in harbours and in docking facilities. Because of this contrast, there are grounds for believing that the current negative view on coastal trade has been grossly exaggerated.

The paper is divided into five sections. Section II discusses to what extent coastal shipping was successful in fighting the challenge posed by railways. It will be argued that coastal shipping and railways were complementary rather than antagonistic except for a portion of the Mediterranean seaboard. Coasters concentrated on a segment of the demand for transport services which was not adequately satisfied either by road carriers or railways. In a country deprived of inland water transport by river and canal, coastal shipping provided a cheap alternative which made possible the haulage of bulky and low value goods over long distances. It is argued in section III that the contribution of coastal

---

[5] John ARMSTRONG, The role of coastal shipping in UK transport: an estimate of comparative traffic movements in 1910, in: John ARMSTRONG (ed.), Coastal and Short Sea Shipping, Aldershot 1996, Table 6, p. 160.

[6] Along the Mediterranean coastline, Barcelona, Cádiz, Valencia and Sevilla were among the busiest ports. On the Atlantic shore, Gijón, Bilbao, Avilés and Santander. See FRAX, Puertos y Comercio, p. 41.

[7] Ibid., p. 43.

shipping to the formation of the domestic market was more significant than has hitherto been suggested. Coastal shipping developed ahead of demand since it benefited from the ships displaced from seaborne foreign trade. Incapable of meeting the competition of foreign vessels on international routes, Spain's merchant fleet resorted to coastal services under the umbrella of tariff protection. Throughout the period, it had excess capacity which pushed down freight rates. Nonetheless, the potential benefits of this process were checked by a cluster of factors of a geographic, economic and political nature which are examined in section IV.

II

The current view of the inability of coasters to challenge railway competition needs to be qualified.[8] I will use three arguments to cast doubt on such a position. First, the rate of increase of tonnage shipped coastwise increased twice as fast in 1891–1931 as in 1857–91.[9] The major railway trunk lines did not come into full operation before 1890. Second, any inference on the performance of coastal shipping and railways drawn from a comparison of tonnage carried by either operator will undoubtedly be biased in favour of the latter. This is explained by the fact that railways and coasters operated in different markets. Thus, while the former concentrated on short haul traffic, coasters specialized in shipping freight over long distances on account of their lower rates. Estimates of tonnage are not an efficient measure of performance. Output in ton-kilometres is preferable.[10] Third, the star-like configuration of the railway network helps to explain why coasters and railways did not come into competition with each other. Priority was granted by the 1855 Railway Bill to trunk lines connecting Madrid, in the heart of Spain, to the major ports. Except for certain areas of the periphery where the track was laid along the coastline, trains and ships acted as feeders to each other. As a contemporary writer, J. de Bona, noted in 1863: »Just as road carriers have increased in numbers under the powerful spell of the railways ... the latter will exert a strong and prosperous influence on coastal trade. This is why coasters and railways are harmonious and inseparable means of transport rather than antagonistic.«[11]

[8] FRAX/MATILLA, Transporte Comercio, p. 220.

[9] FRAX, Puertos y Comercio, pp. 35–6.

[10] On the advantage of output over tonnage, see Antonio GÓMEZ-MENDOZA, Ferrocarriles y Cambio Económico en España, 1855–1913. Una nueva historia económica, Madrid 1982, Appendix B, pp. 252–3. Also ARMSTRONG, The role, pp. 148–9.

[11] J. de BONA, Los ferrocarriles y la navegación de cabotaje, in: Revista Ultramarina Peninsular de los Caminos de Hierro 8 (1863), p. 351.

In spite of the fact that about 3,500 km of track had been laid by 1863, Bona was not just referring to the many regions of the country still deprived of railway service. No broad gauge railway ever linked seaports on the northern coast owing to the abrupt topography. In that part of Spain, railways and coasters soon became complementary. In that regard, a joint tariff with a coastal liner company was established in 1869 by the Zaragoza, Pamplona and Barcelona Railway (ZPB) in order to carry seaborne merchandise from Vigo, Gijón and Santander to Bilbao and by rail from that point to Barcelona.[12] Until narrow gauge lines were laid west of Bilbao later in the century, no competition developed between rail and water. One of those lines linked La Robla at the heart of the Leon coalfields and Valmaseda, a township close to the Biscayan iron foundries. This line succeeded in attracting coal shipments away from the maritime route. In 1901, the British consul at Bilbao reported that »coastal trade has greatly diminished since railway communication with Bilbao and Santander has been established«.[13] However, except for this particular company, none of these lines ever posed a real threat to the hegemony of coastal shipping along the Atlantic shore. Because they were laid with a narrow gauge, transhipment operations were required at termini stations.

The Mediterranean seaboard was quite a different story. From 1865, trains were rumbling south of Gerona to Alicante. South from this city, however, coastal *sierras* hampered the laying down of railway track. It is thus necessary to distinguish two sections of this coastline. In the northern half, intense competition rapidly developed between the two means of transport. A special rate for the conveyance of nougat from Jijona to Barcelona was soon offered by the Madrid, Zaragoza and Alicante Railway (MZA) in order to avoid it being diverted to the sea route.[14] In the late 1880s, it was observed that »large quantities of goods are still forwarded by the rail lines running along the coast and competition is still carried on against the steam-ship trade«.[15] At the turn of the century, competition had not yet vanished. Attempts were made by MZA to retain the traffic in cotton goods from Barcelona to Murcia.[16] The Norte Railway Company (NORTE) also reacted against low shipping rates between Barcelona and Alcoy by cutting its fares for the conveyance of paper, cotton yarn, iron bars, drugs and mineral oil.[17] On the other hand, »no ship would ever be replaced by a locomotive« along the southern half of the Mediterranean coastline. Shipping provided an efficient alternative for freight

[12] ZPB Railway, Minutes, 29 July 1869.

[13] British Parliamentary Papers (BPP), 1901, LXXXIV, p. 634.

[14] MZA Railway, Rapports du Comité de Madrid, 25 Oct. 1872.

[15] BPP, 1888, CIII, p. 46.

[16] MZA, Comisión Mixta, session 26, 2 July 1909.

[17] NORTE, Comisión Mixta, session 26, 2 July 1909.

travelling to and from Andalusian ports since its rates were much cheaper than overland transport.

Commercial intercourse between seaports located on the Atlantic and Mediterranean shores was possible by either a water or rail route. From the second half of the 1860s onwards, Barcelona and Bilbao were linked by rail. Owing to the star-like rail network, however, any other journey from northern to southern Spain had to change trains at Madrid. In spite of this drawback, railways were able to offer passengers a faster service on account of the shorter distances involved and of their higher speed. Nonetheless, general merchandise was far less demanding than people on travel time. Since traffic over long distances was a profitable source of revenue, railway companies tried hard to divert freight away from coastal shipping. Available evidence shows that competition between trains and coasters remained intense throughout the period. As early as 1865, a contract was agreed between NORTE and neighbouring railway companies to share income accruing from the conveyance of freight from Bilbao to Alicante »pour organiser par chemin de fer, en passant par Madrid, une concurrence contre le cabotage«.[18] In 1871, the rate for moving flour from the heartland of the Castilian grain growing region into Barcelona was greatly reduced to fight the competition of the sea-borne route from Santander.[19] Thirty years later, NORTE still faced competition from the coastal trade on this same route.[20]

In brief, coastal shipping and railways complemented each other along the northern and southeastern coast because railway service was never available in those regions. On the northeastern Mediterranean coastline and on the inter-sea routes (Atlantic-Mediterranean), they competed with each other. Contrary to what has been stated in the literature, shipping was never eclipsed by railways on any of these routes which accounted for the lion's share of the output of coastal trade (see table 1 on p. 107).

III

In contrast to the railway, which gradually specialized in the conveyance of short to medium haul freight traffic, most coastal shipping was medium to long range. For the inter-sea traffic, the average haul amounted to 1,939 kms, nearly eleven times the average distance a ton of freight was carried by the railways. This sharp contrast in the average distance travelled by freight makes

[18] NORTE, Rapports du Comité de Paris, 2 Aug. 1865.

[19] The rail distance from Valladolid to Barcelona was 817 km. Grain travelling to Barcelona via Santander covered a distance of 2,770 km (270 km by rail and 2,500 km by sea). NORTE, Rapports du Comité de Madrid, 14 April 1871.

[20] NORTE, Comisión Mixta, session 27, 7 Oct. 1909.

irrelevant any comparison based on tonnage. An alternative measure of performance based on ton-km is far more accurate. In order to convert the actual tonnage shipped by coasters into output estimates, it is necessary to take into consideration the three trading zones in which coastal shipping performed: (i) Atlantic; (ii) Mediterranean and (iii) Inter-sea. However, coastal trade statistics fail to provide information about the actual freight flows within each zone. I will first deal with the tonnage active in each trading area. Second, an average haul, based upon the nautical distance between the busiest ports for each zone, will be applied to tonnage.

Disaggregated output estimates for the three trading areas can be found in table 1. Coastal trade along the Mediterranean coastline was greater than either of the other two trading zones, 1869 excepted. Inter-sea coastal trade was second to the Mediterranean, in spite of the fact that it ranked last when tonnage is used as a standard of comparison. Of course, this upgrading is explained by the long average hauls involved, almost three and nine times the distance over which freight was shipped on the Mediterranean and on the Atlantic routes respectively. When coastal shipping is matched against railways in terms of output, the picture is markedly different from the one suggested in the literature. From column 5 in table 1, it is clear that coastal trade cannot be described as a minor mode of transport in the period 1868–1885. In particular, railways were inferior to coasters in the years between 1868 and 1876. From 1877 onwards, they prevailed over coastal trade. However, the maximum loss experienced by the latter *vis-à-vis* the railway was quite modest, remaining under one third.

Was coastal shipping able to maintain its relative performance unaltered after 1885? An opinion cannot be readily delivered because of the lack of disaggregated data. As has already been mentioned, the rate of growth of tonnage shipped by coasters accelerated sharply after 1890. From 1.8 per cent per annum in 1857–90, tonnage increased at 4.2 per cent per annum in 1891–1913. This last rate was quite close to that attained by the railways. Assuming that the distribution of coastal trade in 1913 was identical to the one registered in 1881–85, coastal shipping output can be estimated at 2.45 billion ton-km, roughly 77 per cent of railway output in the same year.[21] This last percentage is similar to the average level registered in 1877–85.

[21] In 1881–5, the distribution of coastal trade was as follows: Atlantic 28.4 per cent; Mediterranean 55.5 per cent and Inter-sea 16.1 per cent. If these percentages are applied to a total of 3.25 million tons, coastal shipping output is estimated at 2.45 billion ton-kms provided the average hauls were similar to the ones assumed in table 1.

Table 1: The performance of Spanish coastal trade, 1868–1885
(million ton-km and percentages)

	Atlantic	Med.	Inter-sea	Total (CT)	CT/R
1868	32.7	253.6	183.2	469.5	107.4
1869	29.4	207.3	232.1	468.8	103.3
1870	40.2	389.4	279.4	709.0	146.9
1871	47.3	371.5	224.7	643.5	118.7
1872	48.4	450.0	238.7	737.1	115.9
1873	47.1	405.9	231.9	684.9	109.6
1874	38.2	437.2	267.0	742.4	151.1
1875	54.3	433.8	292.5	780.6	126.7
1876	48.0	385.6	281.3	714.9	101.8
1877	53.7	457.0	293.9	804.6	94.4
1878	54.8	377.3	300.2	732.3	87.2
1879	61.4	380.8	291.4	733.6	88.2
1880	68.0	443.3	314.2	825.5	79.1
1881	61.9	426.1	314.3	802.3	80.3
1882	65.1	364.1	320.1	749.3	70.6
1883	72.1	457.2	343.3	872.6	63.1
1884	72.1	456.7	391.3	920.1	68.8
1885	68.1	430.1	384.3	882.5	67.7

Notes and sources: Output in million ton-km has been estimated from tonnage arriving on each seaboard weighted by an average haul, traffic with the Balearic Islands excepted. For the Atlantic, 213 km was the distance between Bilbao and Gijón. For the Mediterrenean, 685 km was the distance between Alicante and Cádiz. For the inter-sea traffic, 1939 km was the distance between Alicante and Gijón. All these ports were the busiest in 1878. Col (1): Output for the Atlantic seaboard.; Col (2): Output for the Mediterranean seaboard.; Col (3): Output for the inter-sea traffic; Col (4): sum of cols 1–3. Col (5): Col (4) as a percentage of railway output which is not given in this table. *Estadística del Comercio de Cabotaje* (1868–85); Gómez-Mendoza (1982) Appendix B p. 253. I gratefully acknowledge the kind assistance of Dr J. R. García-López, Director of the Maritime Museum of Asturias, for supplying me with the nautical distances between the ports of Spain.

IV

In order to assess the role played by coastal shipping in the formation of Spain's domestic market, it is necessary to ascertain the composition of freight traffic for each of the three trading zones. Unfortunately, coastal trade statistics do not provide that kind of information. We must content ourselves with ingoing traffic for each coast in the period before 1887. It should be noted, however, that such traffic included flows originating on either seaboard, that is both short and long distance traffic.

The composition of coastal trade based exclusively on value data might be misleading. In this regard, three facts must be kept in mind. First, bulk cargoes were relevant whenever they absorbed a large proportion of total shipping capacity at any period of time. Second, official values used in coastal trade statistics were quite unreliable.[22] Finally, the presence of commodities with little significance in terms of tonnage might be overemphasized owing to large price differentials.

Inward traffic for Mediterranean and Atlantic ports between 1860 and 1885 in terms of volume is displayed in tables 2A and 2B. One common feature shared by the two coasts is that the bulk of shipping capacity was devoted to low value cargo. Indeed, high value added goods such as cotton yarn and cloth manufactured in the mills of the Barcelona district were shipped, though in small quantities, to other Mediterranean ports. Their absence on the Atlantic seaboard in table 2B indicates that cotton and wool manufactures were mostly carried overland by rail or road hauliers, to destinations at the heart of the peninsula.[23] Moreover, metals contributed less than 10 per cent of the inward traffic on each seaboard. However, their relative significance was more prominent in the Atlantic owing to the existence of iron foundries in Asturias and Bilbao. Apart from this general similarity, the staples of coastal trade were quite different on the two coasts. While foodstuffs prevailed in the Mediterranean, mineral ores were the dominant cargo in the Atlantic. Grain, flour, fish, legumes and wines accounted for over half of the freight disembarked at Mediterranean ports in 1860. Atlantic ports were supplied mostly with mineral ores and coal. Another striking difference between the two shores is the evolution of these staples in the medium run. Thus, table 2A shows that coastal trade in foodstuffs declined rapidly after 1865.

Ten years later, primary products amounted only to one quarter of the traffic into Mediterranean ports. As shipping capacity was released, it was promptly taken over by salt which represented at a maximum 44 per cent of coastal trade along this coast in 1875. By way of contrast, the relative scale of mineral ore shipments (coal included) was preserved throughout the period along the Atlantic coast. It is inferred from this contrasting evolution that coasters gradually specialized in the shipment of low price bulky commodities such as

---

[22] Price at a destination port was sometimes lower than at the port of origin. In 1880, for instance, outgoing coal shipments from Gijón were priced at 54.2 pesetas per ton. At Bilbao, Asturian coal was quoted at only 30 pesetas. See FRAX, Puertos y Comercio de Cabotaje en España, p. 69.

[23] Antonio GÓMEZ-MENDOZA, Ferrocarril y mercado interior (1874–1913), vol. 2, Madrid 1985, pp. 36 et passim.

Table 2A: Mediterranean coastal freight traffic by volume, 1860–1885 (%)

	1860	1865	1870	1875	1880	1885
Grain	19	20	11	9	9	10
Flour	14	7	4	7	4	5
Legumes	6	7	6	3	4	2
Fish	3	5	4	–	3	2
Wine	12	14	17	6	8	6
Metals	6	5	7	4	4	8
Timber & BM	6	7	5	2	3	3
Textiles	3	–	–	3	2	2
Coal	4	5	8	3	7	2
Minerals	2	3	4	7	4	–
Salt	5	4	4	44	38	36
Sample	80	77	76	90	86	80
'000 tons	515	447	401	662	730	623

Notes and sources: Inward traffic as a percentage of aggregate traffic along the Mediterranean seaboard by class of commodity. »BM« = building materials. *Estadística del Comercio de Cabotaje* (Madrid, 1857–87).

Table 2B: Atlantic coastal freight traffic by volume, 1860–1885 (%)

	1860	1865	1870	1875	1880	1885
Grain	14	8	8	6	5	4
Flour	4	9	6	11	6	5
Fish & Other	–	–	–	6	3	2
Wine	6	6	5	6	3	3
Coal	20	18	19	18	22	21
Minerals	9	9	9	9	18	18
Metals	4	7	4	9	5	10
Timber & BM	10	10	7	6	9	10
Salt	23	15	29	–	19	13
Sample	90	80	87	74	90	86
'000 tons	149	193	276	281	356	415

Notes and sources: Inward traffic as a percentage of aggregate traffic along the Atlantic seaboard by class of commodity. »BM« = building materials. *Estadística del Comercio de Cabotaje* (Madrid, 1857–87).

minerals and salt. More valuable staples such as foodstuffs were deflected to the rail route.[24]

When measured by value, the composition of coastal trade is profoundly altered, see tables 3A and 3B. On both coasts, manufactures (textiles, cotton yarn, shoes, paper, soap and glass) are greatly boosted. The increase is specially significant for the Mediterranean ports. In spite of the increased importance of textiles, foodstuffs (wine included) continued to mean good business for coasters. Actually, textiles and foodstuffs exchanged positions after 1875. Moreover, low priced staples which required large shipping capacity, were literally obliterated.

For instance, salt shipments which amounted to 44 per cent of tonnage in 1875, were virtually nil in value terms. Of course, it would be patently inappropriate to infer from this up-grading of manufactures in coastal trade that a successful industrialisation process was under way. A comparison of tables 2 and 3 merely portrays the wide range of values which were ascribed to each commodity.

Table 3A: Mediterranean coastal freight traffic by value, 1860–1885 (%)

	1860	1865	1870	1875	1880	1885
Grain	10	13	9	4	8	5
Flour	11	5	4	4	4	4
Fish	2	–	5	2	3	–
Oil & Other	4	4	10	11	7	11
Legumes	2	7	2	–	2	–
Wine	11	9	14	6	7	6
Metals	5	4	8	13	3	9
Textiles	27	29	16	43	40	29
Tobacco	5	–	2	–	6	11
Salt	2	–	1	1	1	–
Sample	80	71	71	83	81	75
million pesetas	294	269	148	453	302	290

Notes and sources: Inward traffic as a percentage of aggregate traffic along the Mediterranean seaboard by class of commodity. *Estadística del Comercio de Cabotaje* (Madrid, 1857–87).

[24] Ibid., vol. 1, Madrid 1984.

Table 3B: Atlantic coastal freight traffic by value, 1860–1885 (%)

	1860	1865	1870	1875	1880	1885
Grain	11	6	8	5	6	3
Flour	4	9	11	12	8	6
Wine	12	10	11	12	8	7
Metals	7	8	9	10	5	12
Textiles	15	8	9	7	30	21
Tobacco	3	12	16	5	–	21
Timber & BM	2	–	–	–	2	2
Salt	18	11	–	–	1	–
Other	1	9	16	30	13	9
Sample	73	73	80	81	73	81
million pesetas	51	72	72	92	88	143

Notes and sources: Inward traffic as a percentage of aggregate traffic along the Mediterranean seaboard by class of commodity. Building materials are »BM«. »Other« include lard
and oil, hides, fish and coal. *Estadística del Comercio de Cabotaje* (Madrid, 1857–87).

Commercial intercourse between the major trade partners on each seaboard
shows that long distance freight flows consisted basically of low value
commodities, Barcelona excepted. Indeed, the Catalan capital, which was the
workshop of Spain, exported some textile goods to the Atlantic, but the
remaining ports of the Mediterranean exported olive oil, spirits, rice, soap and
salt. They imported from the Atlantic flour and grain in large quantities
together with coal, iron, glass and tobacco.

Apart from the economic backwardness of Spain, there are two other
reasons to explain why grain and wine growers, millers, coal miners and
ironmasters figured among the best clients of coastal shipping. First of all,
they relied on coasters on account of their relative efficiency in carrying bulky
commodities of low value long distances. Second, coastal shipping remained
the only mode of transport in many areas of the periphery as was explained in
section II. Of these three reasons, I wish to stress the relevance of low freight
rates for the integration of the domestic market. As John Armstrong has
explained, the coaster's labour and capital costs were much lower than those
of the railway. Because it did not have to spend on fuel, the sailing tramp was
able to offer the lowest rates.[25]

One major drawback when dealing with freight rates is that the available
information is rather scant. To the best of my knowledge, there is no
comprehensive source on rates charged by coasters before the advent of

[25] ARMSTRONG, The role, pp. 180–1.

coastal liner services in the twentieth century. Rates charged for Asturian coal shipped from Gijón to a number of ports on either coast have been listed in table 4. Shipping rates were inclusive of harbour dues which both national and foreign vessels had to pay. A charge of one *real* per registered ton was levied for anchorage, another *real* for lights and half a *real* for health dues. Finally, one eighth of a *real* was levied for each Castilian quintal of cargo discharged or loaded.[26] With the exception of Seville, the average rate charged by coasters decreased as the distance increased which coal was shipped in 1867.[27] Like the railway, a lower average rate was thus charged the longer the haul. This negative relationship between freight rates and distance is supported by a high coefficient of correlation. In 1867, the average rate charged by NORTE amounted to 0.095 Ptas per ton-km. This rate is 2.13 times the higher rate charged by coasters for a distance of 161 kilometres which was roughly equivalent to NORTE's average haul. Moreover, road hauliers charged a rate ten times higher than the railway, that is twenty-two times higher than coasters. However, to some extent coal was a special cargo. High discounts were granted to coal mines by the railway companies. Both MZA and NORTE charged 0.02 pesetas per ton-km for coal.[28] At this special rate, the haulage of Asturian coal to Cádiz by rail, had it existed, would have exceeded the corresponding shipping rate by 50 per cent.[29]

It is implied that coasters could not face competition from either overland transport operator. Because of the low rates it could offer, coastal trade made possible the shipping of low value cargo over long distances. In its absence, such traffic flows would have been prohibited. Therefore, it can be concluded that coastal shipping provided the best possible service for the kind of freight which was proper for a backward economy like the Spanish. On the other hand, cotton yarn and textiles were able to stand the high rates charged by road carriers who provided the door to door distribution network which was required by consumer goods.

V

In spite of the substantial price advantage in favour of coastal shipping, light and shade intermingled in its performance over the nineteenth century. It has

---

[26] This tax on goods loaded or discharged at the quay amounted to 0.68 Ptas per ton. One Castilian quintal is equal to 46 kgs: BPP, 1862, LIV, p. 68.

[27] The higher rate charged for coal shipped to Seville was probably explained by the extra cost involved in sailing upstream on the Guadalquivir river.

[28] MZA, Comité de Paris, 11 Dec 1885; for NORTE, Una tarifa notable de transporte, in: Revista Minera 42 (1890), pp. 52–3.

[29] The railway distance between Gijón and Cádiz was 1,322 km.

already been noted that the tonnage shipped by coasters remained quite modest by international standards throughout the period. What are the factors accounting for this apparent paradox? Why was coastal shipping unable to trigger off an earlier integration of the home market? In my opinion, the potentialities of coastal shipping were hindered by three factors.

Table 4: Rates for coal shipments from Gijón in 1867

Route	Rate	Distance	Average rate
Santander	28.70	161	0.04457
Bilbao	32.85	213	0.03856
La Coruña	36.50	265	0.03443
Cádiz	70.70	1,287	0.01373
Sevilla	81.50	1,398	0.01489
Málaga	81.50	1,500	0.01358
Almería	80.75	1,663	0.01214
Cartagena	81.50	1,828	0.01115
Alicante	81.50	1,940	0.01050
Barcelona	107.90	2,343	0.01151

Notes and sources: Col (1): Rates in reales per ton, 1 real = 0.25 pesetas. Col (2): Distances in kilometers. Col (3): Average rate in pesetas per ton-km. *Información sobre el Derecho Diferencial de Bandera y sobre las Aduanas exigibles a los hierros, el carbón de piedra y los algodones* (Madrid, 1867) III p. 23.

I will, first of all, discuss geographical factors. As part of the Iberian Peninsula, Spain is endowed with one of the longest coastlines on the Continent, with access to the Atlantic (Guipuzcoa to Pontevedra) and Mediterranean (Huelva to Gerona) through the Straits of Gibraltar, in total, 3,167 km of seaboard.[30] Two features left their imprint on coastal shipping. One is the open character of the coast bereft of natural inlets except for Galicia in the northwestern part of the Peninsula, a land well endowed with estuaries. The other is the close relationship between the linear configuration of the coast and the inner mountain ranges. Because of the proximity of rough terrain to the sea, the coastal landscape is rocky and uneven.[31] Furthermore,

[30] 1,663 km for the Mediterranean, 770 km for the Cantabrian Sea and 735 km for the two fragments of the Atlantic coast on either side of Portugal. Luis SOLE SABARIS, Las costas españolas, in: Manuel de TERAN/Luis SOLE SABARIS [et al.] (eds.), Geografia General de España, Barcelona 1981, p. 126.

[31] SOLE SABARIS, Geografia General, p. 127.

seaports were deprived of easy connection with the markets of the interior. Since the Enlightenment, vast sums of capital were allocated to improve transport with the periphery. Unfortunately, the outcome was quite meagre.[32]

Second, economic factors were also present to prevent coastal trade from fostering economic growth. Indeed, the absence of natural ports implied that additional resources were required to create a network of artificial harbours. With 364 million pesetas of public money invested during the second half of the nineteenth century, maritime works lagged well behind railway or highway building.[33] After 1868, improvements in port facilities were assigned to an independent body, *Juntas de Obras de los Puertos,* which managed public funds. The lion's share was allocated to only eight ports, some of them among the busiest in Spain.[34] They were all connected to the inner markets by rail. It is not clear whether those ports were equipped with modern quays, wharfs, or cranes which were meant to accelerate loading and unloading operations. According to A. Navarrete, an acute observer of the future of coal mining, the actual condition of most ports remained precarious at the beginning of the twentieth century: »Because the docks of those [Asturian] harbours are not equipped with adequate machinery, ship loading is performed at a rate of 300 to 350 tons per day and vessel. Whenever there is a boom in activity, steamers must queue to dock. When they come to a standstill, the coal mine owner has to cover the extra cost of demurrage or the increase in freight rates«.[35] Operating costs were thus inflated as a result of unproductive performance while in port. The docking of vessels of large size was restricted to those ports which had been dredged. In that regard, it would be interesting to enquire whether the poor condition of Spanish harbours was responsible for the prevalence of sailing ships longer than in other European countries.

Third, let us concentrate on political factors. On the one hand, communications along the Atlantic seaboard were interrupted by Portuguese sovereign waters. Because coastal trade is defined as »commercial intercourse or traffic

---

[32] For the Canal of Castile, see GÓMEZ-MENDOZA, Europe's Cinderella: inland navigation in nineteenth-century Spain, in: Andreas KUNZ/John ARMSTRONG (eds.), Inland Navigation and Economic Development in Nineteenth-Century Europe, Mainz 1995, pp. 131–45.

[33] Public investment in maritime works took 39 and 12 per cent respectively of capital formation in railways and highways: GÓMEZ-MENDOZA, Las obras públicas, 1850–1935, in: Francisco COMÍN/Pablo MARTÍN-ACEÑA (eds.), Historia de la Empresa Pública en España, Madrid 1991, Tables 2 and 3, pp. 192 and 196.

[34] Bilbao, Barcelona, Sevilla, Málaga, Santander, Tarragona, Valencia and Gijón. See FRAX/MATILLA, Transporte comercio, p. 220. For the improvement of Bilbao, see Natividad de la PUERTA RUEDA, El Puerto de Bilbao como reflejo del desarrollo industrial de Vizcaya, 1857–1913, Bilbao 1994, pp. 55–100.

[35] Adolfo NAVARRETE, Información de la Liga Marítima, Madrid 1909, p. 38.

along the coast from cape to cape or from harbour to harbour«, the existence
of 700 km of foreign coastline meant a formidable obstacle to sailing craft of
small size.[36] The substitution of steamers for sailing ships in the mid 1880s
was a big step forward in encouraging long distance traffic between the two
seaboards. On the other hand, coastal shipping was a haven reserved to the
domestic merchant fleet under the provisions of the 1829 Commercial Law.
Shipment of bulky cargoes such as minerals, timber, coal, organic fertilizers
and hydrated lime was extended to foreign bottoms after navigation acts were
partially repealed in 1869. This liberalization benefited northern ports to a
higher degree than southeastern ports because the former concentrated on the
trade in bulky commodities. It has already been stated in table 2B that the
traffic in coal, minerals, timber and building materials accounted respectively
for 35 and 16 per cent of the aggregate tonnage moved along the Atlantic and
Mediterranean coastlines.[37]

The domestic shipping interest bitterly complained about unfair competition
from foreign vessels.[38] British steamers offered unbeatable freight rates because they counted on a return cargo. Evidence suggests that there was probably a significant amount of idle capacity in the shipping industry. Joaquín
Costa acknowledged that: »... only one quarter of Spanish ships are able to
find cargoes, the rest is in ballast (with gravel or stones)...«. This was a prime
cause in the stagnation of the shipping trade.[39] It was frequently denounced
that it was not possible to »agree on a freight rate for a round trip since return
cargoes are extremely scarce in Spain«.[40] Foreign vessels were said to have
undercut freight rates by 40 per cent.[41]

In spite of the evidence provided, I suspect that the actual impact of the
liberal measures of 1869 was rather limited. Although confirmation is pend-
ing, I suggest that partial liberalization led to a segmentation of the market for
coastal services. On account of their larger size, foreign steamers were
probably used for long distance traffic visiting harbours which had undergone
modernization.[42] Spanish craft, on the other hand, probably serviced small

[36] For the legal definition of coastal trade, see Marcelo MARTÍNEZ ALCUBILLA, Diccionario de la Administración Española, Madrid 1892, vol. 2, p. 184.

[37] Frax's estimates for 1878 bring this share down to 22 per cent in the total. See FRAX,
Puertos y Comercio, footnote 3, p. 11.

[38] Evidence provided at a parliamentary enquiry was published in: Información sobre la
Supresión del Derecho Diferencial de Bandera, Madrid 1879, vol. 1.

[39] Joaquín COSTA, Dictonen sobre el estado de la Marina Española, in: Congreso de
Geografía Mercantil y Colonial, Madrid 1883, p. 301.

[40] Reply to the enquiry on navigation acts provided by Junta de Agricultura, Industria y
Comercio de Barcelona in: Información sobre el Derecho Diferencial ..., vol. 1, Madrid
1867, p. 93.

[41] Reply to the enquiry on navigation acts provided by Retortillo and Hos (Cádiz), ibid.,
p. 100.

[42] Reply to the enquiry on navigation acts provided by NORTE, ibid., p. 105.

harbours where no return cargoes could be secured owing to faulty market integration. A far-reaching liberalization of the shipping industry was welcomed by railway companies in an attempt at stimulating foreign trade and domestic growth.

9

COASTAL SHIPPING IN ITALY FROM UNIFICATION TO THE FIRST WORLD WAR, 1861–1915

ANDREA GIUNTINI

Definitions

The Italian maritime tradition and long established shipping rights helped shape the definition of the concept of coastal shipping in Italy. Coastal shipping refers, as reported in the many volumes concerned with this subject, to commercial shipping, from port to port, along the coasts.[1] The difference between coastal and international shipping is clear, and this distinction is reflected equally clearly in surveys of the data, so confusion of the two is avoided.

Clarity in the Italian case is due principally to, firstly, the historical importance of maritime activity for the Italian peninsula. It took place mainly within a closed and relatively small sea, namely the Mediterranean, and was thus easily regulated. Secondly the shape of the country, being entirely surrounded by sea and with a large number of ports, although obviously they were not all used to the same degree. In addition, the data collected by public bodies, on which this chapter is based, distinguished clearly between coastal shipping and international shipping.

The principal sources

Italian students of coastal shipping are particularly fortunate. In contrast to the sources for the study of other transport, the data relating to coastal shipping, and indeed shipping in general, are particularly rich and complete. There is a series of volumes of ministerial origin that provides very detailed information and is therefore of great historical value. Particularly valuable is the collection of statistics relating to the period 1861–1880 produced by the Ministry for Industry, and that for the subsequent period leading up to the First World War,

---

[1] As noted also in a work fundamental to the understanding of the subject during the period immediately following unification, G. BOCCARDO, La navigazione di cabotaggio e gli interessi marittimi dell'Italia, Genoa 1862.

compiled by the Finance Ministry, both entitled *Navigazione Italiana* (Italian Shipping). The criteria used for collecting the statistics were kept constant and therefore allow a trustworthy, long-term comparison.[2]

The statistics cover the minor ports as well but only twelve are considered in this essay[3], those described by the original compiler as the principal ports. They are subdivided by coast. The volumes published by the two Ministries record, as well as the number of boats and tonnage, facts about the different countries of origin of the ships using the ports, and the composition of the crews.

One thing that stands out when researching the ministerial volumes is the great importance, in terms of both ships and tonnage, of coastal shipping compared to international shipping in the period indicated. Another element that can be clearly seen in figure 1[4] is the increase in tonnage, despite the progressive reduction in the number of boats. This was such that by the eve of the war there were only half the number of boats compared to the years following Unification. The capacity of steamboats rose relative to that of sailing boats; this increase in the capacity of steamboats is more marked for those registered abroad than those flying an Italian flag.

Also fundamental to understanding the characteristics of coastal shipping in Italy in this period, is the slow diffusion of steam power, and the persistence of the use of sailing boats at least until the end of the 1910s, seen in figure 2. This gives an insight into the technological level of the sector. In the Italian case there is a clear backwardness in this sector, notwithstanding the by no means negligible size of the fleet.

Other sources that have been used in this work are the acts of the numerous commissions appointed during this period by the government or the parliament, and charged with the study of issues pertaining to shipping and the development of ports. Again, this deals with material that is only slightly familiar to historians, who have rarely used it, and often not for the purpose of analysing issues relevant to coastal shipping.

The record of and prospects for the study of coastal shipping within the discipline of history in contemporary Italy

Shipping has long been a subject of great importance, above all for a previous generation of historians. It has been generally restricted to those with an

---

[2] The only exception is the period 1896–1905 during which the method of compilation of the statistics varied from those adopted in the years before and after this time.

[3] The ports are: Ancona, Bari, Brindisi, Cagliari, Catania, Genoa, Leghorn (Livorno), Messina, Naples, Palermo, Savona, Venice. See also map 1 on p. 10.

[4] All figures appear at the end of the chapter.

interest in the medieval and pre-modern periods. Even a brief look at the discipline confirms the large number of works, often of high quality. There is, however, a lack of work focusing on the two centuries closest to us, a welcome exception being a volume from a recent conference.[5] Although too little is devoted to the modern era, it lends itself to further study and greater depth.

Among the many directions that research could take there are two areas of study in particular that ought to be considered. First, assessment of the contribution made by coastal shipping to the economic development of the country, a consideration up until now ignored by economic historians, which merits attention. To this topic it would not be out of place to apply the historical ideas, adopted with some success for the railways, based on the synergy of forward and backward linkages. It would also be interesting to assess the extent to which the various industries active in the shipbuilding sector benefited. Second is a detailed and contextualised analysis of the birth and development of infrastructure in Italy. This first collection of data cannot adequately provide this, but it should still be considered as of crucial importance. Coastal shipping represented an important part of the Italian infrastructure, but its importance can be seen only when considered alongside other systems of transport, in particular, at this time the railways. This period saw the formation of a national market, capable of overcoming the regional fragmentation inherited from the previous pre-unification states. Thus, it is a very interesting case, and in many ways paradigmatic with respect to the role played by infrastructure in the economic development of a »late-comer« country.

The main thrust of this paper is limited to indicating comparisons between road and rail transport, and attempting a realistic evaluation of the relative weight of coastal shipping. A contribution to the knowledge of this sector can however be made through a deeper study of the following subjects: the major ports in this epoch[6]; the shipping companies that existed; the type of goods transported; the politics of tariffs and costs; policy-making and parliamentary lobbies; and finally maritime insurance.

The problem of infrastructure at the dawn of the new kingdom.

Italian historians who have tackled the question of the birth and development of an infrastructure network in Italy have expressed a common opinion that

---

[5] T. FANFANI (ed.), La Penisola italiana e il mare. Costruzioni navali trasporti e commerci tra XV e XX secolo, Naples 1993. Studies of emigration also look at shipping; these are rather numerous in Italy and tend to be of high quality.

[6] Still the most important work is that of G. DORIA, Investimenti e sviluppo economico a Genova alla vigilia della prima guerra mondiale, Milan 1973.

can be compressed into the following dry formula: infrastructure was not decisive in Italian industrial development. The judgement applies to shipping, even though, as mentioned above, nobody has really considered the subject in depth, or sustained their arguments with detailed research.

One of the first problems that the new state had to face, and which had to be resolved as quickly as possible, was the construction of a transport network. This would serve both to link the different areas of the country, and to integrate Italy with the rest of Europe. A task of this scale never appeared simple. Its realisation was impeded by numerous negative factors. First, the dreadful condition of the road system, lacking, among other things, appropriate border crossings. Second, the limited coverage of the rail network and third, the obsolescence of the port system. All these scraps of infrastructure had to be sewn together, despite their very different histories. This was without counting the more general economic and social problems that characterise a recently-unified country.

The Italian economy at the time of unification exhibited one peculiarity – the limited level of integration of the various regional economies.[7] The construction of the infrastructure network was considered a necessary precondition for the integration of the economy. At the time of its birth, it appeared that only transport, in particular rail, was capable of uniting the Italian state, far more so than common borders or the idea of a separate nation. The establishment of infrastructure assumed in the Italian case a particular importance, as it ended up defining the very concept of a nation itself.

Thus, the road and railway networks, the creation of shipping and canals, both for irrigation and industrial drainage, the redevelopment of unproductive areas, the development of commercial ports, all became an integral part of the aspirations of Italy's national bourgeoisie. They created a network of pressure groups that sought to respond to the problem of financing infrastructure. This led to a clash between the public interest and the specific interests of powerful groups, both financial and entrepreneurial.

There is the question of the imbalance between the North and the South of the country that has to be carefully evaluated, even with regards to infrastructure. There is no doubt that infrastructure in the South was significantly limited in comparison to the North. However, as we shall see, albeit briefly, coastal shipping activity had for a long time reached appreciably high levels. This was such that probably the role of coastal shipping in the economic development of the South of the country was not inferior to, and possibly superior to that played by rail.

---

[7] Here we fundamentally accept the argument of G. FEDERICO, as summarised in I fattori della distribuzione, in: Storia dell'economia italiana, vol. 3: L'etá contemporanea: un paese nuovo, Turin 1991, pp.181–200.

A factor of prime importance is that the first governing class of the new kingdom did not fully comprehend all aspects of the phenomenon of infrastructure. They did not understand the need to work within a wider picture, to contextualise the question of infrastructure. This led to serious problems, some of which continue to be linked to the question of infrastructure in Italy today, primarily the lack of integration of the various networks.

The position of the ports

The number of ports and landing places of differing sizes spread out along the Italian coasts when the first governors of the new Kingdom came to power was very high. There was a constellation of small ports uniformly distributed along the coast to serve as landing places for coastal shipping and fishing activity. One statistic from the time indicates that there were a good 298 such ports, most of which were on the Mediterranean.

The inheritance of a glorious past was evident, but the role of shipping in ensuring the mobility of men and objects was no less important than in past times. In 1861 coastal shipping represented the only way to link the two extremities of the peninsula, given the fragmentary nature of the existing regional rail networks.

The top-level ports, substantially those analysed in this study, entirely absorbed international shipping, and a good part of coastal shipping. The structures were, however, generally rather antiquated. The diversity of existing structures and the many problems pertaining to the different ports rendered difficult the job of the state as it attempted to pursue a unitary policy. The law of 1865 sanctioned administrative unification. Enacted as Law no. 2248 on 20 March 1865, the law divided the ports into four categories, and was the first law concerned with public works that was universally applicable. Thanks to this law the administrative assets of the state came to be codified and the criteria for technocratic and bureaucratic action were fixed.

Thus the route towards decisive intervention on the part of the state was opened. Between 1861 and 1878, fifty three laws were passed leading to a total allocation of 141 million lire, an impressive sum, nonetheless incongruities and delays were not completely avoided. Acts of modernisation were not lacking, but in general intervention was characterised by limited efficiency.

In the following decade the task did not become easier. The cost of new work on ports between 1871 and 1880 rose to 46.5 million lire. In order to complete construction a further 63 million was assigned, under the law of 1880. Overall, these figures are very relevant. They provide testimony to the effort of the state to modernise the ports of the peninsula. The problem was not the level of investment, but rather the efficiency of financial investment.

Policy on the ports in the twenty years following unification was not adapted to the situation because it was fragmentary, full of gaps, and in the final analysis, badly managed by the government of the time. A serious, clear programme for the development of the ports was never outlined, thus intervention was directed towards demands as they emerged, a constant stemming of leaks, wherever they appeared in the overall structure of the system. Even the job of assessing the strategic position of Genoa, Venice and Brindisi within the sphere of international transport had only limited success. As with the successive allocations of resources from 1880, the hoped for effect did not transpire, and the shipping infrastructure remained in a critical situation. This was due to the excessive number of ports, the limited evaluation of differences between the ports, and the weakness of the shipbuilding industry and national shipping.

Coastal shipping in the twenty years following unification

Bearing in mind the question of European economic integration, the new Italian state decided to focus on shipping, even though development of rail continued to be a prime objective. This explains the interventions that sought to give the sector a common legal order. This was the fruit of a compromise between the legislation in the various pre-unitary states. Although characterised by a certain discontinuity, and by high levels of fragmentation, the policy adopted by the Italian rulers after 1860 was geared towards strengthening the sector by means of state subsidies, tax relief and awards for the shipping companies who went into ship-building. The whole sector in the first decades of the life of the kingdom, gained conspicuous advantage from state intervention, realised also through the supply of incentives to the main private shipping companies, in particular Florio, Rubattino and Adriatico-Orientale.

Overall the trend that appears in this period is an upward one. The many problems, including those of structure, and the backwardness of technology, exemplified by the persistence of sailing ships, did not impede the growth of coastal shipping, as figure 1 clearly demonstrates. This resulted from an increase in cargo, despite a decrease in the number of vessels from the beginning of the 1870s, and thanks also to the greater number of boats Registered as Italian rather than foreign.

At the time of unification, the maritime industry in Italy was characterised by deep contradictions. On the one hand, the fleet was well endowed which allowed it to occupy a high position in international terms. On the other, there was persistent backwardness consisting of the clear predominance of sail over steam, as we have already seen in figure 2. This led to a delay in technological development in this sector which persisted even to recent times. Beyond the continued preference for sailing boats, we should also mention the difference between the tonnage of the Italian steamboats used for coastal shipping, and those registered overseas. The former averaged, 243 net tons, considerably lower than the latter at 293 net tons.

The liberal economic policy practised by the right fostered the performance of the major Italian ports in the post-unification period. Such a policy, on the other hand, did not stimulate industrial development. It was very rare, except in the case of Genoa for the governors to be convinced that maritime activity could influence industrial policy. The development of coastal shipping in the course of these initial years, had only limited impact on the industrial growth of the country. The negative role of political interference should also be underlined. Local bias led to political intervention that favoured certain ports to the detriment of others, harming the overall fate of the sector, which needed a plan for development with no political conditions attached.

The ports of the northern Mediterranean

The permanent technical inadequacy of the port of Genoa, in terms of mechanical equipment and the structure of the docks, impeded a decisive take-off (see figure 3). The relative importance of the principal cargo port of the country, and natural outlet of the so-called industrial triangle, diminished, after having peaked in the fourteen years that followed unification. Genoa then, still internationally pre-eminent, faced competition not only from Marseilles, but also from the other main Ligurian ports of Savona and La Spezia.

Comparison with Marseilles is telling when attempting to gain a thorough understanding of the nature of the structural problems of the Italian ports. The technical endowment of the French port was superior to Genoa. Marseilles covered an area of 152 hectares, compared to 136, it had a good 12,616 metres of wharves, 8,500 of which were used for transhipment, against the 3,200 of Genoa, almost of all of which were straight; often the ships were unable to moor due to the lack of depth of water. Also, in terms of the speed of loading and off-loading cargo, the comparison was humiliating for Genoa. The railway network that served the French port added up to 20 km, while in the case of the Ligurian port there were only 2 km of railway. 6000 railway wagons per day supplied Marseilles, while 600 was the maximum for Genoa.

The position of the industrial triangle, an important area in the economic development of the country, made the system of ports in Liguria an obvious point of sale for industrial goods, and supply of fuels. Half of the coal imported into Italy in this era was unloaded in the three ports mentioned. In 1907 the three ports of Genoa, Savona and La Spezia alone dealt with around 38 per cent of the goods transported by rail in the three areas of Turin, Milan and Genoa, plus around 20 per cent of the entire national figure. These statistics underline the importance of the Ligurian coast in Italian commercial shipping. In addition it should be mentioned that half the international traffic and international connections took place in the ports of Savona, Genoa and Leghorn taken together.

The port of Leghorn (Livorno), despite the unfavourable relationship between sailing ships and steamboats, managed to renew the glories of a past era; the decisive decline of this port happened at a later time. Coastal tonnage arriving and departing rose steadily from the 1860s to the First World War as is shown in figure 4.

Behind Leghorn on a scale of national importance came Naples, which was to surpass the Ligurian port in the mid-1870s, as shown in figure 5. It also became important in transporting passengers, in particular emigrants leaving for America for whom Naples was the favourite port of departure. Looking at trade flows between southern Italy and the rest of the world, Naples did not reach the point of competing with Genoa, which operated on a different level. Due to the very different economic conditions that pertained in southern Italy compared to the North, maritime traffic was based on primary materials that were produced in the region. The good performance of coastal shipping in the South of Italy was, according to some historians, the basis for the scarce attention paid by the government to railway construction in this area. According to this thesis, coastal shipping served, to some degree, as a substitute for railways in this part of the country.

The Sicilian ports also contributed notably to the high level of coastal shipping in the South, see figure 6. Altogether Sicily accounted for 55 per cent of national traffic, exceeding by far the southern Mediterranean and the Adriatic. Messina in particular was important as the leading place for the export of citrus fruits.

The Adriatic ports

The dynamism of the Adriatic ports was, during our period, inferior to that of the Mediterranean, due in no small measure to a drastic change in international flows of traffic. This was such that the Austrian port of Trieste managed to attract a notable quantity of traffic from the Mediterranean that was heading towards central Europe. The problem lay in the inability of the Italian ports to present themselves as candidates for international traffic, in particular for goods coming from the two large German-speaking countries which continued to focus on Trieste.

Venice, where 70 per cent of the net tonnage was linked to international movements of goods, was the most active port before the annexation of Trieste by Italy at the end of the First World War. The leap forward predicted in the case of Brindisi never arose; the prospect of trade with the East had led to hope for extraordinary levels of traffic. Once again, notwithstanding the expansion of the Pugliese port, the lack of steam proved an obstacle to the decisive growth of this port, and substantially impeded the other ports of the Adriatic in seizing the opportunity constituted by the opening of new routes of communication towards the East. Ancona based its activity predominantly on small coasters, which in statistical terms translated into a higher number of boats passing through the port, the quantity of goods carried was not proportionally as high.

Coastal shipping during the last twenty years of the nineteenth century

In the 1880s Italy's rulers became convinced that to continue to shower the various ports with financial resources was not productive, and that such dispersion of funds would not aid the Italian ports to increase their levels of trade. The numerous commissions established by the government during the course of the last twenty years of the century shed light on this fact. They noted also that the national railway network developed without taking into consideration that it could have been integrated fruitfully with the coastal shipping industry. In practice the two systems moved forward in parallel, without exploiting the possible synergy at their disposal. This did not lead however to a reduction in the investments in the infrastructure of the ports: from 1880 to 1890 on average 14.5 million lire per year were spent, compared to the 7.2 million of the preceding decade. In the following decade the figure fell but the average was still 11.1 million lire per year.

Thus something changed in this period, albeit slowly, in terms of perception of an integrated system of infrastructure. The measures were still insufficient, but for the first time coastal shipping was studied within the broader question of the infrastructure of the country.This was a unitary vision which had been lacking up until then.

The picture of the merchant navy in the enquiry of 1881 demonstrated clearly the inadequacy of the ports. For this reason a different system of classification of ports was suggested which would take into consideration the differing nature of trade in the various ports, and allow for more direct financial participation by the state. Some indicators of this were contained in the law of 1885, of Minister Brin. It proposed a new classification of ports and the launch of a series of initiatives to support naval construction and shipping lines. The law was crucial to the survival of the sector, but had the fault of not pushing sufficiently hard the wider adoption of steam in place of sail. This condemned the country to lasting technical inferiority. In Europe this sector saw a profound transformation due to the increased use of steam, greater transport co-ordination, and the increasing size of vessels. Italy began to lose its position of importance in the sphere of coastal shipping.

In this way the oligopoly of the large companies, increasingly supported by the state to the detriment of smaller companies, was strengthened. This was in line with a belief that they were the only ones capable of conquering new markets. The increase in the merchant fleet was still supported, despite the intensive construction of railways. This was crucial to the expansion of maritime traffic at a time that was particularly delicate in general economic terms. This confirmed that the end of liberal trade policies extended to the maritime sphere, with the consequent disappearance of the small companies. It was not by chance that the two main shipping companies, the aforementioned Florio and Rubattino, decided in 1881 to merge, creating *Navigazione Generale Italiana*, an outcome of fundamental importance for the understanding of coastal shipping in Italy in the fifty years from unification to the First World War.

The new century

The Giolitti era saw a decisive recovery in the fate of coastal shipping. On the eve of the First World War, there was a strong upward trend which brought a figure of more than a million tonnes of goods loaded and unloaded not just in Genoa (7.40) but also Venice (2.8), Naples (2.4), Savona (1.8) and Leghorn (1.6). Compared to the first years of Italian unity, trade in Italian ports had multiplied tenfold. This crucial period of industrial take-off in Italy finally saw the beginning of modernisation of the port structures, and the new century also witnessed a transformation of the technical structure of the maritime industry. From the introduction of electricity to the opening of the first depots for petrol, to the work of strengthening the ports, and the long-awaited, vast, expansion of the use of steam, the face of the Italian merchant navy finally assumed more distinctly modern contours. It was no coincidence, therefore, that the share of coastal sailing ships fell during the first years of the century to under 10 per cent of total cargo.

In terms of state action, the Commission created in 1904 for the study of the condition of the ports, represented the last great state plan in favour of shipping. A decidedly innovative aspect of this period was that the state took over certain lines. In the years preceding the First World War the intention of Prime Minister Giolitti was to create a large shipping company through the participation of the major shipping companies of the Peninsula. This project, however, did not reach a positive conclusion, and the emergence of hostilities led to its permanent postponement.

Figure 1: Coastal shipping in Italy, 1861–1915,
arrivals and departures (tonnage)

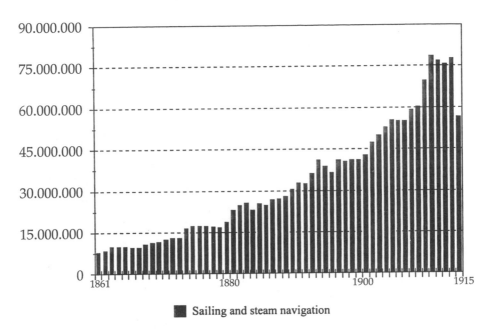

■ Sailing and steam navigation

Figure 2: Coastal shipping in Italy, 1861–1915,
arrivals and departures (number of ships)

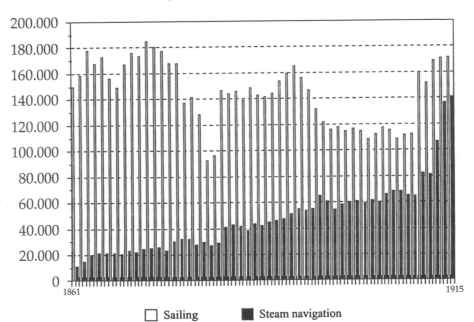

☐ Sailing   ■ Steam navigation

Figure 3: Coastal shipping in Genoa and Savona, 1860/65 – 1911/15, arrivals and departures (tonnage)

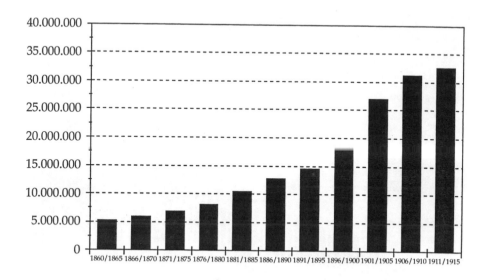

Figure 4: Coastal shipping in Leghorn (Livorno), 1860/65 – 1911/15, arrivals and departures (tonnage)

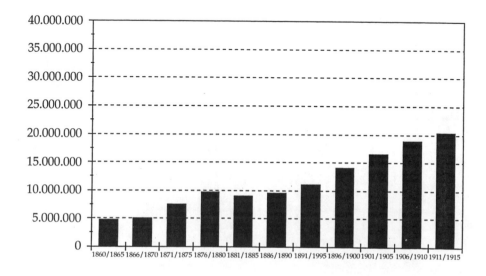

Figure 5: Coastal shipping in Naples, 1860/65 – 1911/15,
arrivals and departures (tonnage)

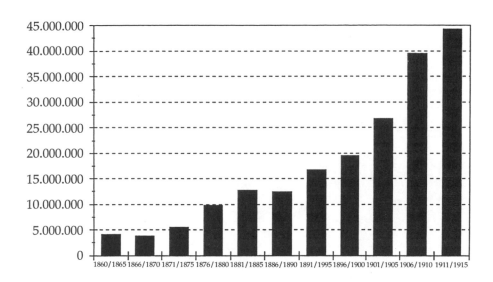

Figure 6: Coastal shipping in Catania, Messina and Palermo,
1860/65 – 1911/15, arrivals and departures (tonnage)

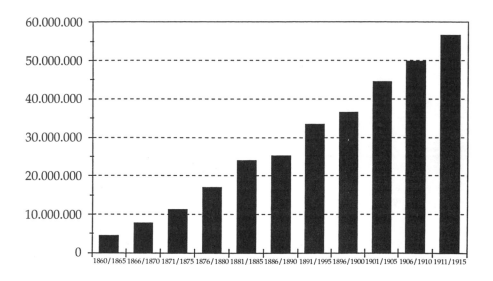

Map 4: The eastern Mediterranean in the early twentieth century
          (Ports shown are those mentioned in the text)

10

THE COASTAL TRADE OF THE OTTOMAN EMPIRE, FROM THE MID-EIGHTEENTH TO THE EARLY NINETEENTH CENTURIES

ELENA FRANGAKIS-SYRETT

This chapter analyses the Ottoman coastal trade, also referred to as internal maritime trade, from the second half of the eighteenth to the early nineteenth centuries. At the time, the Ottoman Empire was immense, spread over three continents – Europe, Asia and Africa – and bordering parts of the Mediterranean, Black and Red Seas. Its economy was basically merchant capitalist with a high degree of monetization in its urban areas and in particular in the western parts of the Empire which bordered the Mediterranean. This was also the region that included the biggest urban centres of the Empire at that time: Istanbul, Izmir, Alexandria, Salonica. In the eighteenth century, internal maritime trade served to connect such urban centres and their hinterland more efficiently and cost-effectively than any other means.

In such an economy, coastal trade served an important function primarily in contributing to the commercialization of agriculture, the monetization of the economy and to the further growth and greater unification of the domestic market. Through coastal trade, goods, people, capital and information were moved more efficiently and cost-effectively than would have been possible through land transport. It was the maritime regions of the Empire that were most affected. For the land mass that made up a large part of the Empire, caravan routes, despite their shortcomings, were still the most frequent means of communication. Moreover, established fairs and caravan routes linking inland markets helped create internal commercial zones which contributed to not only the external trade of the Empire but also the coastal trade of its maritime regions.[1]

---

[1] Archives Nationales de France, Paris, AE Biii 243, Inspection générale du Levant, 1817. Hereafter, these archives will be cited as ANF. See also Eugen WIRTH, Alep dans la première moitié du XIXᵉ siècle: un exemple de stabilité et de dynamique dans l'économie ottomane tardive, in: Revue du Monde Musulman et de la Méditerranée 62 (1991–94), pp. 137–49.

The second half of the eighteenth century was a period of considerable economic growth for the Ottoman Empire.[2] It was part of the general growth of the Mediterranean which affected primarily the Empire's maritime regions. Within the Ottoman economy the internal and external commercial sectors and other associated sectors such as shipping, experienced particular growth. Within the commercial sector, coastal trade played a major role in this economic development, linked as it was with external trade. For the external trade of the Ottoman Empire with western Europe, reflecting the expansionist phase of international trade at the time, grew very considerably in this period contributing in part also to the growth of internal trade.

In the Ottoman Empire, as elsewhere, coastal shipping was synonymous with *cabotage* or internal trade. In essence, it included all maritime trade that was carried out within its territorial boundaries. It was distinct from, although closely related to, the external maritime trade of the Empire. The latter was carried out primarily with Europe through the Mediterranean to the west and with the Far East through the Red Sea and the Indian Ocean to the east. Due to the considerable distances involved, even when taking into account only the Mediterranean – given that the Empire covered nearly two-thirds of the Mediterranean coastline – Ottoman coastal trade, by necessity, included some deep-sea navigation. This was the case for ships that crossed the Mediterranean but still remained within home waters. Thus the definition of coastal trade as internal maritime trade was the most apt for the Ottoman case. The term most used in the primary sources at the time to denote Ottoman coastal trade, particularly in the Mediterranean, was *caravane maritime*.[3] In secondary literature, which is often francophone, both the terms *grand* and *petit cabotage* are used to denote longer and shorter distance coastal trade although here, too, *caravane maritime* is the term most used to define Ottoman coastal shipping.

Given the geographical expanse of the maritime regions of the Empire, and the considerable body of water thus covered, there was bound to be a proliferation of traffic patterns and ports of call if one were to include all the minor markets, in islands or coastal towns, that coasters could have stopped at, in any given voyage. In actual fact, however, the principal routes and the ones

---

[2] Given the paucity of direct data, one way of measuring the rate of economic growth is through the trading activity of the great port-cities of the Empire with France, its most important trading partner. From the middle of the eighteenth century to the eve of the French Revolution imports to Izmir, Istanbul and Salonica increased by well over 30 per cent, while their exports to France grew over 100 per cent, led by Izmir which registered almost double this growth rate: Elena FRANGAKIS-SYRETT, The Commerce of Smyrna in the Eighteenth Century, 1700–1820, Athens 1992, pp. 259–60.

[3] E.g., ANF, AE Biii 271–277 États des bâtiments (1756–1787). Moreover, French sources constitute some of the most important archives on the subject, given the dominant role of French shipping in Ottoman coastal trade at the time.

most used in coastal trade were fewer in number and mostly reflected the size and economic importance of the centres they linked. Despite the problems of transport and communication the internal Ottoman maritime world was quite well-connected. Given its size, it also tended to be divided into a number of regions, each region dominated by one or more economic centres, which were also city-ports and linked the regions with each other. In this respect, three city-ports, rising to an importance which went well beyond their regions, contributed greatly to linking the Empire together: Istanbul, whose political importance and demographic size made it the biggest consumer in the Empire[4]; Izmir, whose pivotal role in the Ottoman external as well as internal trade allowed it to dominate both the Empire's internal and external commercial networks; Alexandria, because it played a crucial role in the trade in certain commodities within the Empire.

The Black Sea formed an important maritime region of the Empire. Since the creation of the Empire, the Ottoman government, conscious of the need to supply the capital[5], had rerouted trade in this region to benefit Istanbul. Indeed until 1774 the Black Sea was closed to all non-Ottoman maritime traffic.[6] Even after 1774 Istanbul remained the most important purchaser and consumer of goods in the region. Given the size of the capital in the eighteenth century, the coastal trade that was centred around supplying Istanbul with grain was a complex operation, mostly undertaken or at least directed by the state. It was also an important part of Ottoman internal trade. Furthermore, given the perishable nature of this type of cargo and the shortness of the season for optimum weather conditions as well as the political pressures likely to arise from grain shortages in the capital, the state devoted considerable resources and organizational effort to this sector of the coastal trade. This included the hiring of private – Ottoman and European – merchant ships with an official shipping broker acting as a middleman between the state and the shipowners. It also necessitated the creation, as far as possible, of an infrastructure that could ensure regular and timely unloading of the grain once the ships reached Istanbul.[7] In view of the overall consumption needs of the

[4] Istanbul was by far the biggest city in the Empire. In the eighteenth century the population of the city was thought to be between 300,000 and 350,000, while Greater Istanbul, which included the surrounding regions, was estimated at 600,000 to 700,000: R. MANTRAN, Histoire d'Istanbul, Paris 1996, pp. 253–4; W. ETON, A survey of the Turkish Empire, London 1799, p. 287; J. McCARTHY, The Ottoman Turks, London 1997, p. 257.

[5] Mehmet GENÇ, Osmanli Imperatorlugu'nda Devlet ve Ekonomi, in: Besinci Milletlerarasi Türkiye Sosyal ve Iktisat Tarihi Kongresi Tebligleri, Ankara 1990, pp. 13–25.

[6] The treaty of Kücük-Kainarci in 1774 gave merchant ships under a Russian flag the right of passage through the Straits.

[7] The complexity and size of such operations can be gauged from the following example: in 1748, a convoy was organized by the head of the Istanbul customs, on behalf of the state, of sixty ships from various Aegean ports to carry grain to Istanbul from Alexandria. The convoy included some triple masted ships of c. 300 tons capacity. Rhoads MURPHEY,

capital, the entire maritime trade of Istanbul, which included both internal and overseas trade, carried a negative balance. Istanbul was able to cover such deficit by being the recipient of the Empire's tax revenue as well as of some of the trade surplus registered by important commercial centres such as Izmir. An elaborate system of bills of exchange transferred such funds to the capital from such economic centres as Izmir, Aleppo or Salonica.[8]

At the other end of the Empire, the city-port of Alexandria and the port of Suez, in Egypt, as well as the port of Djedda, in Arabia, dominated the internal trade of the Red Sea. Goods went along the coast from Djedda to Suez. After a short land journey by caravan to Cairo they were then sent to the main ports in the mouth of the Nile to be subsequently transported to directions east and west. Cargoes were sent to Rosetta and Alexandria where ships could either take them north-west to the island of Crete in the eastern Mediterranean and/or proceed with the merchandise further north to ports in the Greek mainland and the Aegean and/or the Black Sea. Alternatively, commodities could be sent from Alexandria west along the North African coast to major and minor ports in that region. Goods could also be taken in an easterly and north-easterly direction from the port of Damietta on the mouth of the river Nile to ports along the Syrian and Palestinian coasts, including the port of Alexandretta, Cyprus and/or along the Caramanian coast (south western Turkey).

In-between the Red and Black Sea maritime regions, there was the Mediterranean which linked both regions, and thus the entire Ottoman maritime internal trade. Within the Mediterranean, the most frequented axis was the Istanbul-Izmir-Alexandria route. Within this axis Izmir was the most important link. This was because Izmir not only united the various Ottoman maritime regions, from Istanbul to North Africa, with each other, but also a great part of the interior with the maritime regions of the Empire. At the same time, Izmir also linked large parts of the Empire with Europe.[9] In the course of the second half of the eighteenth and early nineteenth centuries, Izmir emerged as the biggest importer and exporter of goods in the trade of the Ottoman Empire with Europe surpassing by far even the larger Ottoman ports.[10] In the process,

Provisioning Istanbul: the state and subsistence in the early modern Middle East, in: Food and Foodways 2 (1988), p. 253.

[8] FRANGAKIS-SYRETT, The Commerce of Smyrna, pp. 147–54; see also Edhem ELDEM, Le commerce français d'Istanbul au XVIIIᵉ siècle, unpublished, Université de Provence, Ph.D. thesis, 1988.

[9] ANF, AE Bi 1053, Consul Charles de Peyssonnel, Mémoire, Izmir, 22 Nov. 1751.

[10] France was the biggest European trading partner of the Ottoman Empire in the second half of the eighteenth century. An average of 35 per cent of all Ottoman exports were annually sent to Marseilles from Izmir, while the ports of Salonica, Alexandria and Istanbul averaged annually 10, 9.3 and 5 per cent respectively of Ottoman exports. Archives de la Chambre de Commerce de Marseille, I, 26 & 28, États des marchandises venant du Levant et de Barbarie (1750–1789). Hereafter, these archives will be cited as ACCM. As far as the import trade was concerned, an average of 30 per cent of all goods coming into the Empire

Izmir drew goods from, as well as distributed goods to, a vast hinterland which included the interior of Anatolia (Turkey) and parts of the Greek mainland and stretched into Syria, Palestine, Iraq and Iran. It also included the western Anatolian coastline and islands in the Aegean and the Mediterranean, from Chios to Crete, while its extensive commercial networks brought it into constant communication with Istanbul, Salonica, Alexandria and the principal ports in the Maghrib.[11] Thus Izmir was not only the port with the most extensive contacts with Europe but also the port with the largest network of commercial contacts within the Ottoman world, including the maritime world.[12] By the early nineteenth century, given its spectacular commercial growth, Izmir dominated absolutely both the internal and the external Ottoman commercial networks.[13]

Notwithstanding the role of Izmir as a central, pivotal pole for the Empire, a sort of *plaque tournante,* Alexandria also dominated a number of maritime routes within the Ottoman world. To start with, a cluster of traffic patterns was formed around Alexandria and the island of Rhodes, and its near-by Caramanian region, in the southern part of the eastern Mediterranean, with a number of axis emanating as a result: namely, Rhodes-Alexandria; the Caramanian coast-Cos-Alexandria and the reverse. Another important cluster of coastal trade activity was formed between Alexandria and Crete. Then there were the routes leading mostly to major port cities. To the east there was an active coastal trade route between Alexandria and the Syro-Palestinian coast, which included also the Alexandria-Cyprus route, while another route, to the west, linked Alexandria with the North African ports. Going north there was an active route leading to Istanbul primarily, as well as to ports along the Macedonian and Thracian coastline, (in northern Greece), to ports such as Salonica or Cavalla, although the former took the greatest share of that region's coastal trade. The single most frequented route, however, was the one between Alexandria and Izmir which included Izmir's feeder ports on the western Anatolian coast and the Aegean islands.[14]

from Marseilles went through Izmir, while the annual share of the other ports was for Istanbul 20.8 per cent, for Alexandria 10.5 per cent and for Salonica 8.7 per cent. ACCM, I, 19–20, États des marchandises envoyées en Levant et Barbarie (1750–1789). See also FRANGAKIS-SYRETT, The Commerce of Smyrna, pp. 257–60.

[11] ANF, AE Biii 242, Consul Fourcade, Mémoire sur le commerce de Smyrne, c.1812.

[12] For a commercial history of Izmir in the eighteenth century, see FRANGAKIS-SYRETT, The Commerce of Smyrna, *passim;* see also idem, Trade between the Ottoman Empire and Western Europe: The case of Izmir in the eighteenth century, in: New Perspectives on Turkey 2 (1988), pp. 1–18.

[13] ANF, AE Biii 243, Felix de Beaujour, Inspection générale du Levant, Izmir, 5 July 1817.

[14] Daniel PANZAC, Affréteurs ottomans et capitaines français à Alexandrie: la caravane maritime en Méditerranée au milieu du XVIIIᵉ siècle, in: Revue de l'Occident Musulman et de la Méditerranée 34 (1982), pp. 23–38.

The port of Alexandria was of paramount importance for the internal maritime trade of the Empire and complemented that of Izmir in a number of ways. The difference between Izmir and Alexandria was, primarily, in the type of goods they moved and the geographical areas they took goods from or sent goods to. In other words, Izmir mainly brought in western and colonial goods and collected goods for the external market from practically the whole of the Ottoman Empire. Alexandria took goods that originated in certain regions and sent them to the appropriate markets within the Empire and vice-versa. For instance, Alexandria took coffee from Yemen, Indian textiles, and herbs. It sent these valuable and popular commodities, together with its own rice, to major markets such as Izmir, Istanbul and Salonica partly for local consumption and partly for further distribution.[15] As a result, Alexandria had a deficit in its trading relations with some regions of the Empire and a surplus with others. For instance, it sent more goods from its own and Red Sea areas to the markets in the Balkans and Asia Minor (Anatolia) as well as to North Africa than it received from them. At the same time Alexandria received more goods, important raw materials that originated in the Syrian and Palestinian regions necessary for Egyptian manufacture, than it sent to those regions, since the latter could also get goods from the Red Sea region by land. Its deficit with the Red Sea region and Syria was thus covered by the surplus Alexandria registered with the other regions of the Empire.[16]

The fact that the Ottoman Empire had a surplus in its trade with Europe in the eighteenth and early nineteenth centuries meant that at least some of this surplus was used in its trade with India and the Far East with which the Empire had a deficit. Izmir regularly used at least some of its surplus from its trade with Europe to buy goods from Alexandria;[17] the latter port, in turn, used its surplus with Izmir to buy goods from India and the Far East. Through the Empire's internal and external trade, Izmir and Alexandria became important links in the flow of the silver going east to India and, finally, to China.

Apart from the principal axis centred around major markets, and in particular emanating from, and centred around, Istanbul, Izmir or Alexandria, there were a number of other smaller traffic routes among coastal ports or islands.[18] The latter, in particular, being scattered in the eastern Mediterranean, were natural stopping places for coastal trade. For instance, ships frequently stopped at islands such as Cos (on the Alexandria-Rhodes route), Lesbos or

---

[15] Michel TUCHSCHERER, Activités des Turcs dans le commerce de la mer Rouge au XVIIIᵉ siècle, in: D. PANZAC (ed.), Les villes dans l'Empire ottoman: activités et sociétés, Paris 1991, vol. 1, pp. 322–4, 327.

[16] André RAYMOND, Artisans et Commerçants au Caire au XVIIIᵉ siècle, Damas 1974, vol. 2, pp. 184–92.

[17] ANF, AE Biii 243, Beaujour, Inspection, 1817.

[18] Olga KATSIARDI-HERING, I Elliniki Parikia tis Teryestis (1751–1830), Athens 1986, vol. 2, pp. 547–8.

Samos (on the Alexandria-Izmir or Izmir-Istanbul-Salonica routes). The surplus production, often in foodstuffs or in other goods particular to an island, were usually sent to the large urban centres, as were some of the more expensive manufactured goods, such as silk stuffs from the island of Chios, for these were the markets that could best absorb such goods.

Goods were also traded locally within the smaller markets of the region especially among the bigger islands. Among them, Chios was an important port of call for most ships crossing the eastern Mediterranean on the north-south axis. The particular prominence of the island of Chios as a stopping place in the coastal trade of the eastern Mediterranean was primarily because of its good location rather than its potential as a major market.[19] Situated in the middle of the Aegean sea, ships tended to stop there to get provisions, fresh water, the current news concerning piratical activity or the outbreak of plague in near-by ports.[20] As one of the more prosperous islands in the region, it also traded with other Ottoman markets, both major and minor ones. Its own market was mostly, although not exclusively, supplied from Izmir with goods that included some of the city-port's more up-market western manufactured imports.[21] Another prosperous island economy was that of Crete. Olive oil, wine and currants were some of the goods that Crete sent to other markets in the Empire. The existence of a local industry, soap making, coupled with an active overseas trade, based primarily on the export of olive oil[22], meant that despite its size, Crete had a local market that enabled it to purchase from major markets, such as Izmir and Alexandria, apart from potash for its soap-making industry, other goods such as rice, coffee, tobacco or western manufactures. Crete was also an important link in the trading routes between Alexandria and Izmir or Istanbul.

The specific needs of the various regional markets for certain commodities and the goods that the various regions produced for the internal and external trade of the Empire greatly affected the pattern and type of coastal trade activity. For instance, Rhodes had contacts, through the coastal trade, with a number of small regional markets such as Cos, Cyprus, Chios, Crete, ports in the Peloponnese and the Syrian coast. However the principal markets with which it carried out most of its trade were fewer: Alexandria, Izmir and, to a

[19] ANF, AE Bi 1013, Consul Jouvin, Chios, 15 May 1763 to Minister, Paris.

[20] Daniel PANZAC, L'escale de Chio: un observatoire privilégié de l'activité maritime en mer Égée au XVIIIe siècle, in: Annales 4 (1985), pp. 541–61. This study, while interesting, tends to exaggerate the importance of Chios since no distinction is made between ships stopping there to trade or simply to get provisions or information.

[21] For a commercial history of the island of Chios in this period and of the international trading activities of its merchants, see Elena FRANGAKIS-SYRETT, I Chiotes Empori stis Thiethnis Synallages, 1750–1850, Athens 1995.

[22] Yolande TRIANTAFYLLIDOU-BALADIE, To emporio ke i ikonomia tis Kritis (1669–1795), Iraklion 1988, p. 62.

lesser extent, Istanbul. Moreover, there was a distinct pattern of trade between
the island and these markets: Alexandria received more goods from Rhodes
than it sent to it, and more ships from Alexandria, while on their coastal trade
voyage, made a stop at the island, than ships left Rhodes for Alexandria. The
goods that were sent to the Alexandrine market were mostly foodstuffs, such
as, citrus fruits, raisins, figs, honey, wine as well as other goods, such as,
tobacco or wood from the forests of the region. Alexandria sent to Rhodes
some of its principal staple goods, such as, coffee, for which there was a mass
market in the eighteenth-century Ottoman Empire, rice as well as salt and, in
limited qualities, flax seed.[23] As far as the Caramanian region, as a whole, was
concerned, Izmir supplied it, primarily through Rhodes and secondarily
through Cos, with European goods, such as cotton cloth, thus competing with
local manufacture.[24] It was to Izmir also that coasters carried the region's
lucrative cargo of sponges where it was bought by Europeans and exported to
major western markets.[25] Some foodstuffs, such as fruit, were also sent
primarily from Rhodes both to Izmir and Istanbul, for local consumption while
certain other goods, such as wine, were sent to the Ottoman capital for export
to Russia.[26]

Given the demographic growth experienced in the Ottoman Empire in the
eighteenth century, one of the most important commodities in the internal
maritime trade, were foodstuffs and, in particular, cereals and grain.[27] At
times of bad harvests and famine, which could hit any part of the Empire at
any time, wheat and cereals had to be sent to the affected area by sea while the
large urban centres, led by Istanbul, had an on-going need for foodstuffs,
including cereals. It was such needs that were being met by the coastal trade
that carried, for instance, cereals for local consumption from ports in Syria or
Anatolia to the ports of North Africa. While rice was a staple commodity in
the trade of Alexandria with all the principal Ottoman markets, olive oil, often
sold for ready cash as opposed to barter or on credit[28], was another valuable
foodstuff, both for the external and the internal trade of the Empire. Areas that
produced olive oil, such as Crete or Mitylene, were integrated into some of the
most active coastal trade routes.

Ottoman coastal trade was also important in the supplying of local industries
with raw materials as well as in distributing finished products. A case in point

---

[23] Maria EFTHYMIOU-HADZILACOU, Rhodes et sa région élargie au 18ème siècle: les
activités portuaires, Athens 1988, pp. 193–228.

[24] ANF, AE Biii 242, Fourcade, Mémoire, 1812; see also AE Biii 415, Picard, Notice
sur l'île de Stancho (Cos), c. 1801.

[25] ANF, AE Bi 1068, Consul Amoureux, Izmir, 3 June 1778 to Minister, Paris.

[26] ANF, AE Biii 242 Fourcade, Mémoire, 1812.

[27] MURPHEY, Provisioning Istanbul, p. 220.

[28] ANF, AE Bi 1052, Consul Charles de Peyssonnel, Izmir, 29 Jan. 1749 to Minister,
Paris.

was the soap industry of Crete.[29] Potash was sent to Crete from Tripoli in Libya, the Syrian ports, Alexandria, Izmir and Salonica.[30] The most important finished goods carried in the coastal trade were local and western textiles. Western textiles were sent principally from Izmir to a number of markets within the Empire. There was also an active internal trade in local textiles. For instance, although North Africa had well-established commercial links with Europe by then, and could thus be easily supplied with western cloth, there was still demand in the region for locally produced textiles which were sent there principally from Izmir and Alexandria.[31] This is not as contradictory as it may first appear. Certainly the trade of the Empire with Europe, based mainly on the exchange of Ottoman raw materials and foodstuffs for western textiles, was growing at the time. However, given the territorial expanse of the Empire there were many Ottoman regions, as well as sectors of regional markets, that the international market could not yet reach and which were still being supplied through the internal market. Moreover, given that we are still dealing with pre-Industrial-Revolution Europe, certain types of Ottoman textiles were still able to compete, under certain market conditions, with western manufactures.

Although Ottoman coastal trade was *de facto* open to *all* nationalities, in theory the situation was more complicated. Based on the Capitulations, the European states claimed the right to participate in the Ottoman coastal trade.[32] They cited, for instance, article 75 of the Capitulations signed in 1740 between the Ottoman Empire and France which gave, quite clearly, the right to the French to participate in the Ottoman coastal trade:

»Lorsque les musulmans ou les rayahs, sujets de ma Sublime Porte, chargeront des marchandises sur des bâtiments français pour les transporter d'une échelle de mon empire à une autre; il n'y sera porté aucun empêchement.«[33]

Throughout the eighteenth century, internal Ottoman government decrees tried to secure coastal trade either in Ottoman hands only or, at least, have Ottoman ships be given priority in coastal trade. Such decrees could not be enforced either because local authorities, such as customs officials, had an interest, due to the revenues that would thus be accrued, in allowing an active

---

[29] Yolande TRIANTAFYLLIDOU-BALADIE, L'industrie du savon en Crète au XVIIIe siècle: aspects économiques et sociaux, in: Revue des études balkaniques 4 (1975), pp. 75–87.

[30] N. SVORONOS, Le Commerce de Salonique au XVIIIe siècle, Paris 1956, pp. 270–1.

[31] Daniel PANZAC, Le commerce maritime de Tripoli de Barbarie dans la seconde moitié du XVIIIe siècle, in: Revue d'Histoire maghrebine 69–70 (1993), pp. 149–50, 153–4; see also RAYMOND, Artisans, pp. 191–2.

[32] The Capitulations were legal agreements made between the Ottoman government and a number of European powers granting non-reciprocal trading privileges to the Europeans in the Ottoman Empire; these agreements also regulated all aspects of the economic activities of the Europeans in the Empire.

[33] George YOUNG, Corps du droit ottoman, Oxford 1905, vol. 3, p. 63.

coasting trade to go through their offices, or because local brokers, who chartered the ships, or local merchants, whose goods were thus being transported, were reluctant to follow such decrees. This was either because the European ships were the only ones available or because, compared to Ottoman ships, they were considered safer for the transport of the merchants' goods.[34] The superior design and construction of European ships was accepted by the Ottomans.[35] They were also aware that there were not enough Ottoman carriers, especially in view of the growth of the internal maritime trade at the time. So that, although there were specific sectors where local – Arab, Greek or Turkish – carriers predominated, within the coastal trade of the Empire, overall, European ships filled the existing and growing needs. The result was not only the active participation of a number of European flags in Ottoman internal trade, but the dominance of this coastal trade by European captains and ships and, in particular, by the French.[36] They were the single most important group, especially in the earlier part of our period, in all routes – except for the Red Sea, in Ottoman coastal trade.[37] There was a tendency for French and other European carriers to be primarily active in the longer routes, or *grand cabotage*, while Ottoman carriers tended to be active in the shorter coastal routes, or *petit cabotage*. Ottoman small craft also dominated the lighterage sector of the coastal trade.

There were a number of advantages that European ships enjoyed in the coastal trade which helped them acquire and maintain their dominance. These were: an advantageous position, based on the Capitulations, as far as customs dues were concerned: on entering and leaving ports in the Empire they paid lower dues than Ottoman ships. European captains were also less likely to be harassed by demands for extraordinary payments, called *avanias*, by local port authorities than local captains were, for the Europeans always enjoyed the protection of a western consular authority. This authority was based on and reflected not only the prestige of the European country in question but also the terms of the Capitulations signed between that country and the Porte. Indeed, as we saw above, it was the Capitulations that gave the European powers the right to claim participation in the internal Ottoman maritime trade for their nationals.[38] The Capitulations, together with a vigorous exercise of consular authority, resulted in greater security and protection for the European captains in the eastern Mediterranean and hence in greater safety for the cargoes they

[34] RAYMOND, Artisans, pp. 170–1.

[35] MURPHEY, Provisioning Istanbul, p. 223.

[36] Although the coastal trade related primarily to the transport of goods, European ships also carried passengers. This included merchants and local officials, pilgrims and Ottoman troops.

[37] ANF, AE Bi 1062, Consul Charles-Claude de Peyssonnel, Izmir, 22 July 1775 to Minister, Paris.

[38] YOUNG, Corps du droit, p. 63.

carried. This factor, coupled with the superior construction and bigger size of the European ships, cited above, which allowed them to withstand the weather better, made them preferable to Ottoman ships. Finally, another asset that the Europeans enjoyed, and which should not be underestimated, was their immunity from the Maltese corsairs which their Ottoman rivals, to their detriment, did not have. Periodic attacks on Ottoman shipping from Maltese corsairs, throughout the period under study, made local merchants and brokers turn even more to European captains.[39]

For the French, the Ottoman coastal trade was considered a lucrative occupation.[40] Compared to the overseas trade of the French with the Ottoman Empire, considerable resources, in terms of ships, were put into the Ottoman coastal trade. Almost three-quarters of the French ships in the eastern Mediterranean at that time were engaged in the coastal trade. Moreover, coastal trade was as important to Ottoman ports as blue water. For instance, in the 1750s and 1760s, almost half of the French ships that arrived in Izmir had originated from other Ottoman ports, while the rest came from Marseilles. The ratio was lower for the departures, with more French ships leaving for Marseilles than for other Ottoman ports[41], although the proportion of French captains having another Ottoman port as their destination was still more than a third in overall departures.[42] As for Alexandria, the share of ships active in coastal trade within its total port activity was even higher.[43]

There were a number of reasons why the French merchant marine preferred the coastal trade to the set routes of Marseilles-Izmir or Marseilles to Italian ports and then onto Izmir and the reverse. Participation in the coastal trade gave them the opportunity to be at sea for at least two years, with a single quarantine at the end of the voyage. In contrast, a normal voyage between Marseilles and Izmir took six months, including a quarantine of up to ninety days, but the sailors were paid for only the four and a half months they were at sea. In the coastal trade even the longest voyages, that is when ships went directly from Salonica or Istanbul to Alexandria or from Alexandria to Tunis, which was rare for ships usually stopped at other ports along the way, only lasted between fifteen and twenty-five days. The coastal trade was also rela-

---

[39] Peter EARLE, Corsairs of Malta and Barbary, London 1970, pp. 141–67.

[40] E.g., ANF, AE Bi 1012 in Hélène PEGNIÉ, Exoteriko ke dianisiotiko emporio sti Chio ton 18° eona, in: Ta Historika, vol. 5, no. 8 (1988), p. 117; see also Report of the Chamber of Commerce of Marseilles in H.A.R. GIBB/Harold BOWEN, Islamic Society and the West, Oxford 1950, vol. 1, pt. I, p. 309.

[41] ANF, AE Biii 271–274; see also Elena FRANGAKIS-SYRETT, Izmir – An international port in the eastern Mediterranean in the eighteenth century (1695–1820), in: Actes du II⁰ colloque international d'histoire, Athens 1985, vol. 1, pp. 124–8.

[42] Captains who had no specific Ottoman port as their destination left Izmir to look for cargo along the way among ports in the eastern Mediterranean.

[43] RAYMOND, Artisans, pp. 168–9.

tively inexpensive to run. On leaving Marseilles, the captain was given two months' provisions and a relatively modest sum (100 piastres) in cash.[44] As an additional recompense, the captain was allowed to keep his return cargo, of wheat or even better of rice, which he had acquired from the profits made on the freight he had carried during his voyage(s) and from monetary trans-actions, usually changing different currencies, western or local, that he in-variably dealt in along the way.[45]

The participation of the French in the Ottoman coastal trade was closely related to their overseas trade with the Empire. For French ships coming from Europe, from Marseilles or an Italian port, usually stayed for a period of up to two years in Ottoman home waters, carrying goods from port to port, before picking up cargo for the return journey to Europe. Usually the return cargo to Europe was provided by the French merchants who had freighted the ship for the initial journey to the Ottoman Empire. In the case of a major port, such as Izmir, the loading could be done on the spot with, at most, the possibility that certain goods, such as olive oil or wheat, might be loaded from a near-by port. However, in the case of smaller ports, such as those in the Peloponnese or Syria, the captain might have to go to a number of ports where, with the co-operation of the French merchants established in those ports, he collected cargo for his return journey to Europe. As far as the coastal trade was concerned, however, the captain had to find freight himself.

Ships active in the Ottoman coastal trade did not belong to shipping compa-nies, nor did they sail up and down specific routes. Instead French captains, like their rivals in the Levant, had to be prepared to change ports and routes frequently according to the charter they could secure, or even to call in ports in the hope of finding cargo. This was due to the uncertainty of the market as well as to the strong competition among carriers. In reality, most captains tended to repeat a number of ports and routes for this was where they had established contacts with charterers or local merchants. This did not mean that ships could not potentially undertake a number of voyages in any given year. Voyages lasted quite a while, with safety being more important than speed. For navigating Ottoman coastal waters was not particularly easy while bad weather and insecurity at sea, due to pirates or privateers, could force them to

---

[44] By contrast, the master of a British ship carrying goods from London to Izmir, for instance, was paid £ 100 worth of foreign currency or bullion, nearly ten times more than his French counterpart and given, as part of his salary, trading privileges that were allocated at a rate of 40 shillings per ton of the ship's burden. Public Record Office, London, SP 105/211, The Printed Orders of the Levant Company, 1744. Hereafter these archives will be cited as PRO. However, captains of French ships were compensated almost entirely by trading privileges. This was considered fair pay since these ships, most frequently engaged in the coastal trade too, were smaller than those used by the British and their journey was much shorter. ANF, AE Bi 1013, Consul Jouvin, Chios, 15 May 1763.

[45] FRANGAKIS-SYRETT, The Commerce of Smyrna, p. 91.

make additional stops for refuge, thus delaying their journey even more. Moreover, loading and unloading were done at a rather leisurely pace with the ship staying in port for a long time. For instance, in the 1760s, the average time that a ship stayed in the two main ports of the island of Crete, for unloading or loading of merchandise, was two and four weeks respectively. In fact the smaller the port the longer the ship might be obliged to stay. Other times, the stay of a ship was influenced by the captain's efforts to get more or new freight.[46] Indeed, time taken up with loading and unloading, as well as with stopping at various ports on the way to the final destination, accounted for a considerable amount of the overall length of the voyage. Actual time at sea was relatively short since distances were not great. Therefore demurrage clauses did not seem to be part of such charters. The exception to this were ships freighted for the transport of grain for Istanbul, or of a region affected by famine. Here tight schedules had to be met and demurrage clauses were part of the contract.[47]

In chartering ships, single voyages predominated by far while return voyages, or what the sources call *fermés*, were much less frequent. Indeed the lack of charters at any given point in time, due to the volatility of the market, led to the widespread practice of coasters setting out from a port, as we saw earlier in the example of Izmir, with no fixed destination, in search of cargo, or what the sources call *en aventure*.[48] Ships were chartered either for a period of time, often four to six months, or for a specific, mostly single, journey. Although ships were usually chartered for their entire cargo capacity, there were also space charters. In the mid-eighteenth century, a ship going to Izmir from Alexandria could be freighted in its entirety for a sum from 400 to 1,500 piastres, according to the dimensions of the ship.[49] Sometimes the freight rate was arrived at by an itemized rate for each type of good loaded on a ship. For instance, 100 *ardebs* (18.6 tons) of rice were carried from Alexandria to Izmir

---

[46] Robert PARIS, Histoire du Commerce de Marseille, vol. 5: Le Levant de 1660 à 1789, Paris 1957, pp. 168–79.

[47] MURPHEY, Provisioning Istanbul, p. 225.

[48] ANF, AE Biii 271–277, États des bâtiments (1756–1787).

[49] Throughout the eighteenth century, the basic Ottoman silver currency, called piastre or gurush, stayed at a fixed rate of 3 livres tournois per piastre for the French currency. However, this rate had to be further adjusted when calculating the exchange rate vis-à-vis the French currency in order to reflect the loss in value that the Ottoman currency underwent in the latter part of the eighteenth and in the early-nineteenth centuries. This becomes more evident in the exchange rate vis-à-vis the British currency which ranged from c. 7 piastres per £ in mid-century to 11 piastres per £ by 1790 and to over 20 piastres per £ by the end of the Napoleonic Wars. Elena FRANGAKIS-SYRETT, The Ottoman Monetary System in the Long Eighteenth Century, paper delivered at the Colloquium on Money and Mints in the Ottoman Empire, 1680–1850, held at the French Institute of Anatolian Studies, Istanbul, Turkey, 28–30 Nov. 1997.

for 90 piastres, to Salonica for 100 piastres and to Istanbul for 120 piastres.[50] In the grain carrying trade, the freight rate could also be arrived at by taking a fixed percentage of the value of the cargo and adjusting it according to the length of the voyage.[51] Often, the captain was paid part of his freight money at the beginning of the journey receiving the balance after the safe delivery of his cargo. Normally the freight was paid, or ultimately settled, mostly in silver specie of either Ottoman or European currencies for both types of coinage circulated in the Ottoman Empire at the time.[52] The latter coins, mostly Dutch dollars or Maria-Theresa thalers, were often preferred. In this respect, the coastal trade was in line with other sectors of the Ottoman economy.

Not everything went smoothly between the European captain and the local merchant or shipbroker when freighting a ship and problems often arose. A reason for this was the endemic monetary scarcity which was a feature of the Ottoman economy even in the prosperous maritime regions. This made it, at times, difficult for the shipbroker to pay all the expenses, such as part of the freight, port dues and other expenses, before the goods had reached their destination and the proceeds from their sale had been realized. As a result, credit, which featured very strongly in all commercial transactions in the Empire at the time, was used in the coastal trade. It was also often the cause of subsequent disputes between the captain and the broker.[53] At the same time, the strong competition that existed in the coastal trade between various shippers made European captains willing to enter into, at times, even dubious freight contracts.[54]

Information concerning the total tonnage of the merchant fleets involved, or the tonnage of types of ships, or of individual ships active in the coastal trade is either incomplete or lacking. It is thus impossible to tell the overall tonnage of these fleets. There is also no complete data concerning the movement of ships, European or Ottoman, leaving or entering Ottoman ports that would allow us to quantify the number of ships involved in the coastal trade. It is equally impossible to tell the global amount of goods carried, even on the principal routes, by either the French or any other group of shippers, within

[50] Daniel PANZAC, Négociants ottomans et capitaines français: la caravane maritime en Crète au XVIIIᵉ siècle, in: H. BATU/J.-L. BACQUE-GRAMMONT (eds.), L'Empire ottoman, la République de Turquie et la France, Istanbul/Paris 1986, pp. 78–9, 82–5 and idem, Affréteurs ottomans, pp. 65–6.

[51] MURPHEY, Provisioning Istanbul, pp. 226–8.

[52] For reasons for such practices, see FRANGAKIS-SYRETT, The Commerce of Smyrna, pp. 139–54; see also Edhem ELDEM, La circulation de la lettre de change entre la France et Constantinople au XVIIIᵉ siècle, in : H. BATU/J.-L. BACQUE-GRAMMONT, (eds.), L'Empire ottoman, la République de Turquie et la France, Istanbul/Paris 1986, pp. 87–97.

[53] ANF, AE Bi 1060, Extraits des minutes de la Chancellerie, Izmir, 12 April 1772 to Minister, Paris.

[54] ANF, AE Bi 1052, Consul Charles de Peyssonnel, Izmir, 5 March 1749 to Minister, Paris.

the period under study. For even when the type of ship is given, there is no certainty as to its tonnage. Differing tonnage figures are given in the sources for the same types of ships.[55] Nevertheless, from data on the *types* of ships involved, we can draw some overall conclusions as to the *range* of their tonnage. Some of the most popular types of merchant ships used in the Ottoman coastal trade had the following range of tonnage: *tartanes* 30–125 tons; *barques* 90–150 tons; *brigantins* 60–190 tons; *pinques* 60–150 tons; *senau(lts)* 60–170 tons; *corvettes* 140–235 tons; *polacres* 60–200 tons; *bombardes* 100–145 tons.[56] We also have some indications concerning the productivity of Ottoman coastal trade, that is, the number of men per ship. Here, there is concurrence in the sources for the French, for whom the data is more complete, that indicates that the man-to-ton ratio was just over ten tons per man.[57] Other nationalities, such as the Venetians, Ragusans or Russians, seem to have had a higher ratio of men per ton than the French. Given the limited data, these figures can only be indicative. Productivity was also affected by other factors as the case of the Ottoman Greeks makes clear. Despite their much lower man-to-ton ratio, which averaged about six tons per man, they were nevertheless very competitive, a fact reflected in the growth of the Ottoman Greek merchant marine in this period. Lower wages and cheaper provisions for the crew contributed to lower overall costs, despite the larger crew sizes.[58]

Despite the stiff competition that the French faced from other European and Ottoman carriers lucrative freight rates made up, as far as the French captains were concerned, for the infrequency and length of charter. This was probably true for other European captains. Moreover, European ships tended to carry more expensive goods, making their freight rates more worthwhile. So that even when the numbers of European ships involved in a certain route were small, the tonnage thus represented, and even more the value of the cargo carried, were higher. By contrast, in the transport of less expensive bulkier goods, covering shorter distances, smaller local, Turkish, Greek or Arab, ships were preferred. For instance, Ottoman shipowners predominated in the coastal trade between Alexandria and the Caramanian coast, including Rhodes, as

[55] Yolande TRIANTAFYLLIDOU-BALADIE, Transports maritimes et concurrence en Méditerranée orientale au XVIIIᵉ siècle: L'exemple de la Crète, in: Actes de IIᵉ colloque international d'histoire, Athens 1985, vol. 1, p. 24.

[56] The data has been taken from a number of sources, namely: TRIANTAFYLLIDOU-BALADIE, Transports maritimes, pp. 23–4; Charles CARRIERE, Négociants Marseillais au XVIIIᵉ siècle, Aix-en-Provence 1973, vol. 2, pp. 594–9; Vasilis KREMMYDAS, To emporio tis Peloponnisou sto 18° eona (1715–1792), Athens 1972, p. 254.

[57] E.g., Murat CIZAKÇA, A Comparative Evolution of Business Partnerships. The Islamic World and Europe, Leiden 1996, p. 129; KREMMYDAS, To emporio tis Peloponnisou, p. 254; TRIANTAFYLLIDOU-BALADIE, Transports maritimes, p. 29.

[58] KREMMYDAS, To emporio tis Peloponnisou, pp. 254–6; TRIANTAFYYLLIDOU-BALADIE, Transports maritimes, pp. 27–9.

they did in the trade between the Ionian islands and the western coast of Greece while the lighterage sector was also in Ottoman hands. Small craft under the Ottoman flag were used for the local traffic connecting Istanbul and Galata (the Asiatic and European shores of the Ottoman capital).[59] At the same time, the coastal traffic of small ports, situated near a major port, such as those in the gulf of Salonica or along the Syrian coast, which acted as feeder ports for the external trade of the major port in the area, was also in the hands of Ottoman shippers.[60] Equally the coastal trade between Izmir and Istanbul, closely related to the external trade, was in the hands of Turkish shipowners.[61]

Among the major European economies of the time, only the French participated so actively in the Ottoman coastal trade: the Dutch did not participate in it and the British did so only to a limited extent. The British tended to be more active at times of war, as for instance during the Seven Years' War (1756–63) when the regulations of the Levant Company concerning the trading activities of its members as well as of non-members, were more relaxed. Although in the second half of the eighteenth century, the Levant Company was no longer able to control shipping between Britain and the Levant, as it had done earlier[62], the British did not become, even then, prominent players in the Ottoman coastal trade. Like their French counterparts, British captains were not averse to utilizing their time, while waiting for cargo to be collected by the European merchants for their journey home, to go coasting. In such a case, the captain might get the help of the British merchant(s) who had initially chartered him from London, either with some freight for near-by ports or with recommendation letters.[63] When a certain Ottoman port could not offer enough cargo for the return journey to London, like his French counterpart, the British captain continued his journey to a number of other coastal ports in the vicinity picking up cargo on the way.[64] Although these goods were destined for the external market, it was also possible for other transactions to

---

[59] E.g., RAYMOND, Artisans, p. 168; Efthymiou-Hadzilacou, Rhodes, pp. 282–6; George B. LEON, The Greek merchant marine (1453–1850), in: S.A. PAPADOPOULOS (ed.), The Greek Merchant Marine, Athens 1972, pp. 20, 27, 29, 31.

[60] Amnon COHEN, Ottoman rule and the re-emergence of the coast of Palestine (17th-18th centuries), in: Revue de l'Occident Musulman et de la Méditerranée 39 (1985), p. 165.

[61] E.g., PRO, SP 105/188, Ambassador Sir Robert Ainslie, Istanbul, 11 & 16 May 1782; 3 Feb and 2 Dec. 1783; 27 Jan. 1786.

[62] E.g., PRO, SP 105/116, Levant Company, London, 13 Aug. 1719 to Consul Cooke, Izmir; SP 105/117, Levant Company, London, 26 Sept. 1729 and 1 Sept. 1730 to Consul Boddington, Izmir; ibid., Levant Company, London, 13 March 1739 to Treasurer Tooke, Izmir.

[63] Elena FRANGAKIS-SYRETT, Trade practices in Aleppo in the middle of the eighteenth century: the case of a British merchant, in: Revue du Monde Musulman et de la Méditerranée 62 (1991), p. 126.

[64] PRO, SP 110/36, Th. Lansdown, Aleppo, 17 Jan. 1760 to Captain C. Wilson, Iskenderun.

be made and for some goods to be carried locally while the captain was undertaking such a coastal route.

Other European participants active in the Ottoman internal trade were the Danes, Swedes, Ragusans, Venetians and those of Imperial Germany. While the French faced strong competition during peacetime, it was primarily maritime wars between France and other European powers that caused them their biggest problems and led to the erosion of their dominance. During such wars, the commerce raiding activities of their enemies affected them adversely and severely compromised the safety of their cargoes. As a result, local merchants and charterers alike tended to avoid French ships during wartime. With business falling sharply, French captains even resorted to selling their ships on the spot to their erstwhile local or other western rivals and to temporarily withdrawing from the coastal trade.[65] Other nationalities filled the gap left by the French. During the Seven Years' War, the Ragusans became the single most important carriers of the coastal trade along the western Anatolian coast and the Aegean Sea.[66] Moreover, in the aftermath of the War, the Ragusans emerged probably as the biggest competitors to the French.[67] In the last quarter of the eighteenth century and onwards, due to a number of factors, among them being the economic prosperity cited above, Greek and Turkish shipowners were able to benefit most from the problems of the French.

The upheaval of the French Revolution, coupled with the destruction of the French merchant fleet by the British navy during the French Revolutionary and Napoleonic Wars, allowed the local shipowners, the Greek more than any other group, to make even greater inroads, in the late-eighteenth and early-nineteenth centuries, into the French carrying trade than the Ragusans ever had. A number of reasons account for such developments. The general commercial prosperity of the eastern Mediterranean was particularly evident among the Greeks of the Ottoman Empire. It was reflected in their active and increasing participation in the overseas trade of the Empire, particularly that between the eastern Mediterranean and the Italian ports, as well as in the growth experienced by the Greeks in the carrying trade.[68] In this sector they were increasingly active in both the overseas and the internal Ottoman maritime trade. Greek ships started carrying goods not only between Ottoman and Italian ports or Marseilles, but also among islands and ports in the eastern

[65] PANZAC, Négociants ottomans, pp. 79–80.

[66] ANF, AE Biii 271, États des bâtiments, 1756–1762. For Ragusan competition to French coastal trade following the Seven Years' War, see AE Bi 1062, Consul Charles-Claude de Peyssonnel, Izmir, 22 July 1775 to Minister, Paris.

[67] Francis W. CARTER, Dubrovnik (Ragusa). A Classic City-State, London 1972, pp. 421–41.

[68] ANF, AE Bi 859, Consul L'Allement, Messina, 20 March 1784, 3 Sept. 1785, 4 Feb. 1786 and 14 Jan. 1788 to Minister, Paris.

Mediterranean.[69] Thus the Greeks, from the outset, were active both in commerce and in shipping.[70]

At the same time, the specialization of the Greeks in the commerce and transport of certain key products in the overseas trade of the Empire, such as Ottoman wheat and European cloth, gave them an important asset which in turn contributed to the increase of their merchant marine.[71] The Greeks also enjoyed a number of other assets which their local Turkish rivals in the coastal trade did not. They carried out privateering activities during a number of European or Ottoman wars in the second half of the eighteenth and in the early-nineteenth centuries.[72] For instance, during the Russo-Ottoman War (1768–74) Russian-protected Greek privateers were very active in the Aegean Sea to the detriment not only of their Turkish but even more of their Ragusan rivals. During this war the Ragusans were badly hit by the Russians who considered them Ottoman.[73] When there were no wars, the Greeks often reverted to piracy, which was rife in the Aegean Sea in the late-eighteenth and early-nineteenth centuries.[74] Such activities contributed to their capital accumulation and overall economic growth, including their share of the internal Ottoman maritime trade. There were certain exceptions to this. For instance, an area of coastal trade where Turkish shipowners maintained a clear dominance over their Greek and European rivals, in the late-eighteenth century, was the carrying trade between Izmir and Istanbul.[75] Yet, even after a sharp decline in French trade activity in the Levant, in 1812, the coastal trade in the

---

[69] ANF, AE Bi 1087, Consul Fraunnery, Trieste, 27 Jan. 1789 to Minister, Paris.

[70] Elena FRANGAKIS-SYRETT, Greek Mercantile Activities in the eastern Mediterranean, 1780–1820, in: Balkan Studies 28 (1987), pp. 73–86.

[71] E.g., Archives du Ministère des Affaires Étrangères, Paris, CCC, Vol. 8, Vice-Consul David, Chios, 17 Oct. 1824 to Minister, Paris. Hereafter, these archives will be cited as AMAE. See also FRANGAKIS-SYRETT, The Commerce of Smyrna, pp. 101–2, 110–4 and LEON, Greek Merchant Marine, pp. 30–2, 41–2.

[72] M.S. ANDERSON, Russia in the Mediterranean, 1788–1791: a little-known chapter in the history of naval warfare and privateering, in: Mariner's Mirror 45 (1959), pp. 25–35.

[73] However, they subsequently recovered to become once more active in the Ottoman coastal trade in the 1800s; see, CARTER, Dubrovnik (Ragusa), pp. 439–41.

[74] E.g., ANF, AE Bi 168, Consul Benincasa, Ancôna, 24 Feb. 1785 to Minister, Paris; PRO, SP 105/128, Consul Werry, Izmir, 1 Feb. 1802 to Levant Co., London; PRO, SP 105/129, Consul Werry, Izmir, 2 May 1803 to Levant Co., London; PRO, SP 105/132, Consul Werry, Izmir, 19 May, 9 July & 20 Nov. 1809 to Levant Co., London; PRO, SP 105/135, Consul Werry, 6 April 1815 to Levant Co., London; PRO, FO 78/136, W. Hamilton, Istanbul, 2 July 1823 to Consul General Cartwright, Istanbul; AMAE, CCC, Vol. 8, Vice-Consul David, Chios, 17 Oct. 1824 to Minister, Paris. See also C. G. PITCAIRN JONES, Piracy in the Levant, 1827–8, London 1934, passim; D. THEMELI-KATIFORI, I dioxis tis piratias ke to thalassion dikastirion kata tin protin Kapodistriakin periodon, 1828–1829, Athens 1973, vol. 1, pp. 47–54.

[75] Bashbakanlik Osmanli Arshivi in Mehmet Genç (forthcoming); see also PRO, SP 105/188, May 1782, Feb. & Dec. 1783.

Aegean Sea alone was considered profitable enough to warrant the continuation of French trade in the area.[76]

Given the pre-industrial nature of the economy, the internal maritime trade of the Ottoman Empire fulfilled an important function by circulating goods, mostly agricultural, that were necessary either for local consumption or for local industries. It also circulated, perhaps to a lesser extent, goods of local manufacturers. Coastal trade thus directed the output of a specific region to the market needs of another region, primarily maritime, within the Empire in the most cost-effective manner. In the process, it contributed to the further commercialization of the Empire's agricultural production and to the further monetization of its economy. For the Europeans, and particularly the French, it was a lucrative part of their extensive trading activities with the Ottoman Empire in the eighteenth century. Their participation in the Ottoman coastal trade, which went against the trend of protection of a country's coastal trade mostly in force in Europe at the time, was an economic necessity for the Empire given its territorial expanse, cost of land transport and inadequacy of the Ottoman merchant marine. The participation of the Europeans was also a natural extension of the growing integration of the Ottoman Empire into the international market and the growing commercial links that were being forged between the Empire and Europe. The close ties between the internal and external trade of the Empire further reflected such trends. Finally, the nature and organization of Ottoman coastal trade and of European participation in it were also the results of wider trends in economic growth that the world economy experienced, in the second half of the eighteenth and in the early-nineteenth centuries, and of which the Ottoman Empire was also part.

[76] ANF, AE Biii 242, Jumelin, Commerce du Levant en général, c. Sept. 1812.

Map 5: Mecklenburg and Western Pomerania in 1814

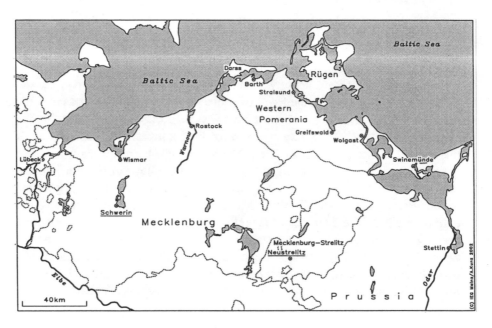

Map: IEG-Maps (http://www.ieg-maps.uni-mainz.de).
Cartography: Joachim Robert Moeschl

11

THE COASTAL SHIPPING OF MECKLENBURG AND WESTERN POMERANIA, 1750–1830

DANIEL A. RABUZZI

Coastal shipping was important to the economic development of northern Germany and the Baltic region generally during the period prior to industrialization, c. 1750–1830. It may be that growth in coastal shipping was one of the necessary preconditions for industrialization. I will explore this hypothesis by examining coastal shipping during the said period within and originating from the neighbouring north German provinces of Mecklenburg and Western Pomerania (*Vorpommern*). Judging from secondary evidence, it appears that the maritime experiences of these two territories were similar to those of other Baltic and North Sea areas.

We cannot fully understand the rise of the transoceanic Atlantic economies from the seventeenth century on without understanding the internal feeder traffic of Europe's two older seas, the Baltic in my example as well as the Mediterranean. Baltic capillaries of trade, along which grain and naval stores were collected and tropical goods were distributed, may have been as important to the continent's economic development as the arteries connecting Europe to Asia and the Americas. The case of Mecklenburg and Western Pomerania supports the growing consensus that coastal and regional trade was at least as important to Western Europe's economic development between c. 1650 and c. 1850 as the more dramatic (and much more intensively studied) long-distance trades.[1]

---

[1] John ARMSTRONG/Philip BAGWELL, Coastal shipping, in: Derek H. ALDCROFT/Michael J. FREEMAN (eds.), Transport in the Industrial Revolution, Manchester 1983; Simon VILLE, Transport and communications, in: Derek H. ALDCROFT/Simon P. VILLE (eds.), The European Economy 1750–1914, Manchester 1994; Lex HEERMA VAN VOSS, Trade and the formation of North Sea culture, in: Northern Seas Yearbook 1996; T. C. BARKER, Transport: the survival of the old beside the new, in: Peter MATHIAS/John DAVIS (eds.), The First Industrial Revolutions, Oxford 1989; David PINCKNEY, Cabotage, France's forgotten common carrier, in: French Historical Studies 16 2 (1989); Dwight ROBINSON, Secret of British power in the age of sail: Admiralty records of the coasting fleet, in: The American Neptune 48 (1988). For late medieval background, see: Richard BRITNELL, The Commercialisation of English Society 1000–1500, Manchester 1996, pp. 86–8; Maryanne KOWALEWSKI, Local Markets and Regional Trade in Medieval Exeter, New York 1995, chap. 6. For related comments on inland navigation, see: Andreas KUNZ/John ARMSTRONG

To capture the extent and frequency of traffic *within* the Baltic, we will need to examine the records of the lesser Baltic ports individually; our central source for Baltic trade, the Danish Sound Toll Records, was not designed to document coastal trade within that sea.[2] I have used a variety of primary sources, in particular the customs (*Zulageregistern*) and port clearance (*Schifferbücher*) records for the West Pomeranian capital of Stralsund, held in the Stralsund City Archive (*Stadtarchiv*), as well as reports found in Denmark's National Archive (*Rigsarkivet*) from the Danish consul in Mecklenburg's leading port Rostock.[3] I also used evidence from documents in the

---

(eds.), Inland Navigation and Economic Development in Nineteenth-Century Europe, Mainz 1995; Malcolm WANKLYN, The impact of water transport facilities on English river ports, c. 1660 – c. 1760, in: Economic History Review 49 (1996). For similar comments about colonial North America, also emphasizing the relative lack of research on coastal trades: John MCCUSKER/Russell MENARD, The Economy of British America, 1607–1789, Chapel Hill, 2nd ed. 1991, p. 109.

[2] The literature on Baltic trade is enormous, but the primary focus has been on movements through the Sound. See Maria BOGUCKA, The role of Baltic trade in European development from the XVIth to the XVIIIth centuries, in: Journal of European Economic History 9 (1980); J. A. FABER, The decline of the Baltic grain-trade in the second half of the seventeenth Century, in: W. G. HEERES [et al.] (eds.), From Dunkirk to Danzig: Shipping and Trade in the North Sea and the Baltic, 1350–1850, Hilversum 1988; Hans Christian JOHANSEN, Shipping and Trade between the Baltic Area and Western Europe 1784–1795, Odense 1983; Herbert KAPLAN, Russian Overseas Commerce with Great Britain during the Reign of Catherine II, Philadelphia 1995; Jake KNOPPERS, Dutch Trade with Russia from the Time of Peter I to Alexander I, Montreal 1976; J. Thomas LINDBLAD, Sweden's Trade with the Dutch Republic 1738–1795, Assen 1982. Concentrating on the Baltic's internal trade are: articles in this volume by Hans Christian Johansen, and Jari Ojala; Robert BOHN, Das Handelshaus Donner in Visby und der Gotländische Aussenhandel im 18. Jahrhundert, Cologne 1989; Edmund CIESLAK, Aspects of Baltic sea-borne trade in the eighteenth century: the trade relations between Sweden, Poland, Russia, and Prussia, in: Journal of European Economic History 12 (1983); Elisabeth HARDER-GERSDORFF, Handelskonjunkturen und Warenbilanz im lübeckisch-russischen Seeverkehr des 18. Jahrhunderts, in: Vierteljahrschrift für Sozial- und Wirtschaftsgeschichte 57 (1970); Aage RASCH, Kopenhagen und die deutschen Ostseestädte 1750–1807, in: Hansische Geschichtsblätter 82 (1964); Rolf ENGELSING, Die Häfen an der Südküste der Ostsee und der Ostwestverkehr in der ersten Hälfte des 19. Jahrhunderts, in: Vierteljahrsschrift für Sozial- und Wirtschaftsgeschichte 58 (1971).

[3] For shipping and trade generally in Mecklenburg and Western Pomerania c. 1650–1850: Thomas BRUECK, Korporationen der Schiffer und Bootsleute: Untersuchungen zu ihrer Entwicklung in Seestädten an der Nord- und Ostseeküste vom Ende des 15. bis zum Ende des 17. Jahrhunderts, Weimar 1994; Werner BUCHHOLZ, Öffentliche Finanzen und Finanzverwaltung im entwickelten frühmodernen Staat: Landesherr und Landstände in Schwedisch-Pommern 1720–1806, Cologne 1992; Hans-Joachim HACKER, Zum Schiffs- und Warenverkehr Stralsunds im 17. Jahrhundert, in: Studia Maritima 3 (1981); Stefan KROLL, Die Sozialstruktur der Städte Stade und Stralsund in der Endphase der schwedischen Grossmachtzeit (1700–1715), PhD Diss., Hamburg, 1995; K. F. OLECHNOWITZ, Handel und Seeschiffahrt der späten Hanse, Weimar 1965; Daniel A. RABUZZI, At Home in the Market: Stralsund Merchants and their Families, 1740–1830, PhD Diss., Johns Hopkins, 1996; Alfred RUBARTH, Stralsunds Segelschiffe,ihre Kapitäne und Schicksale 1800–1920, Hamburg 1992; Walther MÜLLER, Rostocks Seeschiffahrt und Seehandel im Wandel der Zeiten, Rostock 1930. A modern maritime history of Rostock is badly needed.

Greifswald City Archive, the Western Pomeranian Provincial Archive, the Provincial Archive of Sealand, the Lübeck City Archive, and the Stockholm City Archive. The period in question was a proto-statistical age, that is the data are neither as comprehensive nor as reliable as today's numbers, meaning that my findings can only be suggestions.

Rostock (population c. 11,000 in 1800) was a sizeable exporter of grain to destinations both within and beyond the Baltic. Wismar (population c. 6,500) also exported primarily grain; located in the Duchy of Mecklenburg, it was held by the Swedes until 1803. Western Pomerania was held until 1815 by Sweden, thereafter by Prussia, which already held Eastern Pomerania with its great port-city Stettin. (Mecklenburg and Western Pomerania today combined form the northeastern-most *Land* within the Federal Republic of Germany; Eastern Pomerania is the northwestern-most region of Poland.) Stralsund (population in 1800 c. 11,000) was Western Pomerania's largest commercial centre and an important shipbuilding site; it was one of Europe's leading exporters of malt. Wolgast (also the site of shipyards), Greifswald, and Barth were smaller West Pomeranian ports, and, like Rostock, Wismar, and Stralsund, all were former members of the medieval Hanseatic League.

Mecklenburg and Western Pomeranian coastal shipping consisted of two sorts: west-east trade along the littoral; and south-north hauls across the Baltic to Sweden and Finland. The former included the dense network of routine traffic between Stralsund, its Western Pomeranian sister ports, and ports along the south Baltic coast ranging from Jutland to East Prussia. Archival records suggest that this trade was both lively and extensive, with what looks like regular packet services for some ports. Not infrequently, a coaster made multiple stops, loading and discharging cargoes along the way like a modern liner. The list of connections was very long, ranging from major ports such as Stettin, Danzig and Königsberg to mid-size ports (e.g., Rostock, Wismar, Lübeck, Kiel) to myriad smaller places such as Zingst, Olthagen, Wolin, Leba, Ueckermünde, Damgarten, Demmin, Loitz, and Anklam (the last three being river ports). Rostock's networks looked similar, with greater contact as well to Lübeck and to Denmark.

In 1755, for example, 25 per cent of the laden vessels departing Stralsund were destined for ports along the adjacent Baltic coast.[4] By 1786, the range had expanded: for instance, some 14 per cent of laden outbound ships were headed to ports in Schleswig-Holstein alone (Ärösköbing, Kappeln, Neustadt,

---

[No eds.], Rostock im Ostseeraum in Mittelalter und früher Neuzeit, Rostock 1994. For eighteenth-century East Prussian maritime history: Heinz HINKEL, Schiffsbestand und Schiffer in den Häfen Pommerns, in: Baltische Studien, new ser., 53 (1967); Gottfried LOECK, Pommerns Schiffahrt im Jahre 1744, in: Deutsches Schiffahrtsarchiv 11 (1988); Wilhelm. BRAUN, Zur Stettiner Seehandelsgeschichte, 1572–1813, in: Baltische Studien, new ser., 51 (1965) and ibid., 52 (1966).

[4] Stadtarchiv der Hansestadt Stralsund (hereafter SAHS) 15-242, *Schifferbuch* for 1755.

Sonderburg).[5] The pattern was probably similar for Rostock. For example, in the twelve-month period beginning in August 1806, 176 ships averaging some fifteen *Commerzlast* (CL) in size arrived at Rostock coming from twenty-nine micro-ports in Denmark/Schleswig-Holstein.[6]

The cross-Baltic haul meant the routes from Mecklenburg and Western Pomerania to southern Sweden and Finland included therefore much sailing along the Swedish and Finnish coasts and within their archipelagoes. Rønne on the Danish island of Bornholm was also a destination. Besides Stockholm and Gothenburg, Swedish destinations included Malmö, Ystad, Karlshamn, Karlskrona, Kalmar, Vaestervik, Norrköping, Nyköping, and Gaevle as well as Visby on Gotland.

The coastal routes were the workhorse runs that shaped the Mecklenburg and Western Pomeranian merchant marine. The same captains made these runs throughout the sailing season, year in and year out, perfecting their knowledge of the shoals, islets and winds, and learning the ways of local trade. The Pomeranian coastline is especially treacherous, well known for shipwrecks, with its many lagoons, straits, spits and shallow bays. Captains made monthly trips from Wismar and Rostock to Lübeck already in 1700, almost certainly continuing traditions begun centuries earlier in hanseatic times.[7] In 1755, one captain made five and one-half round trips from Stralsund to Gothenburg within 189 days, which is seventeen days per leg including layover time.[8] One Danish captain made at least seven trips between Copenhagen and Rostock, plus a trip to Stettin, between March 1815 and July 1816.[9] Another Danish captain made twenty-four trips from Copenhagen to Rügenwalde and Stettin in Eastern Pomerania between September 1814 and May 1819.[10]

---

[5] SAHS 15-248, *Schifferbuch* for 1786. For remarks about Dano-Baltic trade, see: Lars HENNINGSEN, Provinsmatadorer fra 1700-aarene, Flensborg 1985, pp. 37–9, 47–52, 80, 154–62; Jørgen MIKKELSEN, By-Land-Oevrighed; Studier i sjaellandske koebstaeders oekonomi og administration ca. 1740–1807, Ph D Diss., Copenhagen, 1995, chaps. 5–7; Anders Monrad MØLLER, Fra Galeoth til Galease, Esbjerg 1981; RASCH, Kopenhagen.

[6] Rigsarkivet, Copenhagen (hereafter RA), *Kommercekollegiet* 1797–1816, no. 1746 »Handels- og Konsulatsfagets sekretariat; Rapporter fra konsulatet i Rostock aarene 1806–09.« Includes ships in ballast. Not counting ships from Norway or Iceland, then under Danish rule. Data for Feb. 1807 missing, but would have no material impact because few, if any, ships typically arrived in that month. CL = c. 2.6 metric tons.

[7] Archiv der Hansestadt Lübeck (hereafter AHL) *Zulagebuch* no. 16 (1700–2), see movements of captains D. Burmester, P. Runge, A. Griese, and others.

[8] N. Pehrson between 1 May and 5 November; see SAHS 15-242, *Schifferbuch*.

[9] Landsarkivet for Sjaelland, Copenhagen (hereafter LA), København Waterskout-Waterskouts protocol, 1814–1816. Captain is Jesper Praest with *Jagt* Kristine Magdalena of 9 CL.

[10] Ibid., plus same source, next volume covering 1816–1819. Captain is Herman Holm.

The coastal routes plied by ships from Mecklenburg and Western Pomerania were thus characterized by the same sort of regularity and probably had the same kind of economic importance as short-sea trades better known to historians. Examples of the latter, and good cases for comparison, include: the *Boertfahrt* between Hamburg, Bremen and Amsterdam; the trade between Denmark and Norway; the Newcastle-London coal run; the East Anglian and Kentish grain trades to London; the English cross-channel grain trade to the Netherlands; the trade in building lime in southern Wales; the Irish Sea trades; and the coastal traffic in colonial New England.[11]

Mecklenburg and Pomerania sent grain and wool to Sweden, receiving herring, fish oil, tar, iron, and colonial goods; they exported the same to Denmark, and returned primarily with colonial goods. Wood and wine they fetched from Stettin; hemp, flax, sailcloth, tallow, leather, and iron they took from Riga and St Petersburg. The archival records hint at fairly extensive arbitrage and multilateral cross-trading, suggesting a relatively sophisticated, integrated set of markets capable by about 1800 of calibrating supply with demand within the Baltic more or less efficiently. (We have to use so many qualifying phrases because the sources are limited). In 1765, for example, Stralsund ships cleared for Rostock, Reval (today Tallinn), and Königsberg with what was specifically designated as »Swedish« herring, raising the question of why Swedish merchants did not sell their product directly to the final consumers instead of shipping via the Pomeranian middleman.[12]

Likewise, in the grain trades, one finds numerous examples that indicate complex arrangements: for example, rye transshipped at Stralsund from Wolgast to Lübeck; oats or wheat shipped from Stralsund to Wismar or Wol-

---

[11] Ludwig BEUTIN, Nordwestdeutschland und die Niederlande seit dem Dreißigjährigen Kriege, in: Vierteljahrsschrift für Sozial- und Wirtschaftsgeschichte 32 2 (1939); Hans Christian JOHANSEN, København-Norge, en handels- og skibsfartsakse i slutningen af 1700-tallet, in: Soefart, Politik, Identitet tilegnet Ole Feldbaek, Kronborg 1996, and idem, Sejlads og handel mellem Norge og Danmark i 1700-tallet, in: B. BASBERG [et al.] (eds.), I det lange loep [Festschrift Fritz Hodne], Oslo 1997; Simon VILLE, English Shipowning during the Industrial Revolution, Manchester 1987; Dennis BAKER, The marketing of corn in the first half of the eighteenth century in northeastern Kent, in: Agricultural History Review 18, pt. II (1970); John A. CHARTRES, City and towns, farmers and economic change in the eighteenth century, in: Historical Research 64 (1991); David Ormrod, English Grain Exports and the Structure of Agrarian Capitalism 1700–1760, Atlantic Highlands, N.J., 1986; R. J. MOORE-COLYER, Of lime and men: aspects of the coastal trade in lime in south-west Wales in the eighteenth and nineteenth centuries, in: The Welsh History Review 14 (1988); Robert SINCLAIR, Across the Irish Sea, London 1990; Benjamin LABAREE, American colonial commerce, in: John HATTENDORF (ed.), Maritime History, vol. 2: The Eighteenth Century and the Classic Age of Sail, Malabar, Florida, 1997.

[12] SAHS 15-242, *Schifferbuch* for 1765 [sic], outbound voyages nos 12, 27, 32, 42. Gothenburg merchants often sold or consigned large amounts of herring to Greifswald or Stralsund merchants in return for grain; it is still not clear why the Swedes did not always sell directly to, say, Danzig or Riga, and use the proceeds to pay for their Pomeranian grain. See Arne MUNTHE, Slaekten Ekman, Gothenburg 1958, pp. 205–45.

gast (normally grain exporters themselves); rye imported into Lübeck from Stockholm, the latter itself a huge importer of rye from Mecklenburg and Western Pomerania; rye sent from Riga, Danzig, Rostock, or Wolgast to Stralsund, itself a sizeable rye exporter (such shipments were thus akin to »sending coals to Newcastle«); rye and wheat sent frequently in small lots from Denmark to Rostock, presumably as Rostock merchants assembled large cargoes for shipment to Sweden or through the Sound to Hamburg, London or Amsterdam.[13] Sometimes these shipments followed wartime deprivation, such as when 15 per cent by volume of Stralsund's grain exports went to Stettin in 1765; Prussia rarely allowed Western Pomeranian imports but must have been constrained to do so after the Seven Years' War.[14] At other times, such as in the rye trade between 1796 and 1806, merchants and shippers were responding to record grain prices, and to public unrest by hungry crowds. Whatever the reason, many of the grain-exporting cities along the southern Baltic traded regularly with one another; hitherto we have tended to see them, incorrectly it appears, primarily as competitors and not as trade partners.

The sources also outline for us the distribution channels through which many industrial raw materials, finished industrial products, and tropical goods flowed. Rostock sent salt to Stralsund (Stralsund took much larger shipments directly from Liverpool).[15] Wismar forwarded sizeable quantities of citrus fruit and silks to its Swedish metropole; in 1774, for example, one-fifth of the citrus imported into Stockholm came from Pomerania, and between 1767 and 1770 nearly 60 per cent of Sweden's silk imports did the same.[16] Wolgast, for at least a while, exported fairly large amounts of tobacco to Lübeck, the origins of which are unknown, Pomeranian perhaps Brandenburgian or Ukrainian?[17] Despite heavy competition from St Petersburg, Copenhagen, Hamburg, Amsterdam, London and Bordeaux, Lübeck continued to play a not inconsequential role as Baltic entrepot at least as late as 1800. Around that time, for instance, Stralsund merchants imported from Lübeck fairly large

---

[13] Stadtarchiv Greifswald (hereafter GSA) 5-3027 *Kornausfuhr,* petition from the Western Pomeranian cities to the Swedish Crown, 26 Feb. 1796; GSA 5-6210: Hiesige Handlung und Schiffahrt, Greifswald trade statistics 31 Dec. 1806; numerous advertisements in the Stralsund newspaper (*Stralsundische Zeitung*) between 1799 and 1806; SAHS 15-251, *Schifferbuch* for 1796, outbound voyage nos 95, 157; SAHS 15-248, *Schifferbuch* for 1786: see, for example, outbound voyages nos 102, 107 (entered by clerk in error, is actually 108), 120, 131, 201, 219, 222, 252, 296, 297, 298; RA *Kommercekollegiet* 1797–1816, no. 1746, letter 20 Sept. 1806; no. 1748, ship-list 27 June – 30 July 1814; AHL *Zulagebuch* no. 25 (1800), p. 114.

[14] SAHS 15-242, *Schifferbuch.*

[15] The Rostock consular reports to Copenhagen frequently mention Danish ships averaging about 8 CL arriving in ballast and departing with salt for Stralsund.

[16] Erik SEFSTROEM, Handels-Bibliothek, Stockholm 1772–5, part I, p. 144 and part III, pp. 113–38. See LINDBLAD, Sweden's Trade, pp. 92, 109.

[17] AHL *Zulagebuch* no. 24 (1790), pp. 17, 99, 131.

cargoes of tobacco, hemp, sailcloth, soap, sugar, raisins, and vinegar, as well as some ceramics and miscellaneous »East India goods«, besides large supplies of French wine and rum.[18] Stralsunders, of course, also imported wine at first hand from Bordeaux, and other goods from the colonial powers directly; the key point is that importing at second hand via Lübeck still made sense, and that Lübeck could therefore still be competitive despite the dominance of the imperial Atlantic ports.

Stralsund in turn routinely re-exported to the smaller Western Pomeranian cities of Greifswald, Wolgast, and Barth large quantities of, *inter alia*, unslaked lime, coal, sawn boards, leather, flax, hemp, tar, ceramics, iron, linen, nails and hardware, paint, glass, furniture, and bleach as well as salt, tobacco, sugar, coffee, and rice.[19] Merchants in neighbouring Greifswald (population c. 6,000 in 1800) challenged the Stralsunders and by the Napoleonic era Greifswald had become a local entrepot for colonial goods and *Materialwaaren* on its own account.[20] (Greifswald even on occasion sold grocery items to Stralsund). Here we see most clearly the links between the Atlantic commercial revolution and the importance of Baltic markets: consumers in places like Greifswald and its hinterland played a not inconsiderable role in building merchant capital in Copenhagen, Hamburg, London and Amsterdam.

Coastal trade in quotidian items may also have instigated capital formation locally; fortunes could be made from Baltic products as well as from sugar and coffee. Shipmasters, hailing from Marstal, Rudkøbing and many other small harbour towns, shuttled Danish cheese to Rostock; Stralsunders distinguished between the Dutch »sweet-milk cheese« and local varieties, suggesting that the latter was what they ate routinely. There was a steady trade in locally produced pottery, though Dutch and English ceramics gradually took over the market. Regardless of provenance, pottery had to be shipped by coaster to the widely dispersed population of the southern Baltic. So, for example, we see two shipmasters from Ärö in Denmark making three trips in 5 CL ships to Wismar in the summer of 1807 with cargoes consisting only of pottery.[21]

---

[18] SAHS 35-476 *Zulageregister* for 1796, incoming goods, see entries for Bartels, Wolter, J. H. Israel, Voelger, Bevernis, Pagenkopf, J. C. Wallis, Harloff, Volckmann, Reimer, Grimm, Schlueter, F. B. Müller, Stender, and Paepke.

[19] The Stralsund records are thick with references to the local coastal trade. For example, see SAHS 15-242, *Schifferbuch* for 1765, outbound voyages nos 23, 31, 33, 36, 45, etc.; and SAHS 15-251, *Schifferbuch* for 1796, outbound voyages nos 72, 75, 111, 124, 133 etc.

[20] Vorpommersche Landesarchiv, Greifswald 10-2428: Navigation, vol. I (1810), 'Tabelle über die bei Kaufleuten und Krahmer vorräthige und Colonialwaaren'; P. L. POGGE, Geschichte der Familie Pogge in Greifswald, Greifswald 1913.

[21] RA *Kommercekollegiet* 1797–1816, no. 1746: Handels- og Konsulatsfagets sek., ship-lists for Wismar 1–31 July 1807 and for 1–31 August 1807 (see 6 July, 16 July, 2 August); Wolfgang RUDOLPH, Poetter-Schiffer, ein Beitrag zum maritimen Kulturaustausch im Südlichen Ostseeraum während des 18. und 19. Jahrhunderts, in: Handels- og

Bricks and tiles were other favoured articles in the Baltic's internal trade:
Flensburg and Sonderburg exported large amounts of bricks coastwise to
Rostock, for example.[22] There was a regular trade between Stralsund and
Lübeck in copper and brass (the ultimate source for the former was Sweden,
which sent much of its copper to Lübeck); interestingly, Stralsund copper-
smiths shipped old copper back to Lübeck as well, in what looks like an early
form of recycling.[23]

Finally, we should note the wide range of miscellaneous non-bulky items
shipped coastally or across the narrow stretches of the Baltic to adjacent areas.
Some are unidentifiable, appearing in the records only as »piece goods«,
»merchandise«, or »packages« (*Stückgüter, Kaufmannsgut, Fässer/Kisten*).
Others are listed; for example, Stockholm sent to Western Pomeranian ports
such niceties as clocks, mirrors, claviers, tea-tables, portraits, window glass,
and, presumably from one of Linnaeus' apostles and intended for the university at Greifswald, several cartons of preserved insects.[24] In return, Stralsund and Wismar acted as conduits of European culture for their Swedish su-
zerain, exporting many books and even boxes of writing pens (56,000 quills in
one shipment) to Stockholm.[25]

Western Pomeranians and to a lesser extent Mecklenburgers, controlled
their own coastal and short-sea trades using locally owned and managed
coasting fleets. The ships deployed in Stralsund's Swedish grain trade about
1800 were primarily one-and-a-half-masters locally known as the *Brigantine*
and the *Galleasse*, with the *Schalup,* the *Schalup-Galleasse,* the *Huker,* and

Soefartsmuseet paa Kronborg, Aarbog 1981; Gesine SCHULZ-BERLEKAMP, Stralsunder
Fayencen, Putbus 1993.

[22] RA *Kommercekollegiet* 1797–1816: Konsulatsfagets sekr., ship-lists for Rostock and
Wismar for all years show many cargoes of bricks and tiles arriving (as distinct from bricks
being used, as they often were, for ballast). At the Hamburg Workshop, Ulrike Albrecht
noted that Flensburg was well-known c. 1800 for its extensive brickyards; likewise, John
Armstrong and Skip Fischer commented generally that building materials constituted a
large though unheralded percentage of coastal freight. Cf. R. BOHN, Handelshaus Donner,
on trade of Gotland lime and stone within the Baltic; and H. H. WORSOE, Tiden 1721 til
1814, in: J. HVIDTFELDT/P. K. IVERSEN, Aabenraa Bys Historie, vol. 2 (n.p., 1967), pp. 93–
9 on brick trade from Aabenraa (Apenrade) to Copenhagen and northern Germany.

[23] AHL *Zulagebuch* no. 20 (1760), p. 16, and no. 25 (1800), pp. 18, 86; SAHS 15-248
Schifferbuch for 1786, outbound voyage no. 244 and for 1787, outbound voyages nos 7,
190; SAHS 15-251 *Schifferbuch* for 1796, outbound voyage no. 284; SAHS 35-476
Zulageregister »Einkommende«, see entries for Wichmann, Boeckenhagen, Hasenburg.

[24] Culled from Stockholm Stadsarkiv (hereafter St.S) *tolagsjournaler* for 1756, 1778,
1786, 1796, 1806 and 1817. For the insects, see 1806 outbound voyage nos 93 & 243.

[25] Uno WILLERS, Ernst Moritz Arndt och hans Svenska Forbindelse, Stockholm 1945,
pp. 91–6; St.S *tolagsjournal* for 1799 incoming voyage no. 437, and for 1806, pp. 1407
and 2346 verso; cf. HEERMA VAN VOSS, Trade, pp. 14 ff. for comments on trade and culture
around the North Sea.

the *Huker-Galleasse* used too.[26] The *Galleasse* had steadily replaced the *Galiot* from about 1760 onwards, a development seen elsewhere in the northern seas as well. The Stralsund grain ships averaged about 35–40 CL. These same vessels also worked the west-east routes, supplemented by the *Jagd* (averaging some 10–15 CL). In 1796, for example, the average size of the cargo (also grain as it happened) carried from Stralsund to ports in Schleswig and Holstein was around 6 CL equivalent. In that same year wheat cargoes shipped from Barth to Stralsund (and from there »to the North Sea«, i.e., Hamburg or Bremen) ranged in size from 4 1/2 CL to 19 CL. The average size of 132 Stralsund-owned ships built between c. 1795 and 1816 was 60 CL, approximately 20 CL higher than the average size of the Baltic fleet, because Stralsund also had much larger vessels engaged in West European and even Mediterranean trades.[27]

Stralsund's harbour could not accommodate vessels above 45 CL; ships of that size were said to »sit upon the bottom for days« in the early 1780s.[28] The inner harbour was no more than 10–15 feet deep, and perhaps as little as 6–7 feet in places; the roadstead, the *Reede*, was 17–29 feet deep.[29] The Stralsund port records do not include movements of barges, skiffs, riverine craft, or the smallest sloop/cutter-type ships (the vessel designations »Kähne« and »Ewer« do not appear), but scattered references in other sources imply a steady flow of traffic from immediately proximate areas such as Darss and Rügen. Grain was often brought from Rügen in small open boats (*Schuten*), for example, causing complaints that it was ruined by rain and mist.[30] Open carriage of grain was not peculiar to Stralsund by any means; many observers noted the same for the great exporting centres such as Danzig too.[31] Grain was shipped to Stralsund from coastal hamlets on Rügen (Ralswiek, Schaprode, Zudar, and Spycker) that could have provided little more than a slip or landing, and must therefore

---

[26] For general description of these vessel types, see Alfred DUDSZUS [et al.], Das große Buch der Schiffstypen, Augsburg 1995, pp. 44, 67, 120, 123, 137, 235; and R. GARDINER (ed.), The Heyday of Sail: The Merchant Sailing Ship 1650–1830, London 1995, chap. 3.

[27] Average derived from data in RUBARTH, Stralsunds, agrees generally with G. ZETHELIUS, Handelsfartyg, typer och byggnad, in: G. HALLDIN (ed.), Svenskt skepps-byggeri: En oeversikt av utvecklingen genom tiderna, Malmö 1963, pp. 203, 211.

[28] Johann David von REICHENBACH, Patriotische Beytraege zur Kenntniss und Aufnahme des Schwedischen Pommerns, vol. 4, Greifswald 1785, p. 79.

[29] For good eighteenth-century descriptions of harbours in the Baltic, see: J. J. ODDY, European Commerce, London 1805, *passim*; Jonas HAHN, Den Namnkunnige Aalder-Styrmanens...Sjoe-Maerkes-Bok oefwer Farwatnen inom Oester-Sjoen, Stockholm 1748; Gustav af KLINT, Beskrifning om Kusterne vid Oestersjoen, Stockholm 1827; G. P. H. NORMANN, Ueber Wismars Handelslage..., Rostock 1803, pp. 7–9.

[30] REICHENBACH, Patriotische, pp. 67–68. See also SAHS 3-3267 *Kammergericht*, Streit zw. Kfm. Bevernis u. dem Pächter Willmer (1795).

[31] ODDY, European Commerce, p. 248.

have been served by boats and very small, flat-bottomed ships.[32] By the early 1820s there was so much harbour activity, especially in the newly opened grain trade to Stettin, that Stralsund's authorities allowed small craft to load and unload at a quay previously reserved for the wood trade.[33]

Rostock's situation was probably similar (as a riparian port, Rostock was presumably plagued by silting even more than Stralsund was). The Danish consul in Rostock cast some light on north German coastal traffic in the early nineteenth century, describing what sounds like a primitive form of multi-modal transport: »There is only a little supply of unsold rye here. Significant shipments [of rye] have been sent overland to Ribnitz and from there along the inner waters [*Binnen-Wasser*] to Stralsund and then further to Stettin, where the price has risen to 160–162 *Reichsthaler*«.[34] Of course, wartime exigencies, such as blockades and privateers, forced Rostock's merchants in this case to avoid open waters and seek the shelter of dry land and lagoon, but it shows nevertheless what could be accomplished with small craft. The consul also refers two years later, in 1810, to open pilot-boats carrying syrup from Copenhagen to Rostock and then to Stettin.[35]

The reference to road haulage reminds us that, as Pierre Jeannin has observed, we know little about overland transport networks for northern Europe in this period, let alone about how road and waterway fit together.[36] What we do know is that a surprising number of active Baltic ports had no major river to supply them (and in some cases had no river whatsoever), including not only smaller ports such as Barth, Greifswald, Wolgast, Wismar, Stralsund, Windau, Narva and Reval but also larger exporters to western Europe such as Pernau and Libau. The Western Pomeranian records refer to grain being carried to town in wagons and by sledge in winter, but we are all aware of the steep cost curve for bulk goods being hauled overland, a curve which the state of Pomeranian roads around 1800 would have steepened even further. The roads may have been better than their reputation, but that would not be saying much. Using cliches standard in most travel accounts of the time, for instance, one writer claimed: »It is impossible for an Englishman who has never left his

[32] SAHS 3-3190 *Kammergericht*, Klage Kfms A. B. Brandenburg gegen Kfm C. F. Brandt wegen Eindrangs in seine vertraglichen Kornlieferungen aus Ralswieck, 1768– 1770; Guenther LAU, »Seestadt« Bergen, in: Rügener Heimatkalender 1994.

[33] SAHS 15-279a: Acta Senata Sundensis betr. die Langenbrücke 1739–1842, letter 26 April 1823 to Königl. Preuss. Regierung.

[34] RA, *Kommercekollegiet* 1797–1816, Handels- og konsulatsfagets sekr., no. 1746, letter of 20 June 1808. The inner waters in question must be the lagoons (*Bodden*) protected from the Baltic proper by the Darss peninsula and the island of Zingst right up to the strait leading to Stralsund.

[35] Ibid., no. 1747, letter of 18 June 1810.

[36] Pierre JEANNIN, The sea-borne and the overland trade routes of northern Europe in the XVIth and XVIIth Centuries, in: Journal of European Economic History 11 (1982), pp. 28–9.

own country to form any notion of the Prussian roads in general.«[37] Western Pomerania did not get its first *Chaussee* (turnpike) until 1836; its roads could hardly have been much better than the muddy tracks and sandy wastes of Prussia. In short, with road carriage a dubious proposition for individual travellers, not to mention for freight, and with fluvial options small or unavailable, coastal shipping assumed critical importance for many parts of the southern Baltic.

No comprehensive ownership statistics are available, but I have pieced together enough evidence to state that Western Pomeranian and Mecklenburg ships were fairly widely held by residents of those provinces.[38] Unsurprisingly, merchants held a large percentage of the tonnage, concentrated especially in the larger ships; more surprising, when compared to eighteenth-century ownership patterns in larger German ports such as Hamburg, Bremen, and Königsberg, shipmasters (*Schiffer*) retained significant minority shares, and were often majority owners in vessels of less than 25–30 CL.[39] Sole ownership was unusual except for the smallest vessels – a *Partenreederei*, joint-liability partnership with three to eight partners was typical. Noteworthy was the degree of ownership outside the immediate mercantile and shipping circles, among both estate-owning nobles and urban artisans. Few foreigners held shares in Western Pomeranian ships, and those few were invariably merchants of German descent living in Sweden and engaged in the grain trade with the province. There was a vibrant market in ship-shares.

In addition, many Mecklenburg and Pomeranian farmers, fishermen, and other coastal folk owned boats and small ships that were used in local trades. Operating illegally, that is, outside the scope of the shipmasters' and merchants' corpora, these country people drew the constant ire of their urban rivals.[40] Here we see the bias inherent in our dependence on city-centered records: since shipping of whatever kind was defined by and in terms of the city shipmasters' guild, the rural interlopers officially could not exist and were never enumerated. Nevertheless, exist they obviously did. We may well, therefore, have seriously under-estimated the aggregate size of tonnage used

[37] John CARR, A Northern Summer, Hartford 1806, p. 303.

[38] SAHS 3-3121 *Bielbriefe* 1696–1776; SAHS 3-7559: Eidesstattliche Verklärungen von Partenreeder über die Höhe ihrer Schiffsanteile (1798); a large number of bankruptcy and post-mortem inventories; numerous advertisements in the Stralsund newspaper.

[39] Cf. Walter KRESSE, Materialien zur Entwicklungsgeschichte der Hamburger Handelsflotte 1765–1823, Hamburg 1966; Andrzej GROTH, Die Handelsflotte von Köningsberg, Pillau und Memel in den Jahren 1725, 1732 und 1781, in: Heide GERSTENBERGER/Ulrich WELKE (eds.), Das Handwerk der Seefahrt im Zeitalter der Industrialisierung, Bremen 1995.

[40] SAHS 13-1912: Die Schiffahrt der Darsser Bauern 1739–1771; GSA 5-5243: Die Nichtbefugnis der Landschiffer zur Seeschiffahrt und ihre Verbindlichkeit zur Einziehen in die Seestädte 1771–1804; Wismar Stadtarchiv Abt. III Ratsakten Tit. IX;B: Kaufmanns-Kompagnie (1): Vorstellung betr. das Loeschen...

along the Baltic coasts, since the farmer-shipmaster phenomenon was wide-spread at that time.[41]

In conclusion, if the Western Pomeranian and Mecklenburg examples are at all representative, coastal trade *within* the Baltic in the late eighteenth and early nineteenth centuries may have been much livelier and more extensive than we have hitherto imagined. In fairness, the »we« may refer here to West European and American historians rather than to our colleagues from countries on the Baltic. We have been dazzled by the long-distance trades since the sixteenth century; in c. 1596 Shakespeare opened *The Merchant of Venice* (I.i. 9–14) with: »your argosies with portly sail/Like signiors or rich burghers of the flood/Or as it were the pageants of the sea/Do overpeer the petty traffickers/That cur'sy to them, do them reverence/As they fly by them with their woven wings.« Yet it may be that the »petty traffickers«, the carriers of routine coastal freight, played as significant a role in European development as their deep-water counterparts. Maritime historians need to investigate such a claim further, to see whether we need to alter our Atlanticist conception of European development centred on the grand and exotic trades.

---

[41] Yrjo KAUKIAINEN, Suomen Talonpoikaspurjehdus 1800-Luvun Alkupuoliskolla, Helsinki 1970 [English summary and charts]; Wolfgang RUDOLPH, Maritime Kultur der südlichen Ostseeküste, Rostock 1983, pp. 13–15, 34 ff., 45–60; Hermann KELLENBENZ, Bäuerliche Unternehmertätigkeit im Bereich der Nord- und Ostsee vom Hochmittelalter bis zum Ausgang der neueren Zeit, in: idem, Wirtschaftliche Leistung und Gesellschaftlicher Wandel (= Kleine Schriften III), Stuttgart 1991.

12

FRENCH ATLANTIC COASTAL TRADE IN THE EIGHTEENTH CENTURY: THE CASE OF BORDEAUX

PETER VOSS

French research on maritime trade ranks among the finest in the field. The great works by Pierre Dardel on Rouen, Jean Meyer on Nantes, Charles Carrière on Marseille, Jacques Bernard, Christian Huetz de Lemps and Paul Butel on Bordeaux, or André Lespagnol on St Malo have contributed greatly to the reputation of French historical research.[1] In addition, the history of the large state-owned trading companies has been investigated by Philippe Haudrère and Gérard Le Bouëdec.[2] In the last few years, research by the Parisian historian Alain Cabantous on the social and cultural history of seafarers and coastal dwellers has generated great interest, as well as what he and others have called, the history of maritime mentality.[3]

One research focus of French economic history is still the fast growing maritime trade, the trade with European countries and the colonies or territories overseas, the history of the large sea ports, of the patrician merchant community or the maritime officer corps.[4] Against the backdrop of this

---

[1] Pierre DARDEL, Navires et marchandises dans les ports de Rouen et du Havre au XVIIIe siècle, Paris 1963; Jean MEYER, L'Armement nantais dans la deuxième moitié du XVIIIe siècle, Paris 1969; Charles CARRIERE, Négociants marseillais au XVIIIe siècle, Marseille 1973; Jacques BERNARD, Navires et gens de mer à Bordeaux (vers 1400 – vers 1550), Paris 1968; Christian HUETZ DE LEMPS, Géographie du commerce de Bordeaux à la fin du règne de Louis XIV, Paris 1975; Paul BUTEL, Les Négociants bordelais, l'Europe et les Îles au XVIIIe siècle, Paris 1974; André LESPAGNOL, Messieurs de Saint-Malo. Une élite négociante au temps de Louis XIV, Rennes 1997.

[2] Philippe HAUDRERE, La Compagnie française des Indes, Paris 1987; Gérard LE BOUËDEC, Le Port et l'Arsenal de Lorient, de la Compagnie des Indes à la Marine cuirassée, une reconversion réussie XVIIIe – XIXe siècle, Paris 1994.

[3] Alain CABANTOUS, Gens de mer à Dunkerque aux XVIIe et XVIIIe siècles, Dunkirk 1977; idem (ed.), Le Ciel dans la mer. Christianisme et civilisation maritime, XVIe – XIXe siècles, Paris 1990; idem, Dix mille marins face à l'océan. Les populations maritimes de Dunkerque au Havre (vers 1660–1794), Paris 1991; idem, Les Côtes barbares. Pilleurs d'épaves et sociétés littorales en France, 1680–1830, Paris 1993.

[4] The educational programme »Les Européens et la mer, 1690–1790«, which forced thousands of students preparing for the teacher examinations *CAPES* and *Agrégation* between 1996 and 1998 to study maritime history, produced a large number of studies and surveys on maritime history. See for example: Alain CABANTOUS, Européens et espaces

knowledge, the French historian Gérard Le Bouëdec recently argued for an intensified interest in smaller ports, shipyards, seamen and other unknowns of the »*sociétés littorales*«. Cabotage, too, figures among the deficits of this new maritime »micro-storia«.[5]

In the late 1980s, Paul Butel and Robert Richard demanded more thorough research into the topic of cabotage twenty years after Christian Huetz de Lemps had characterised cabotage as the least well known topic in Bordeaux's trade history.[6] Huetz de Lemps deserves much praise for his research on cabotage, but nonetheless his 1970 statement is still valid in the overall French context. We can concur with Huetz de Lemps that the difficulty in doing research into French cabotage is rooted in the silence of contemporary sources. While the detailed *Mémoires* of the Intendants of Guyenne mention cabotage, they do not specify its importance. The scarcity of written testimony can be attributed to the lack of prestige that cabotage enjoyed compared to international and colonial trade. Furthermore, this may be a result of the usually unproblematic nature of cabotage, which did not require elaborate legal procedures, accompanying memoranda, and disputed documentation, which could inform us today about the exact process.[7]

The first part of this article examines the changes in, and the extension of the definition of cabotage in France over the course of two centuries. It is followed by a brief discussion of fundamental works on cabotage. A third section, provides an overview of trade and shipping in the Atlantic port of Bordeaux in the seventeenth and eighteenth centuries and of the sources in the

maritimes au XVIIIe siècle, in: Historiens et géographes 353 (1996), pp. 271–82; Paul BUTEL, Européens et espaces maritimes (vers 1690 – vers 1790), Bordeaux 1997; Gérard LE BOUËDEC, Activités maritimes et sociétés littorales de l'Europe atlantique 1690–1790, Paris 1997; Philippe HAUDRERE, Le Grand Commerce maritime au XVIIIe siècle, Paris 1997; Olivier PETRE-GRENOUILLEAU, Les Négoces maritimes français, XVIIe–XXe siècles, Paris 1997; Patrick VILLIERS/Jean-P. DUTEIL, L'Europe, la mer et les colonies, XVIIe–XVIIIe siècles, Paris 1997. See too the contributions of Michel Morineau, Marie-Noëlle Bourguet, Alain Cabantous, Martine Acerra, André Lespagnol, Michel Zylberberg, Marie-Louise Pelus-Kaplan, Denis Woronoff et Gérard Le Bouëdec, in: Bulletin de la Société d'Histoire moderne et contemporaine 44 (1997).

[5] LE BOUËDEC, Activités maritimes, p. 3; see also: idem, Les approvisionnements de la Compagnie des Indes (1737–1770). L'horizon géographique lorientais, in: Histoire, Economie et Société 1 (1982), pp. 377–412; idem, La Compagnie des Indes et le cabotage atlantique au XVIIIe siècle, in: Bulletin de la Société d'Histoire moderne et contemporaine 44 (1997), pp. 140–67. David H. PINKNEY, Cabotage, France's forgotten common carrier, in: French Historical Studies 16 (1989), pp. 471–7.

[6] Paul BUTEL, Le Corpus des navires français au XVIIIe siècle (enquête CNRS). Les navires dans les ports français au lendemain de la Guerre de Sept Ans, in: Bulletin du Centre d'Histoire des Espaces Atlantiques 4 (1988), pp. 45–72; Robert RICHARD, Le fichier international des navires. Etat d'avancement. Observations méthodologiques, ibid., pp. 23–43.

[7] Christian HUETZ DE LEMPS, Le cabotage des vins d'Aquitaine à la fin du règne de Louis XIV (1697–1715), in: Vignobles et vins d'Aquitaine. Histoire, économie, art, Bordeaux 1970, p. 117.

Bordeaux archives. Finally, some results of research into the Bordeaux-Hamburg trade in the late-seventeenth and eighteenth centuries will be presented.

I

The *Encylopédie* defines *cabotage* as »navigation along the coast ... sailing from one port to the other on the same or a neighbouring coast without losing sight of the coastline or of the bottom«. *Caboter* therefore means: »sailing from one cape to another, from one port to the next, navigating along the coast«.[8] As opposed to overseas trade (*navigation propre*), *cabotage* or *navigation commune* requires only a limited competence in technical or nautical affairs. The captain of a *caboteur* relies only on his precise knowledge of the coastal region such as anchoring places, sandbars, currents and tides. The usage of nautical equipment is usually limited to compass and sounding line.

In French maritime law there were two ordinances, the Ordinance of 20 August 1673, and the General Naval Ordinance of August 1681 which distinguished for the first time between overseas trade (*voyages dits de long cours*) and coastal shipping *(voyages dits de cabotage)* with regard to maritime insurance. The Regulations of 13 August 1726, and 23 January 1727 introduced a further distinction between *Grand Cabotage* and *Petit Cabotage*, codified again in the Ordinance of 18 October 1740, the Decree from Ventôse 14, An II, and the Ordinance of 12 February 1815.[9] The Ordinance of 18 October 1740, expanded the jurisdiction of the *petit cabotage*. Article II reads: »Voyages to England, Scotland, Ireland, Holland, Denmark, Hamburg and other destinations as far as the Strait of Gibraltar fall under the category of *grand cabotage*.« Article III expands: »voyages to Brittany, Normandy, Picardie, and Flanders, to the ports of Ostend and Newport, Holland, England and Ireland are to be considered *petit cabotage*«.[10]

---

[8] Encyclopédie, ou Dictionnaire raisonné des Sciences, des Arts et des Métiers, Paris, 1751–65: Cabotage: »navigation le long des côtes (...), celle qui se fait d'un port dans un autre situé sur la même côte ou sur une côte voisine, pourvu que le vaisseau s'éloigne presqu'entièrement de la vue des côtes & ne trouve plus de fond«. Caboter: »aller de cap en cap, de port en port, naviguer le long des côtes«.

[9] Ordonnance du 20 août 1673, Ordonnance générale sur la marine d'août 1681, Règlement du 13 août 1726 (navigation en Provence et Languedoc), Règlement du 23 janvier 1727 (navigation en Guyenne, Saintonge, Pays d'Aunis, Poitou et îles dépendantes), Ordonnance du 18 octobre 1740, Arrêté du 14 ventôse an II, Ordonnance du 12 février 1815; see M. BAUDON, Traité d'Administration de la Marine marchande, vol. 1, Paris 1925, p. 25.

[10] See LE BOUËDEC, Compagnie des Indes, p. 155.

In the nineteenth century shipping which took place within certain boundaries was defined as *cabotage* as opposed to overseas trade. The limits were toward the south: 30°, toward the north: 72°, toward the west: 15° longitude Méridien de Paris; toward the east: 44° longitude Méridien de Paris. Iceland and Icelandic territorial waters also counted as cabotage.[11]

Some other distinctions also existed: *Navigation de cabotage international* was shipping between French and foreign ports, and shipping between foreign ports, as opposed to *Navigation de cabotage national* (or *cabotage français, cabotage réservé*) which was shipping between French ports. *Navigation de Grand Cabotage* was shipping in the North Sea and the Atlantic beyond Texel in the north and La Coruña in the south, as well as shipping in the Mediterranean beyond Naples in the east and Malaga in the west, and shipping along the African Coast, west of Gibraltar and east of Tunisia, as opposed to *Navigation de Petit Cabotage* which was shipping within the boundaries of *Grand Cabotage*. Also included in the area of *petit cabotage* were the British Isles, Corsica, Sardinia, and the Balearics.

The General Naval Ordinance of August 1681 required an annual inspection (*visite*) of all merchant ships by a commission of three members: a sea captain, a shipbuilder, and a ships carpenter. They had to examine the soundness of the ship for sea travel. This regulation also applied to skippers of coasters, who could load their ships and begin the voyage only after having obtained a certificate of survey (*certificat de visite*).[12]

According to French maritime law, only certified masters (*maître au cabotage*) were allowed to navigate coastal ships (*caboteurs*). Because it was difficult to recruit certified boatmen for local coastal shipping (*navigation de bornage*) these restrictions were slowly softened in the course of the eighteenth century. The Regulations of 13 February 1785 excluded small ships involved in local coastal shipping (coastal fishing ships and ships used in local trade, which returned to their home port every day) from the annual inspection. However, these inspections were reintroduced by the Circular of 7 May 1852.[13] In the nineteenth-century, *navigation de bornage* defined ships, with a loading capacity which did not exceed twenty-five tons and which did not travel further than forty-five miles from their home ports. If the tonnage of the ship exceeded twenty-five tons or the distance travelled exceeded the forty-five mile limit, it was automatically considered cabotage.[14]

[11] Décret-Loi du 20 mars 1852, Loi du 30 janvier 1893 and Loi du 19 avril 1906; see BAUDON, Traité d'Administration, pp. 26–8.

[12] Ibid., pp. 347, 350. The Ordonnance générale sur la marine d'août 1681 was supplemented by the Déclaration royale du 17 août 1779, the Règlement du 13 février 1785, the Loi de 9–13 août 1791, the Article 225 du Code de Commerce as well as the Ordonnances des 2 avril 1823 et 17 janvier 1846.

[13] Ibid., p. 352; Réglement du 13 février 1785, Circulaire du 7 mai 1852.

[14] Ibid., p. 30; one Bordeaux ton (*tonneau*) is roughly equivalent to 1000 kg.

The rules of the Ancien Régime appear to be somewhat arbitrary, particularly in the case of the Ordinance of 18 October 1740 which did not clearly differentiate between *petit cabotage* and *grand cabotage*. However, it would be incorrect to take these legal rules at face value. The real reason behind the 1740 definition was the government's intention to reduce the requirements for obtaining a certificate (*maître au cabotage*), to enable as large a number as possible of seamen, most of whom were illiterate and unfamiliar with the French language, to become master of a coaster.[15]

There is no uniform usage of the term *cabotage* in recent historiography. For Normandy, James B. Collins considers the territory between Spain in the west all the way to Hamburg or even Danzig in the northeast as *cabotage normand*. This *cabotage atlantique* was supplemented by *cabotage local*, which was carried on primarily by fishing boats from the Cotentin.[16] Christian Huetz de Lemps defines cabotage nationally.[17] To him the *cabotage atlantique* of the port of Bordeaux in southwestern France was performed only within French borders. Dunkirk in the north and St Jean-de-Luz in the south represented the borders of the Bordeaux cabotage. Voyages from Bordeaux to Ostend or San Sebastián are considered by Huetz de Lemps *commerce international*. In this context the relative randomness of political borders, which did not influence the technology and types of coastal and deep water shipping, especially in the area of the North Sea needs to be pointed out. In 1664, the merchants and shipowners of Dieppe in Normandy labelled trips to England as cabotage.[18] Huetz de Lemps admits that the trade with small ships between Bordeaux and Ireland as well as the trade between Bordeaux and the Spanish and Portuguese coasts was similar to cabotage.[19] The *cabotage national* was generally operated solely by French ships. Foreign merchantmen were, theoretically, excluded from French domestic sea trade. The *caboteurs* were normally ships with a capacity of less than forty tons with a crew of five or six men, which in the case of Bordeaux cabotage normally transported domestic goods (for example, the *petits vins*). Strictly limiting oneself to national borders does not make sense in the case of Bayonne, the other large port in southwestern France, as *caboteurs* from the Spanish Basque country played a decisive role in this city's trade which was highly hispanicised.[20]

---

[15] LE BOUËDEC, Activités maritimes, p. 152.

[16] James B. COLLINS, La Flotte normande au commencement du XVIIe siècle. Le mémoire de Nicolas Langlois (1627), in: Annales de Normandie 34 (1984), pp. 361–80.

[17] HUETZ DE LEMPS, Cabotage des vins d'Aquitaine, p. 118: »Ce terme de cabotage recouvre naturellement tous les transports de vin à destination des ports français du littoral de l'Atlantique, de la Manche et de la mer du Nord«.

[18] COLLINS, Flotte normande, p. 364.

[19] HUETZ DE LEMPS, Géographie du Commerce de Bordeaux, p. 525.

[20] BUTEL, Corpus des navires français au XVIIIe siècle, pp. 46, 56.

II

Recently, Gérard Le Bouëdec has presented detailed research on cabotage. At its heart is a database with 5400 *caboteurs* who frequented the arsenal of Lorient in Brittany between 1737 and 1770.[21] From the perspective of the *Compagnie des Indes* in Lorient, Le Bouëdec views cabotage primarily as supply trade, that is the shipping of a vast variety of different, mostly but not exclusively French, materials needed for building and supplying *Compagnie* vessels. According to Le Bouëdec's calculations, the *Compagnie des Indes* relied on a cabotage fleet of some 170 coasters which brought materials to build three merchantmen for the *campagnie* and provisioned seventeen which were bound for Asia.

According to Le Bouëdec, *cabotage atlantique* extended along the European coastline from the Iberian peninsula to the Baltic sea, from Cadiz to St Petersburg and even to Archangel. In accordance with this view he not only regards the short-haul coastal shippers, but likewise Dutch, Hanseatic or Scandinavian merchantmen as *caboteurs* with their *fluitships* having an average capacity of 150 to 200 tons. Even though the latter were active primarily in international trade, they nonetheless competed in the short-haul coastal trade, for example, against coastal shippers from Brittany. The Dutch and other nations participated in this tramping along the French Atlantic coast as well.

The size of the ships is not a critical criterion for Le Bouëdec, even though the majority of French coastal ships were small craft. About 93 per cent of the fleet of Île d'Yeu which specialized in Atlantic cabotage between Brittany and Spain, consisted of ships with a capacity of not more than thirty tons. On the other hand, the capacity of the three-masted *gabares* deployed for timber shipping from the peninsula of Rhuys in the Gulf of Morbihan ranged from 80 to 200 tons.[22] Furthermore, the average tonnage of the *caboteurs* who frequented the port of Lorient in southwestern Brittany, nearly doubled during the course of the eighteenth century.[23]

Instead of the fuzzy definition of the *Ancien Régime*, which hardly reflected the actual situation, Le Bouëdec favours distinguishing between short-range, national, coastal trade, long-range, national, coastal trade, and international

---

[21] LE BOUËDEC, Activités maritimes, p. 119–67. In September 1998, Le Bouëdec presented a paper on: L'Etat et le cabotage en Europe aux XVIIe et XVIIIe siècles, Colloque international »Pouvoirs et littoraux du XVe au XXe siècles«, Université de Bretagne-Sud (Lorient, France).

[22] LE BOUËDEC, Activités maritimes, p. 150.

[23] 79–89 tons in 1770, LE BOUËDEC, Activités maritimes, p. 148.

coastal trade.[24] This approach includes mixed forms. Generally, Le Bouëdec emphasizes the regional differences with regard to tonnage, the diversity of types of vessels deployed (for example, *double-chaloupe, chasse-marée, barque, gabare, galiotte, senault, brigantin*), the geographic range of activity, merchandise shipped, captains, size of crews, and shipowners.

The emphasis on local traditions, specializations and other particularities turns out to be important, as neighbouring ports active in cabotage took very different approaches. Brittany coasters of Ambon, Île aux Moines and Île d'Arz in the Gulf of Morbihan, for example, engaged in long-range coastal trade and even international cabotage, while the merchants of Quiberon, Arzon, Carnac, Locmariaquer and Ploëmeur were content with fishing and short-range coastal trade.[25] Vessels based in the Brittany port of Le Conquet, for example, employed in the cabotage of Bayonne averaged more than fifty tons. In Le Conquet a group of genuine shipowners existed who must be distinguished from captains. The tonnage of ships of Le Carteret in Normandy, which were also active in Bayonne, usually did not exceed twenty five tons, the shippers were furthermore owners of their coasters.[26] The close proximity of cabotage and fishing is evidenced by the many French coasters which devoted themselves to fishing during the summer (sardines in Brittany, tuna in the case of Île d'Yeu). In other cases, professional fishermen took on occasional cabotage opportunities.[27] This pattern can be seen as related to the distinctive seasonality of French maritime trade, for example in the case of Bordeaux's wine trade.

Generally, one can conclude that all major French ports relied on cabotage fleets in their vicinity. Bordeaux and Bayonne, La Rochelle, Nantes or Rouen made use primarily of *caboteurs* from Brittany, followed by vessels from Normandy, the Saintonge, Aunis or Basque country. Only in rare cases were ships from major ports deployed for coastal trade. They rather specialized in European, overseas and colonial trade according to the strengths of their local merchant communities.[28] International shipping routes like those documented for Rouen by Pierre Dardel (that is Rouen-Cadiz-Marseille-Rouen or Rouen-Lisbon-Marseille-Rouen), had their equivalent in regularly served coastal trade routes, which were generally characterized by short travel time and high turnarounds. Pierre Dumas, for example, completed nineteen journeys aboard the three-masted *pinasse L'Alexandre de Bayonne* between 1763 and 1765 with a cargo of stones and iron from San Sebastián to Bayonne, and back to

---

[24] Ibid., p. 152; cabotage national à petit rayon d'action, cabotage national à grand rayon d´action and cabotage international.

[25] Ibid.

[26] BUTEL, Corpus des navires français au XVIIIe siècle, pp. 59–61.

[27] LE BOUËDEC, Activités maritimes, p. 149.

[28] Ibid., p. 165.

San Sebastián with a cargo of wine, wood and distilled liqueur.[29] Nonetheless, short haul coastal trade did not equate to short journey times and high frequencies. Of the 5400 coasters identified for Lorient in the period 1737–1770, seventy per cent visited the port only once.[30]

Based on an elaborate and detailed analysis of cabotage routes and their average journey time, Le Bouëdec arrives at the paradoxical conclusion that London was further away from Lorient than Newcastle, Dunkirk further than Rouen, Lannion further than Cherbourg. The journey of a *gabare* with a cargo of building timber from Redon or Nantes to Lorient was equivalent to a voyage by a merchantman from St Petersburg or Riga to Lorient in terms of travel time. The type of cargo turns out to be a major reason. While a journey between Nantes and Lorient with a regular cargo typically took two weeks, it increased to a full month, if the cargo consisted of iron; and even two and a half months if the cargo was timber.[31]

The current French discussion takes an increasingly differentiated view of cabotage. Both Gérard Le Bouëdec and Michel Morineau occasionally use the term in plural form and speak of *les cabotages*.[32] It is curious, however, that the term *navigation de bornage* does not have any significance in the modern research on French cabotage or coastal shipping.

III

At the close of the *Ancien Régime*, an increasing interest in recording statistical material relating to the maritime and external trade of France in an organized fashion emerged. A. M. Arnould's *De la balance du commerce et des relations commerciales extérieures de la France dans toutes les parties du globe, particulierement a la fin du règne de Louis XIV et au moment de la Révolution*, dating back to 1791, is a good example.[33] Jean-Claude Perrot, the most knowledgeable expert on the history of statistics in France, had good reason to call the era of the French Revolution »the golden age of statistics«. However, the focus of the statistical work during the Revolution, the Consu-

---

[29] BUTEL, Corpus des navires français au XVIIIe siècle, p. 46.

[30] LE BOUËDEC, Activités maritimes, p. 160.

[31] Ibid., pp. 160–1.

[32] Ibid., p. 152; Michel MORINEAU, L'Insertion de l'histoire maritime européenne au XVIIIe siècle dans le temps et dans l'espace, in: Bulletin de la Société d'Histoire Moderne et Contemporaine 44 (1997), p. 32.

[33] A. M. ARNOULD, De la Balance du commerce et des relations commerciales extérieures de la France dans toutes les parties du globe, particulièrement à la fin du règne de Louis XIV et au moment de la Révolution, Paris 1791, 2 vols. and 1 atlas.

late, and the Empire was primarily on demographics, agriculture, and industry.[34]

This changed with the publication of the Statistique générale de la France. In 1835, the first volume, entitled Documents statistiques sur la France included a Tableau général de la grande et de la petite navigation de la France for the period between 1820 and 1834. There we find not only a description of the maritime trade with foreign countries and the colonies, as well as of the fishing business, but, for the first time, comprehensive statistics on cabotage. Furthermore, the volume includes statistics of port activity by maritime categories, listing the number of ships entering and leaving the ports, their cargo, and their crews.[35]

Over one hundred years, from 1837 to 1939, the French Customs Administrations published an annual table of cabotage movements with details of the departures and destinations of ships, cargoes, number of ships, tonnage, and size of crews. In this official publication, cabotage is defined as the transport of national merchandise between two ports within the kingdom, or as the transport of imported goods from a French entrepôt to another port within France. At the centre of this listing are the different categories of goods and their total tonnage.[36]

This focus on the modern statistical presentations emerging at the beginning of the nineteenth century should not diminish attention on the pre-statistical era, which produced data and sources that allow the reconstruction of maritime and trade movements over an extended period. The Sound Toll Registers are an example, despite the fact that this source must be evaluated with caution.[37]

To my knowledge, no comparable sources exist for eighteenth-century France which would capture national or European trade in a comprehensive manner. However, the efforts of the French Administration to gain an accurate overview of France's maritime and trade matters are reflected in the codifica-

[34] Jean-Claude PERROT/Stuart J. WOOLF, State and Statistics in France 1789–1815, Chur 1984.

[35] Bertrand GILLE, Les Sources statistiques de l'histoire de France. Des Enquêtes du XVIIe siècle à 1870, 1st edition, Geneva, 1964; 2nd Edition, Geneva, 1980.

[36] For example: Tableau général des mouvements du cabotage pendant l'année 1837, Administration des Douanes, Paris 1838. This series of cabotage statistics was published yearly until 1895. From 1896 on, the Tableau général de Commerce et de la Navigation is divided in two volumes; vol. 1 considers the French colonial trade and the French trade with foreign countries, vol. 2 considers the coastal trade. See for example: Tableau général de commerce et de la navigation. Année 1896. Deuxième volume: Navigation (navigation internationale, cabotage français et effectif de la marine marchande), Direction Générale des Douanes, Paris 1897. The last Tableau (years 1937, 1938, and 1939) was published in 1940.

[37] Pierre JEANNIN, Les comptes du Sund comme source pour la construction d'indices généraux de l'activité économique en Europe (XVIe–XVIIIe siècles), in: Revue Historique 231 (1964), pp. 55–102, 307–40.

tion of the maritime and trade law (*Ordonnance générale sur la Marine*, 1681), initiated by Colbert and his successors, and the *Statistiques descriptives de l'Ancien Régime* (*Enquête de Colbert of 1664, Travaux de Vauban, Enquête of 1697*), as they were named by the French historian Bertrand Gille in 1964.[38] Two motivations lay behind these efforts. On the one hand, the lessons from the statistics were to be used to strengthen France's position in international trade, while on the other hand the fiscal element of skimming off profits from maritime trade dominated.

The attempt of the French administration to regulate trade led to close supervision and an increase in tariffs and taxes for the merchants, shipowners, and ships' crews, coupled with a high administrative burden in the form of muster rolls (*Rôles d'équipages*), sea letters (*Passeports maritimes*), master's reports (*Rapports à l'entrée des navires*) or certificates of clearance (*Congés de sortie*). Depending on the political climate, foreign vessels had to pay an additional fee of 50 sous per *tonneau* (*Droit de fret*) when entering a French port. Compared to France, the situation in Hanseatic Hamburg, for example, was characterized by a relative laissez-faire on the part of the port administration, as French observers frequently pointed out in admiration.

Informed contemporaries, like Bishop Fénelon, identified the structural weaknesses of a system, which would later be known as Colbertism or mercantilism. It was viewed as putting such a strong emphasis on gathering statistical information and thereby regulating trade that it hindered trade more than helping it.[39] On the other hand, the zeal of the French administration has created a unique statistical wealth in some ports, like St Malo or Bordeaux, which can be evaluated by modern historians to great benefit.[40] Before introducing some important source material stored in Bordeaux, it seems necessary to present briefly the structure of the port activities of this emporium in southwestern France.

Already by 1968, in his monumental work on *Navires et gens de mer à Bordeaux (vers 1400 – vers 1550)*, Jacques Bernard, the doyen of Bordeaux's maritime history, pointed to the importance of the southwestern seaport as a

---

[38] GILLE, Sources statistiques, p. 80.

[39] »L'Etat ... au lieu d'ouvrir, suivant notre ancienne coutume, ses ports à toutes les nations les plus éloignées dans une entière liberté ... veut savoir le nombre des vaisseaux qui arrivent, leurs pays, les noms des hommes qui y sont, leur genre de commerce, le prix de leurs marchandises et le temps qu'ils doivent demeurer ici. Il fait encore pis, car il use de supercherie pour surprendre les marchands et pour confisquer leurs marchandises. Il inquiète les marchands qu'il croit les plus opulents; il établit, sous divers prétextes, de nouveaux impôts. Il veut entrer lui-même dans le commerce et tout le monde craint d'avoir quelque affaire avec lui«. FENELON, Télémaque, vol. 2, book X, Paris 1927, pp. 88–9; see Henry MECHOULAN, Amsterdam au temps de Spinoza. Argent et liberté, Paris 1990, p. 85.

[40] For Saint-Malo see in particular Jean DELUMEAU, Le Mouvement du port de Saint-Malo, 1681–1720. Bilan statistique, Rennes 1966.

central crossroads of the *cabotage atlantique*.[41] The extremely rich original records of Bordeaux are the foundation of a detailed study by Christian Huetz de Lemps in 1975 on *La Géographie du commerce de Bordeaux à la fin du règne de Louis XIV*. Cabotage plays an important role in this publication, while Paul Butel focused on the Bordeaux merchant elite and colonial trade in the eighteenth century.[42]

Toward the end of the seventeenth century, Bordeaux was the largest port in France with its tributary ports Libourne, Bourg and Blaye. In good years, more than 2500 ships left the port of Bordeaux. In the year 1700/1701 alone, more than 3108 ships with a total tonnage of 143,873 tons were counted. These figures exceeded by far the traffic of Marseille, Nantes, La Rochelle, Rouen or St Malo. The importance of Bordeaux can be explained by its wine trade and its trade in wine derivatives like brandy and vinegar, as well as in other products from the Aquitaine hinterland (chestnuts, plums, walnut timber, paper, etc.). It was not until the beginning of the eighteenth century that these products were supplemented with goods from the French West Indies like sugar, indigo or coffee. In the course of the eighteenth century, Bordeaux developed into the most important French port for the re-export of colonial goods.

The structure of shipping in Bordeaux can be characterized by a number of features.[43] Firstly, the overrepresentation of international trade. Northwestern Europe, especially the Netherlands, represented the largest trading partner for Bordeaux. In 1699/1700, 2280 French ships were counted on the Gironde with a total capacity of 59,369 tons as compared to 63,404 tons for the 550 foreign ships. The latter were usually responsible for more than half of the exports going through Bordeaux. Dutch trade alone represented about forty per cent on average of the total tonnage. Due to the types of goods traded, Bordeaux's trading partners were located almost exclusively in northern Europe, the Netherlands, Great Britain, and the Hanseatic cities. Following the Netherlands, Brittany was the second largest trading partner with twenty-two per cent of outgoing trade until the war of the Spanish Succession. Overall, approximately thirty-five per cent of Bordeaux's wine exports was processed by French coasters within France.[44] Nevertheless, it is amazing to see that the role of the cabotage fleet from Brittany in the Bordeaux trade declined sharply in the years after the war of the Spanish Succession, due to the decline of wine consumption in this northwestern French region.[45]

---

[41] »L'histoire de Bordeaux est dans une large mesure celle de tout le cabotage atlantique«; BERNARD, Navires et gens de mer, p. 3.

[42] BUTEL, Négociants bordelais.

[43] See HUETZ DE LEMPS, Géographie du Commerce de Bordeaux.

[44] Ibid., p. 117.

[45] Ibid., p. 550; Delumeau, Mouvement du port de Saint-Malo, p. XI.

Secondly, the lack of a domestic fleet in Bordeaux. Toward the end of the seventeenth century, local ships made up only six per cent of the tonnage counted in Bordeaux. Trade with other French regions was executed almost entirely by coasters of Saintonge, the Aunis, the Île d'Yeu, Normandy, and especially Brittany. In 1699/1700 there were 1200 ships (27,553 tons) in Bordeaux, whose home ports were located between Olonne and St Malo. 501 *caboteurs* (10,244 tons) came from the Île d'Yeu alone.

Thirdly, the discrepancy between imports and exports. Because of the specific structure of demand in Bordeaux and in the Guyenne, incoming ships usually carried only half a load or were totally in ballast, while the number of ships leaving the port with ballast was negligible. Bordeaux was an international entrepôt and export port.

Finally the seasonal character of trading activities. The dominant position of trade in wine was responsible for the cyclical and fluctuating nature of trade in Bordeaux. The European trading fleets and the *caboteurs* entered Bordeaux every year at the beginning of the wine harvest. The peak of outgoing traffic was therefore in the winter months, especially in the wake of the two fairs during the months of October and March. During the summer months – May to September – trading activity in Bordeaux nearly ceased completely.

Some important source material from the Admiralty of Guyenne stored in the Regional Archives of the Gironde, allows the reconstruction of Bordeaux's trade and port activities. At the centre of this archive are the master's reports (*Rapports à l'entrée des navires, 1640–1792*) and the certificates of clearance (*Registres des Congés, Departs des Navires du port de Bordeaux, 1649–1749*).[46] The certificates of clearance are a series that document the shipping traffic leaving the port of Bordeaux. They cover a period of one hundred years, 1649–1749, but a chronologically complete and continuous record is available for the years 1682 to 1716 only. Individual registers exist for the years 1649, 1671 to 1673, 1718, and 1744 to 1749.[47] The certificates of clearance contain the date on which the master reported the planned departure of his ship, the name of the master and the ship, the home port, the tonnage, type of cargo (wine, liquor, etc., but without an exact record of the quantities) and the destination of the journey. Usually, the name of the ship broker (*courtier*), the most important link between the merchants and the admiralty, was also noted. For the years 1671 to 1673, the name of the Bordeaux merchants whose cargo was loaded on board of the ship is also given. Furthermore, for a number of years, there is a systematic summary listing of the crew (for example: »six men, including the captain, and one boy aged seventeen«),

---

[46] Archives Départementales de la Gironde (ADG), Série 6B: Amirauté de Guyenne; see Répertoire numérique des fonds de l'Amirauté de Guyenne (6B), éd. par Maurice Oudot de Dainville, Bordeaux 1913.

[47] ADG, 6B 282 to 309, Départs des navires du port de Bordeaux, 1649–1749.

and occasionally even the names of passengers, who boarded in Bordeaux. A significant change occurred on 1 October 1698 the cause of which is unclear. From 1698 to and including 1718, the bookkeeper of the Admiralty of Guyenne also noted the exact quantities of the cargo (for example: 100 tons of wine, 12 barrels of brandy, 24 bushels of plums, etc.). It is therefore possible to estimate the volume of the exported goods by destination.

Fraud and exemptions, which cause great problems for other statistical series like the *Sound Toll Registers*, do not really amount to much in the case of Bordeaux. The more than several thousand ships, among those very small coastal ships with a tonnage of less than ten tons, which are found in the annual registers, indicate that all ships which left the port and the jurisdiction of the Admiralty of Guyenne were accounted for. In Bordeaux, the relevant articles of the General Naval Ordinance of August 1681 were conscientiously applied: »No vessel shall leave the ports of our kingdom for the sea without the approval of the Admiralty, registered by the bookkeeper of the Admiralty of its departure port, under the penalty of confiscation«.[48]

The master's reports (*Rapports à l'entrée dans le port de Bordeaux*) document the *incoming* ships. While less complete than the certificates of clearance, the seventeen volumes of the reports document incoming ships for the period between 1640 and 1718, but only a few years present a continuous series. For the years 1721 to 1792, incoming ships are reported in a total of thirteen volumes, but these have many gaps.[49] For the first half of the nineteenth century, however, the port registers have survived fairly completely. An example is the biweekly registration of arriving and departing ships for the years 1811 to 1858.[50]

The master's reports of the seventeenth and eighteenth centuries contain the following data: the date when the master handed his travel log to the admiralty, the name of the skipper and the ship, the tonnage, the home port, the port of departure, the ports called at, the duration of the journey, the cargo in the form of a qualitative description, like »barrel wood, copper, iron rods«, supplemented after 1698 by an exact quantity of the individual goods, as well as the crew listing. In some cases, we also find the name of the shipowner, the recipient in Bordeaux or the names of the passengers. Occasionally, the

[48] J. M. PARDESSUS, Collection des Lois maritimes antérieures au XVIIIe siècle, vol. 4, Paris 1837; Ordonnance touchant la Marine du mois d'août 1681, Livre Premier, Titre X, Article 1er.

[49] ADG, 6B 213 to 281, Rapports à l'entrée des navires dans le port de Bordeaux, 1640–1792. A continuous record exists for the years 1640 to 1646, 1669 to 1670, 1684 to 1699, and 1714 to 1715.

[50] ADG, Série M, Administration générale et économique du Département, 1800–1940, Sous-Série 8M: Commerce; ADG, 8M 197: Relevés des navires entrés et sortis dans les ports du département de la Gironde (Bordeaux, Blaye, La Teste, Libourne) 1818–1820; ADG, 8M 198–239: Relevés bi-mensuels des navires entrés et sortis dans le port de Bordeaux, 1811–1858.

skipper will add a log with special events during the journey, such as storms, loss of anchor, wreckage, encounter with other ships, including warships.

As in the case of the certificates of clearance, we can also assume for the master's reports that all incoming ships, including small coastal ships, were counted. Both series complement each other exceptionally well. For those years for which both the registers of the master's reports and the volumes of the certificates of clearance survive (1682, 1684 to 1699, 1714 to 1715 and 1718), the complete maritime traffic entering and leaving the port of Bordeaux can be reconstructed.[51] For the years 1740 to 1778, the 56 volumes of the muster rolls for the coastal trade and the fishing business provide a more detailed insight into the composition of the crews active in coastal shipping.[52]

These sources allow the reconstruction of details on the route, the frequency of voyages, trade in merchandise, etc. Occasionally, one ship or captain can be traced over a number of years. Source material relating to the jurisdiction of the Admiralty of Guyenne, the Procedures (*Procédures)*, Settlements (*Appointements)* and Judgements (*Sentences*), can also be drawn on for further analysis.[53] This type of documentation permits in some cases insights into the forms of ownership of the shipping companies, the listing of crews by name, or the social life on board with its specific conflicts. Furthermore, these documents, which detail litigation on shipping accidents, conflicts with pilots, and record shipwrecks and convoys, allow a better understanding of the everyday conditions of the sea and coastal trade in the Atlantic and the estuary of the Gironde in the early modern era.

The rich collection of Bordeaux's legal archives containing shipping contracts (*charte-parties*), maritime insurance, ship sales, etc, opens up a further avenue of investigation, like the reconstruction of the shipping activities and interests of the Bordeaux merchants or their role as agents for merchants outside of Bordeaux.[54] Historical investigation is possible of all segments of Bordeaux's maritime trade, the overseas trade as well as the European trade. Based on the sources and materials just introduced, a detailed analysis of the many thousand coastal ship operators who frequented the port of Bordeaux could certainly be done. The Bordeaux documentation may indeed permit a definitive evaluation of the fleets and the seafaring population of the French Atlantic coast between Dunkirk and Bayonne or St Jean-de-Luz.

---

[51] The large series of master's reports and certificates of clearance can also be supplemented by six volumes of the record ADG, 6B 607–612: Divers. Bureau de Libourne. Etat des entrées et sorties de navires, 1729–1764.

[52] ADG, 6B 547–602, Rôles d'équipage pour le cabotage et la pêche (petit cabotage, bateaux pêcheurs côtiers, etc.), 1740, 1741, 1746–1764, 1766, 1768–1775, 1777–1778.

[53] ADG, Série 6B: Amirauté de Guyenne, Attributions Judiciaires: 6B 613–666 Sentences, 1650–1792; 6B 667–868 Appointements, 1643–1792; 6B 898–1933 Procédures, 1642–1792.

[54] ADG, Série 3E: Fonds des Notaires.

The same is true for the fleets of the Netherlands, Great Britain, Scandinavia or the Hanseatic cities.

IV

Hamburg's fleet as well as those of the Hanseatic cities Bremen and Lübeck began trading with France during the late seventeenth century, when the dominant Dutch influence in France began to lose ground due to the wars of Louis XIV. With regard to the importance of Bordeaux's trade with northern Europe, Hamburg began to challenge the Amsterdam entrepot. Relations between Hamburg and Bordeaux bade well for the future. After 1740 Bordeaux exported more colonial goods to Hamburg than to Amsterdam. In the 1780s, a third of all tonnage leaving the southwestern French port was destined for the three German Hanseatic ports.

Using the above mentioned sources we have been able to identify a total of 1126 Hanseatic merchantmen (179,848 tons) in Bordeaux for the period from 1670 to 1718. Of these, 797 were from Hamburg (128,857 tons), 141 from Bremen (17,210 tons) and 188 from Lübeck (33,781 tons).[55] The Bordeaux data was compared with documents from the Hanseatic cities, more specifically lists of Hamburg ships from 1671 and 1674, published by Ernst Baasch and Pierre Jeannin, and lists of Bremen ships from the end of the seventeenth century published by Hartmut Müller.[56] Some complementary research was done in the Lübeck archives pertaining to the *Spanische Collecten*. Finally, the lists of sea letters issued by the Swedish port adminstration of Stade on the Elbe river, published by Claus Tiedemann, contain important additional information.[57] This type of data check allowed a better identification of the masters and their vessels, and led to a significant improvement of the database.

What is surprising regarding the tonnage of the ships is that a medium-sized ship (somewhere between 100 and 200 tons) dominated in European cabotage on the Bordeaux-Hamburg route. There are also extreme cases, like the *Jonas* or the *St Johannes von Hamburg* of thirty-two and thirty-six tons respectively.

---

[55] See Peter Voss, Bordeaux et les villes hanséatiques, 1672–1715. Contribution à l'histoire maritime de l'Europe du Nord-Ouest. Thèse de doctorat, Université Michel de Montaigne – Bordeaux III, 15 décembre 1995. Atelier national de reproduction des thèses, Lille 1996.

[56] Ernst Baasch, Ein Verzeichnis der hamburgischen Kauffahrteiflotte vom Jahre 1672, in: Zeitschrift des Vereins für Hamburgische Geschichte 15 (1910), pp. 39–52; Pierre Jeannin, Zur Geschichte der Hamburger Handelsflotte am Ende des 17. Jahrhunderts. Eine Schiffsliste von 1674, in: Zeitschrift des Vereins für Hamburgische Geschichte 57 (1971), pp. 67–82; Hartmut Müller, Untersuchungen zur bremischen Reederei im 17. Jahrhundert, in: Bremisches Jahrbuch 53 (1975), pp. 91–142.

[57] Claus Tiedemann, Die Schiffahrt des Herzogtums Bremen zur Schwedenzeit (1645–1712), Stade 1970.

At the other end of the spectrum, we find the *Hoffnung von Hamburg* of 436 tons. Research on the Lübeck ships confirms that all categories of the Hanseatic merchant fleet were engaged in the trade with France, except the very large ships with a tonnage of more than 400 tons, which, in the case of Lübeck, were used for trade with Spain.[58] Two thirds of all Hamburg ships arrived in Bordeaux on a direct route. One third of the Hamburg ships took on their cargo at a port on the North sea, primarily in the Netherlands. These numbers are identical for Bremen and Lübeck. However, one third of all Lübeck ships engaged in trade with France, picked up their cargo in a Baltic seaport, primarily in Riga, before heading for Bordeaux. On their journey to Bordeaux, the Lübeck ships also frequently stopped at Roscoff in Brittany, to unload Baltic linseed.

The database reveals that many Hamburg masters travelled frequently to southwestern France. For example, Willem Cloppenburg undertook a total of fourteen journeys between Bordeaux and Hamburg aboard the *Prince Charles* and the *St Peter von Hamburg* between 1701 and 1715. Peter Petersen of Lübeck arrived at the port in France's southwest fourteen times. Johan Beckerhenning of Bremen also called at Bordeaux a total of thirteen times aboard the *Katharina* and the *Susanna von Bremen* in the years 1700, and from 1707 to 1715. In some cases, we find a surprisingly high frequency of trips: between January 1688 and April 1689, Johan Cornelissen embarked on four journeys aboard the *Bleicher von Hamburg* calling at Hamburg, Rotterdam, Bruges, and Bordeaux. Hinrich Lüders achieved eight trips from Hamburg to Bruges and Bordeaux between February 1687 and April 1689. Several members of the Hamburg, Bremen, and Lübeck-based skipper families seem to have specialized in the cabotage trade with Bordeaux. The »enthusiasm« for the trade with France was occasionally even handed down from father to son, like, for example, in the case of Johan Lange and Johan Lange Jr of Hamburg, who embarked on a total of twenty-seven trips to Bordeaux with six different ships between 1669 and 1712.

In the case of Hamburg, there appears to be a link between the maritime trade with France and the traditional trade with Spain and Portugal. More surprising, however, is the presence of Hamburg whalers in southwestern France. We have identified sixty-seven Hamburg ships in Bordeaux, which are documented in a listing of Hamburg whalers aggregated by Wanda Oesau.[59] Here too a close cooperation between cabotage, other areas of the maritime trade and whaling is shown. Johan Lange Jr, for example, undertook six

---

[58] Marie-Louise PELUS, Eine Hansestadt im Planetensystem des Sonnenkönigs. Der Handel mit Frankreich und seine Bedeutung für die lübeckische Wirtschaft in der Epoche Ludwigs XIV., in: Zeitschrift des Vereins für Lübeckische Geschichte und Altertumskunde 65 (1985), pp. 119–42.

[59] Wanda OESAU, Hamburgs Grönlandfahrt auf Walfischfang und Robbenschlag vom 17.–19. Jahrhundert, Glückstadt/Hamburg 1955.

whaling expeditions aboard the galiote *Abrahams Opfer* for the Hamburg shipping company of Peter Jansen Schomaker between 1684 and 1688. Between 1682 and 1689, we find him in Bordeaux ten times aboard the same ship. Even in subsequent years, Johan Lange can be found aboard different Hamburg whalers both in the North Atlantic, off Greenland and Spitzbergen, as well as in the Gironde.

Captain Heinrich Schlichting embodied the four dimensions of Hamburg's maritime trade with the *Freiheit von Stade*, a 260 ton vessel. In February 1693, he engaged in whaling off Greenland. In September 1693, he shipped a cargo of salt from Scotland to the Baltic Sea. In April 1695, he left the port of Bordeaux for Hamburg carrying wine, brandy, plums, paper and walnut wood. He arrived in Hamburg one month later. On July 30 of the same year, he left for Cadiz and Malaga in Spain.

The example of Heinrich Schlichting demonstrates that one shipmaster with the same ship could, to use Violet Barbour's words, undertake the different journeys of European cabotage »from the mouth of the Garonne to Archangel«.[60] Hamburg merchants, the Dutch or the English, however, did not enjoy the privilege of this maritime trade. Even Bordeaux merchants and skippers, who are not really famous for dynamic enterprise, engaged in overseas trade. From 1662 to 1665, for example, Martial Deyles, a shipmaster from the Saintonge region, made eleven journeys from France to Spain and England with the *Marie de Bordeaux*, a small ship of 40–50 tons built in the Bordeaux shipyards of Guillaume Lapeyre. In 1665, he took control of another caboteur, the *Jeanne de Bordeaux*, a vessel also belonging to Guillaume Lapeyre. After several journeys to other French ports, and to Bilbao, Santander and the British Isles, the *Jeanne de Bordeaux* sailed to Lisbon, Madeira and the Canaries in 1668, 1670 and 1671. In 1667 and 1670 Martial Deyles participated in the Newfoundland cod fisheries. Three years later, in 1673, the *Jeanne de Bordeaux*, crossed the Atlantic once again for the French West Indies islands of La Martinique and La Guadeloupe.[61]

It is very important, however, to note that even at the beginning of the eighteenth century, the transatlantic trade was occasionally undertaken with ships of a tonnage of not more than thirty or fifty tons. Shipmasters and ships were recruited from the cabotage or coastal trade of the French Atlantic coast, Normandy, Brittany, the Aunis, Saintonge, the Basque country, and also the estuary of the Gironde. Thus, with regards to the shipmasters and ships, Bordeaux enjoyed a direct link between cabotage and coastal shipping on the one hand, and transatlantic shipping on the other hand.

---

[60] Violet BARBOUR, Dutch and English merchant shipping in the seventeenth century, in: Economic History Review 2 (1930), p. 265.

[61] Peter VOSS, L'Exemple d'un Bourgeois et marchand de Bordeaux au milieu du XVIIe siècle, in: Bulletin du Centre d'Histoire des Espaces Atlantiques 4 (1988), p. 90.

13

BELGIAN COASTAL SHIPPING, 1879–1914:
A SPECIAL CASE?

GRETA DEVOS

As a result of the League of Nations Third Conference on Communications and Transit, held in Geneva in August–September 1927, an enquiry was conducted on the meaning of the term »coasting trade« in the various countries.[1] The organizer was the League's Permanent Committee on ports and maritime navigation. The questionnaire sent in 1930 to the various members contained four different questions. Firstly, which laws outline, limit or define the ships used in coastal trade? Secondly, if coastal trade is reserved to the national flag, is this restriction absolute or are some exceptions (temporary or permanent) allowed in favour of other flags? Thirdly, do coasters under national flag receive special treatment (such as reduction in port dues, towage, pilotage dues, or light dues)? Finally, do the goods transported by these coasters receive any preferential treatment?

The Belgian reply was one of the shortest. There were no special regulations for coastal trade. Article 209 (since 1908 article 232) of the Second Book of the Belgian *Code de Commerce* defined deep-sea navigation only.[2] Consequently coastal trade was regarded as all maritime trade that did not belong to this type of navigation. Coastal trade was not reserved to the national flag. Neither ships under the Belgian flag nor the goods transported enjoyed any special treatment.

To justify this policy, the Belgian Ministries of Foreign Affairs and of Transport argued in their reply that the absence of any regulation was a result of the country's geography, which was not favourable to national coastal shipping, and of the protectionist measures taken by neighbouring countries. The absence of any regulations should, according to the Ministries, not be inter-

---

[1] Société des Nations, Enquête sur la portée de la notion du cabotage dans les différents pays (Commission consultative et technique des Communications et du Transit). ARA (Public Record Office Brussels), Administration de la Marine, 5305. – Some of the data on which this chapter rests were gathered by Bart Lemayeur, my research assistant between 1994 and 1999.

[2] Constant SMEESTERS, Eléments de Droit Maritime Belge, Brussels/Paris 1914, p. 241; Pandectes Belges, vol. 15, Brussels 1885, col. 49–50.

preted as a lack of interest, for Belgium was particularly interested in »international coastal shipping« because of her geographical situation, the Belgian coastline being no longer than 68 km.

That was the situation in 1930. If we look at legislation in the nineteenth century, the area of coastal shipping was limited before 1879 to navigation in the area from the Sound in the north and the Straits of Gibraltar in the south. This definition originated in the French *Code de Commerce*. A distinction between »large« and »small« coastal trade *(le grand et le petit cabotage)* no longer existed as of 1879. This distinction had been introduced by the French, although *petit cabotage* was not clearly defined. It covered shipping in the Scheldt estuary and to all French atlantic ports, and later also other ports such as Hamburg and Hull. The new maritime law of 21 August 1879, article 209, which revised the second book of the *Code* dealing with maritime trade, extended the coastal shipping area to the whole of the European continent and included the coasts of Northern Africa, the Near East and the Black Sea.[3] The definition of overseas trade (that of coastal shipping was not given) was important for insuring the ship, and more specifically for determining when a ship could be considered lost, as no news of it had been received, and the sum insured claimed. It defined deep-sea trade as voyages beyond 30° northern latitude in the south, 72° northern latitude in the north, 15° western longitude and 44° eastern longitude by the Paris meridian. Coastal shipping took place within that area. The text was clearly inspired by the French legislation which defined the same area.[4]

As a consequence, Belgian coastal shipping was indirectly defined geographically and it concentrated on »international cabotage« or short-sea shipping. The definition changed little in the course of the twentieth century. A Royal Decree of 21 May 1958 defined coastal shipping as that within the area geographically contained between 72° northern latitude and 30° northern latitude, in the east by 46° eastern longitude (by the Greenwich meridian) and 25° western longitude.[5] Still this was not the only definition. The old »restricted« definition of the *Code de Commerce* persisted in the twentieth century. The National Labour Agreement of 1967 reserved an even more restricted area for coastal shipping: all Western European ports from Kiel or Copenhagen down to Cape Finistere, including the British Isles. The port of Antwerp, for the determination of port dues, limited coastal shipping to that

---

[3] Although the old definition is still used in literature in the twentieth century: P. VAN DEN BROECK, Trampvaart en Lijnvaart, Antwerpen 1945, p. 28–9; J. VAN BEYLEN (ed.), Maritieme Encyclopedie, vol. 4, Bussum/Antwerp 1971, p. 200.

[4] Victor JACOBS, Le droit maritime belge. Commentaire de la loi du 21 août 1879, Brussels/Paris 1891, vol. 2, p. 449.

[5] Dirk NOLLET, De Kustvaart in Belgisch havenperspectief, Antwerp 1973, p. 10 (unpublished dissertation).

from Spain along the continental Western Coast up to the Sound, again including the British Isles.

In short, Belgian legislation, central and local regulations have different views on coastal trade. It fluctuates between intra-continental, also called »international coastal shipping« or short-sea shipping[6] on the one hand, including the coast of Northern Africa and the Near East and shipping to ports of the western European coastline on the other hand, including the British Isles. The definition of coastal shipping, as interpreted by countries with a long coastline, as navigation from port to port or from cape to cape, was non existant.

Belgian »coastal shipping« in different ports

Antwerp like Ghent and Brussels is an inland port. It has the status of a »commercial port«. The location of Antwerp about 88 km inland offered and still offers a variety of modes of transport. Ostend, Nieuport and Zeebrugge (since 1903) are coastal ports and are considered in documents of the period as »ports de vitesse« more adapted to rapid mailboat services.[7] In the course of the nineteenth century Antwerp developed into an important liner port. On the eve of the First World War Antwerp was linked to almost every important port in the world by 193 regular shipping lines. Shortly after the war no less than 60 per cent of the incoming tonnage was in the liner trade.[8]

Traffic in the port of Antwerp greatly exceeded that of all other Belgian ports. In 1913 it took the lion's share with 76 per cent of total ship movement and 90 per cent of tonnage. Ghent followed with respectively 15 per cent and 7 per cent, and Ostend with 7 and 2.3 per cent respectively. Nieuport had 2 and 0.7 per cent.

Of the smaller Belgian ports, Ghent accounted for most of the coastal liners, all trading to British ports. In 1912 eight regular lines linked this inland port with Britain. The initiative was taken by British shipping companies [9] such as, to London: the Leach & Co. Line; to Goole: the Goole Steamshipping Company, owned by the Lancashire & Yorkshire Railway; to Hull: the Wilson Line; to Leith: the Geo Gibson Line; to Liverpool: the Cork Steam Shipping

---

[6] According to the Belgian Shortsea Sailing List published by the maritime newspaper *De Lloyd*, Antwerp now has 143 shortsea lines. The ports on this list are compatible with the definition of »international coastal shipping« in the definition of 1879.

[7] Répartition entre les ports de Dunkerque et d'Anvers des courants commerciaux du Nord et l'Est de la France, 1911. By kind permission of Prof. F. Caron.

[8] P. VAN DEN BROECK, Trampvaart, p. 163.

[9] Tableau général du commerce de la Belgique avec les pays étrangers pendant l'année 1912, vol. 3, Brussels 1913, p. 746.

Co. Ltd; to Newcastle: the Tyne Steam Shipping Co. Ltd; to Manchester: the
Cork Steam Shipping Co. Ltd; to Dublin: Palgrave, Murphy & Co.

It is not surprising that imports of goods from British ports amounted to 36.4
per cent of the total. The biggest importer was Russia with 40.1 per cent of the
tonnage, most probably timber transported by tramp ships. Thanks to improvements in the Terneuzen lock in 1908, ships drawing 8 metres could enter and
the largest size of coaster that could be catered for rose from 524 tons in 1893
to 705 tons in 1912.[10]

In 1912 regular lines from the port of Ostend also concentrated on English
ports. In addition to the long established Ostend-Dover mailboats, from 1863 a
state owned line, there was a service from Ostend to London run by the General Steam Navigation Company for the transport of passengers and goods and
the ultra-rapid Ostend-Tilbury service for the transport of goods (not only steel
products but also foodstuffs), owned by the Société Anonyme John Cockerill.
British imports in the port of Ostend amounted to 33.7 per cent of the total.
Exports were almost entirely sent (99 per cent) to Great Britain. Nieuport was
not visited regularly by shipping lines, however a large part of the imports
consisted of British coal.

Some characteristics of the port of Antwerp

In Antwerp, the influence of the Ancien Regime remained apparent throughout the course of the nineteenth century. The reopening of the river Scheldt in
1796 restored international ocean navigation, but traffic was during the first
years mostly limited to coasters. The proclamation of Belgian independence in
1830 caused serious damage to the merchant navy as well as to trade.[11]
Merchants and shipowners diversified their interests by founding branch-
establishments in neighbouring ports or simply left Antwerp. As a consequence the Belgian merchant fleet was in a deplorable state. Measures, such as
government aid for shipbuilding in 1837 and subsidies for the organization of
direct transocean shipping lines, reinforced the temporary effects of the law on
differential tariffs of 24 July 1844.[12] Direct foreign trade with ships under the
Belgian flag enjoyed special treatment. On the one hand the government tried
to limit the trade of colonial and other goods through neighbouring countries
such as France, the Netherlands and Great Britain. On the other hand Bel-

---

[10] Ibid., p. 739.

[11] Karel VERAGHTERT, From inland port to international port, in: F. SUYKENS (ed.), Antwerp, a Port for All Seasons, Antwerp 1986, p. 355.

[12] Greta DEVOS, De oprichting van de Hulp-en voorzorgskas voor zeevarenden onder
Belgische vlag, in: Van wieg tot zeemansgraf, Hulp-en Voorzorgskas voor Zeevarenden,
1845–1995, Antwerp 1995, pp. 13–14.

gium's modernised industry was in those years desperately looking for new overseas markets. Although Belgian international trade was largely dependent on these fairly well protected neighbouring markets, with 64 per cent of total imports and 82 per cent of exports in 1840–44, attempts were made to limit dependency on France and the Netherlands for the import of colonial and overseas products. These products entered the country via warehouses in neighbouring foreign ports. As a result shipping, especially to the neighbouring countries, was regarded with suspicion. When the government started to grant subsidies to foreign mailboats from the 1860s, foreign, especially British, companies often threatened to send coasters to Antwerp if no subsidy was granted, instead of ocean steamers outward bound. This was the case in the early 1880s. The Belgian government only subsidised ships that were leaving Antwerp and going directly to transoceanic destinations, which was an obstacle to British shipping companies who generally preferred Southampton as their last European port of call. This British attitude partly explains the very dense traffic to important British ports such as London, Liverpool, and Hull. Coasters, in this case almost all of them under the British flag, often served as feeders to the ocean-going ships departing from British ports. Unlike the situation in the last decades of the twentieth century, this had nothing to do with the size of the ships but with the unwillingness of British companies to send their ocean steamers to Antwerp, especially in the early 1880s.[13]

Thus coastal shipping was never subsidised by the government. The expansion of the port also paid no attention to this section of shipping. Separate docks for loading and unloading of coasters did not exist, with the exception of the timber docks, which were excavated in the 1860s and 1870s. Special equipment for unloading grain, coal, and ore was available in the last decade of the nineteenth century, but the distinction between coasters and deep-sea ships was non existant.

Another inheritance of the past was the presence of foreign merchants, shipping agents and shipbrokers in Antwerp.[14] Calculations based on directories show their importance. So, international competition was extremely fierce. According to some protest voices of the period the activities of these foreign agents stifled the initiative of Belgian shipowners. They suffered from the low

[13] Greta DEVOS, Belgische Overheidssteun ann scheepvaartlijnen 1867–1914, in: Bijdragon tot de internationale maritieme geschiedenis (= Collectanea Maritima IV), Brussels 1988, p. 89.

[14] The most important and well known foreign firms for shipping were: John P. Best & Co., Kennedy, Hunter & Co., Walford & Co., Gellatly, Hankey & Co., Thos Ronaldson & Co., all English with offices in London, the Dutch firm Ruys & Co., the shipping company Adolf Deppe of German origin. See: Antwerp: commercially considered, London 1898, p. 48–59; for coastal shipping Best and Deppe were important in 1880 and Deppe and Walford in 1912. Of the 65 agents and brokers in the late 1890s only 31 were Belgian or partly Belgian. See: A. LECOINTE, Développement de la Marine marchande en Belgique, Ostend 1989, p. 6.

freights for which Antwerp was famous. The abundance of freight, especially from the last quarter of the nineteenth century, attracted big German steamers which came to Antwerp to supplement their cargo before setting sail.

As a consequence, the Belgian merchant navy was small. The transition from sail to steam nearly halved the fleet in the 1860s and 1870s. In 1883 the fleet amounted to 15 sailing ships and 47 steamers.[15] Thirty-two years later the number of steamers had risen to 97 totalling 174,021 net tons and the sailing vessels had fallen to 8 of 7,616 tons. The total tonnage had grown from 83,360 to 181,637 net tons. The share of the Belgian flag in Antwerp traffic was 11 per cent in 1880 and 6.5 per cent in 1913, fairly low in spite of all initiatives. At the end of the nineteenth and the beginning of the twentieth centuries the problem of the Belgian merchant navy was one of the important topics of discussion. There were no shortage of arguments. According to shipping circles, one of the main reasons was the lack of willingness of bankers and entrepreneurs to invest in shipping. Belgian capital, they complained, was always available for investment in industry and even for investments abroad. Another much cited argument was the poor quality of training for officers. It is typical that Belgian shipping companies relied on foreign officers, despite numerous and recurrent protests.[16] As far as the ships are concerned, the situation was not much better. The large majority had been built in British yards. There was no want of basic materials such as steel, but there was a shortage of professionally qualified shipbuilders. Even in the first half of the twentieth century many shipping engineers obtained their training in the Netherlands at the Technische Hogeschool in Delft.

As mentioned before, the role of Belgian shipowners was rather modest. Some of them were at the same time shipping agents, individual merchants, or commercial houses. Only four of them were limited-liability joint-stock companies in the 1880s. Two of the eighteen shipping companies were in that period owned by metalworks such as the well known Société John Cockerill and the Société Royale Asturienne des Mines. They both had their mining companies in the south of Europe and transported the ores on their own vessels. On the eve of the First World War the situation had slightly improved. There were seventeen Antwerp shipping companies in 1912. Important companies were the Red Star Line, and the Compagnie Belge Maritime du Congo. Both were exclusively long-distance lines; the first to the United States, the second to the Belgian colony. Other well known companies were the Armement Adolf Deppe which ran regular services to the Mediterranean, the Black Sea and the Sea of Azov, Léon Dens & Cie to Glasgow, and to Italian, French and Greek

[15] G. BEETEMÉ, Antwerpen, moederstad van handel en kunst, vol. 3, Antwerp 1983, pp. 202–3.

[16] Greta DEVOS/Guy ELEWAUT, CMB 100. A century of commitment to shipping 1895– 1995, Tielt 1995, p. 37.

ports; and the Ligne F. Alexander to Middlesbrough and Grangemouth. At the beginning of the century, newcomers were the shipowners Henry Gylsen, of Danish origin, and Arthur Brys, who was the only one to also operate tramps. Their joint venture, the Antwerpsche Zeevaart Maatschappij organised a monthly sailing to Venice and Bari. In other words, although coastal shipping had not been subsidised by the government, its part in the national merchant navy was dominant.

Coastal shipping and the port of Antwerp

With the exception of a few unpublished dissertations[17] and papers, nothing has been written on the development of short-sea shipping in Belgium or in Antwerp, and consequently very little is known on the subject. Belgian statistics only distinguish between inland shipping and maritime shipping, so it is difficult to deduce information on coastal shipping, in whatever sense, since these figures are included under general sea traffic. Nevertheless, for the port of Antwerp the statistics of the harbour master offer the possibility of extrapolating short-sea shipping. A long-run time series from the 1870s till the 1960s gives twelve pieces of information: the date of arrival, the name of the ship, the name of the captain, the flag, the tonnage in Belgian Moorsom tons after 1884, the port of departure, the local shipping agent or shipbroker, the type of inward cargo, the date of departure, the port of destination, type of outward cargo, and the harbour duties paid.

This rich source of information enables us to separate short-sea shipping from the general maritime traffic. The selection of data on the basis of the port of departure or destination is a rather labour intensive job. Out of a total of 11,000 ships about 7,400 ships were singled out in the two years 1880 and 1912.[18] These years were selected because of their significance in the development of traffic; from the beginning of the 1880s foreign intercontinental shipping lines developed their activities at the port, and 1912 was an average traffic year on the eve of the First World War. These rather poor samples should be seen as a first attempt to distinguish short-sea shipping from the total port traffic.

In addition we consulted the lists of the regular lines that visited the port, so we got more information on the ownership of the vessels used in the intra-continental trade and at the same time we were able to identify a great deal of

---

[17] Dirk NOLLET, De Kustvaart, Diss. Antwerp 1973; Walter WEEMAES, De Belgische kustvaart en haar toekomst, Diss. Antwerp 1962–63; P. STRICK, De Belgische kustvaart in Europees perspectief, Diss. Antwerp 1982–83.

[18] SAA (Municipal Archives Antwerp), Modern Archive, 13.733 and 36.250.

the ships and their voyages. A list of regular steamer lines for the year 1881[19] shows that forty shipping lines out of fifty, i.e. 80 per cent, concentrated on intra-continental shipping. Of the 193 regular service lines in March 1913 only 88 lines, i.e. 45 per cent called at intra-continental ports.[20] So regular short-sea shipping in the period studied fell relatively, but not absolutely. The same trend is apparent in the whole of intra-continental shipping in Antwerp. Its share dropped from 48 per cent of the total incoming tonnage in 1880 to about 31 per cent in 1912. In 1880 15.5 per cent of all incoming tonnage was still sailing ships. Short-sea shipping scored lower with 10.8 per cent. Thirty two years later the share of sailing ships was at its lowest with 1.1 per cent of the total traffic. This development was clearly influenced by the growing tonnage of transoceanic steamers and the technical changes in shipping. If we consider the number of voyages in 1880, 74 per cent were of short-sea shipping against 62 per cent in 1912. The relative importance of the intra-continental navigation had decisively decreased.

On the whole, as might be expected, the participation of the Belgian fleet in short-sea shipping was limited. In 1880 it amounted to 7 per cent (all steam navigation) and to 9 per cent in 1912. In 1880 the British share rose to 62 per cent, see figure 1. For steam navigation it was even higher with 66 per cent. So short-sea shipping, as well as general traffic, in Antwerp was clearly dominated by the British. The German, the Swedish, the Norwegian and the Russian shares were limited on the whole, but scored points in sailing ships with respectively 14, 11, 30 and 10 per cent. Here also British sailing ships did well with 20 per cent. In 1912 the total British share in short-sea shipping decreased by 11 per cent while the German part had more than doubled from 6 to 14 per cent, see figure 2.

Categorised geographically, the lists of regular steam lines give the following results for 1881: seventeen out of forty shipping lines visited British ports, eleven went southwards to Atlantic ports, ten lines connected Antwerp with northern ports and only two regular lines went as far as the Mediterranean and the Black Sea. The situation in March 1913 was quite different: thirty regular lines were counted for the Mediterranean and the Black Sea, twenty five lines to the north, twenty two lines to the U.K., and only eight lines to the southern Atlantic ports. This means that for regular lines the traffic to the Mediterranean and the Black Sea increased because of the growing need for ores and grain. According to the figures of the harbour statistics the situation was much more complicated:

---

[19] ARA, Administration de la Marine, 4209.

[20] Tableau général du commerce, 1912, vol. 3 (1913), p. 697–703. Of these 193 lines no less than 111 visited Antwerp as a terminal port and 82 as a port of call.

Table 1: Incoming short-sea shipping by port of departure, 1880 and 1912

| | 1880 | | 1912 | |
	tons	no.	tons	no.
UK	37.9%	43.1%	41.8%	51.1%
North*	4.7%	5.0%	12.3%	11.5%
Baltic Sea	23.4%	26.1%	11.6%	13.9%
South Atlantic**	9.6%	9.5%	6.7%	7.3%
Mediterranean	10.8%	9.1%	12.3%	9.0%
Black Sea	12.7%	4.8%	14.3%	5.8%
Others***	1 %	2.4%	1.1%	1.5%

* North Sea and Norwegian coast

** France, Spain, Portugal

*** Belgium and undefined ports

Figure 1: Incoming short-sea shipping tonnage by national flag:
Antwerp, 1880

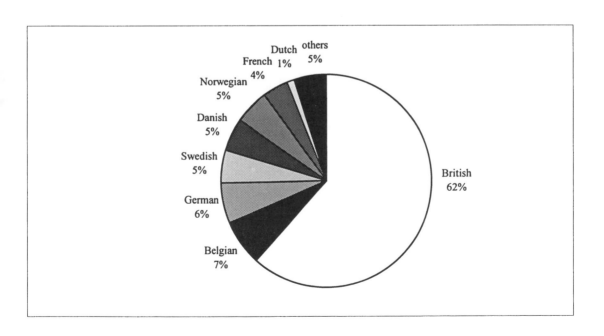

Figure 2: Incoming short-sea shipping tonnage by national flag: Antwerp, 1912

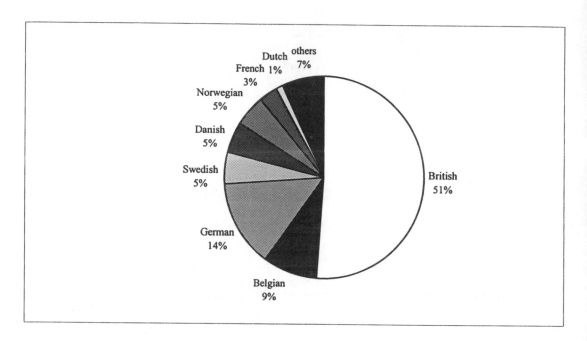

Table 2: Outgoing short-sea shipping by port of destination, 1880 and 1912

	1880		1912	
	tons	no.	tons	no.
U.K.	67.9%	63.3%	58.7%	60.8%
North	6.6%	8.3%	10.6%	11.0%
Baltic Sea	11.6%	14.0%	8.7%	11.0%
South Atlantic	8.3%	9.2%	5.9%	6.4%
Mediterranean	2.7%	2.0%	13.3%	8.7%
Black Sea	2.0%	0.9%	1.9%	0.9%
Others	0.9%	2.3%	0.9%	1.2%

In the first place more research is needed to distinguish between the liner trade and tramp ships. For some ports one should distinguish between a port of departure and the port of destination. For instance the amount and the share of British ships coming from British ports was lower than the ships leaving Antwerp for British ports, very often in ballast. The conclusion is still more valid for ships coming in from the Black Sea with grain and loading for the Mediteranean or the Black Sea elsewhere. Change over time is also of importance. The British supremacy remained important for the whole period. The trade with the Baltic Sea reached a peak in absolute terms, but decreased relatively. The connections with the Mediterranean ports grew constantly. Traffic between the North Sea ports increased, especially the tonnage, but the number of ships did not increase to the same extent. This can be explained by the arrival of large transoceanic, especially German, steamers coming from Bremen, Hamburg or Rotterdam.

Transport to the neighbouring countries of France, Germany and the Netherlands

Movements within the country are nearly all registered in the statistics of inland navigation, as is a large part of the traffic to the Netherlands, the north of France and the Rhineland. Inland navigation and rail traffic can be seen as complementary transport to coastal shipping, although they can also be considered as competitive. The geographical situation of Belgium with its intricate traffic infrastructure is in this respect a highly interesting, but rather complicated research topic. Studies based on the population figures and the distances between the thirteen most important ports between Hamburg and Le Havre show that Antwerp is the most centrally situated port.[21] The development of a solid network of communications of course promoted the already favourable geographical situation of the port 88 km inland.

With regard to the connections with the Netherlands and France, it is remarkable that data on Dutch ports and on harbours in the north of France rarely appeared in the harbour statistics for 1880. All traffic to these ports appeared in the statistics of inland navigation or was included in the railway statistics. The annual tonnages of outgoing barges from Antwerp in the period 1880–1914 showed the rapid revival of inland navigation from around 1890, with a boom period after the turn of the century. According to Van der Herten, the need for cheap bulk transport was generated by the second industrial revolution and played an important part in this development.[22] In our opinion, the intensification of Belgian inland shipping was also inspired by examples abroad, especially in Germany, where the use and construction of waterways connected industrial centres to one another, and the »national ports« Bremen

---

[21] Cf. the report from the Bremer Ausschuß für Wissenschaftsforschung and the Nederlandse Centraal Planbureau (The Hague). Hinterland, 1995, vol. 2, p. 31.

[22] Bart VAN DER HERTEN, Belgian inland shipping 1831–1939, in: Andreas KUNZ/John ARMSTRONG (eds.), Inland Navigation and Economic Development in Nineteenth-Century Europe, Mainz 1995, p. 42.

and Hamburg acted as a catalyst. Another possible explanation was that the depletion of the mines in the southern part of Belgium stimulated in the last quarter of the century, the import of foreign ores and the building of metalworks in the north. Of course, inland navigation benefited from this situation. The competition between rail transport and inland navigation attracted public interest in these years and encouraged discussions on river navigation in parliament from this time onwards. This eventually led to the law on maritime and fluvial navigation of 10 February 1908.

Inland navigation was particularly well represented in transport to Netherlands and Germany, see figure 3, even though the Scheldt-Rhine connection had been neglected by both the Belgian and Netherlands governments.[23] In 1912 only 8.7 per cent of goods leaving the port of Antwerp by ship for Dutch ports were being shipped by sea. The rest was transported by canals and rivers. For German ports the figures in the same year were even more convincing, with 4 per cent by sea and the rest on inland waterways.

Figure 3:   Annual tonnage of outward barges: Antwerp, 1883–1914

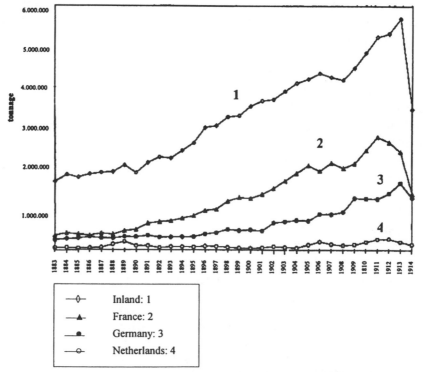

[23] Annuaire statistique de la Belgique et du Congo Belge, Brussels 1884–1919.

For traffic to the ports in northern France, particularly Dunkirk, inland navigation was less important. The railway played a leading role here. Nevertheless, a network of canals existed from the beginning of the nineteenth century, and had been steadily expanded. If we concentrate, for instance, on the port of Dunkirk, it has been established that in 1910 some 400,000 tons of goods annually came from or went to the port of Antwerp.[24] These goods were transported partly by rail, partly by barges. The reason for this journey was of course the limited hinterland to the port of Dunkirk with its poor traffic facilities. It was easier and cheaper to transport goods to Antwerp, with its lower port taxes and speedier cargo handling, its better port facilities and its special railway tariffs for raw materials and export products.

Special rail rates for transport to the national ports certainly have to be taken into account. This mainly applied to the ports between Hamburg and Le Havre, thereby undoubtedly fuelling mutual competition between them.[25] Far too little attention has been paid up till now to this phenomenon. Documents from the end of the nineteenth century in Lorraine, Luxemburg and the Ruhr, for instance, testify to clever manipulation of the special tariffs for the transport of half-finished and finished steel products to North Sea ports. Even in the 1830s the young Belgian government recognised the benefits of a good connection with the Rhineland and other German regions. The opening of a railway to Aachen in 1843, of a connection for freight traffic via Montzen and the installation of a line Antwerp-Mönchen-Gladbach in 1876 over Dutch territory show the government's concern to promote commercial ties with its eastern neighbours. Figures for the transit by rail to the Rhineland and the Ruhr region are unfortunately not available. From Antwerp the goods were mostly shipped by German transport companies with local agencies.

Besides the regular sailings via the Belgian and Netherlands inland waterways that were considered as inland navigation, we also had the lines Antwerp-Bremen and Antwerp-Hamburg. These ships brought in mixed cargo and also left with mixed cargo. The lines were partially run by transoceanic steamer lines such as the Norddeutscher Lloyd which ran in 1913 a service of seven or eight journeys monthly to Bremen. Records show that the ships from these lines continued their journeys from Antwerp to South America, the Far East or Australia, but did not always call at Antwerp on the return journey.[26] Therefore we can assume that these ships brought goods from Bremen to Antwerp and acted as feeder vessels. Regular lines to Hamburg were organ-

[24] Répartition entre les ports de Dunkerque et d'Anvers des courants commerciaux du Nord et de l'Est de la France 1911, p. 16.

[25] Paul EHLERS [et al.], Die Verkehrswirtschaft des Antwerpener Hafens. Eine zusammenfassende Studie, Hamburg/Bremen 1915, p. 66–71.

[26] Greta DEVOS, German Ocean Shipping and the port of Antwerp 1875–1914, in: Proceedings of the International Colloquium »Industrial Revolutions and the Sea« (Brussels 28–31 March 1989) (= Collectanea Maritima V), Brussels 1991, p. 226.

ised by the H.J. Perlbach & Co., Nachf. A. Kirsten line with two services a
week. This shipping company was already active in the early 1880s. The Ver-
einigte Bugsir und Frachtschiffahrtsgesellschaft with services to Hamburg,
other North Sea and Baltic ports was in 1912 another regular.

Special attention should be drawn to the coasters which were put into inland
navigation. They also are incorporated in the Antwerp harbour statistics. Their
impact was rather limited, since the ships leaving Antwerp for an inland port
only represent 0.8 per cent in 1880 and 0.8 per cent in 1912 of the total incoming »coastal traffic« in numbers and respectively 0.5 and 0.1 per cent in
tonnage. The number of these ships was higher in 1880 than 32 years later, but
the total tonnage was lower. The average tonnage rose from 226 to 707 tons
for the inward ships. Sixty ships came from inland ports i.e. 13,537 tons in
1880. Brussels and Louvain scored high with 41 ships. Only 25 ships of 2,939
tons went inward. In 1912 43 coasters of 30,408 tons had an inland port of
departure; 34 coasters left Antwerp for an inland port. Ghent, with respectively 22 and 17 coasters, was an important port of destination, but in comparison to the proper inland navigation by barges these data are definitely
unimportant.

Conclusions

The geographical position of Belgium with its limited coastline of 68 km puts
Belgian coastal shipping in an entirely different light from other European
countries. The terminology used by the legislature can be interpreted in many
ways; it covers stipulations concerning maritime insurance, education of officers and port dues. In statistics the term »coastal shipping« is not specifically
mentioned. Anyway, the definition »coastal shipping« was not much in use in
general, and literature on it is almost non-existant. Coastal shipping, according
to the Belgian government, should be seen as »international coastal shipping«,
»intracontinental shipping«, although navigation to ports on the northern
Africa coast and the Near East is included, and in more recent language is
»short-sea shipping«.

From the statistics of the Antwerp harbour master, short-sea shipping can be
extracted from the general maritime statistics. This job is very labour intensive
and the analysis of the figures, independent of the choice of definition, is
extremely complex. The proximity of other important neighbouring ports such
as Rotterdam, the position of Antwerp 88 km inland and the strongly
developed network of rivers, canals and railways do not facilitate the in-
terpretation. One should at least be conversant with the different lines and
services and with the the ships of the various shipping companies for a better
identification of the different traffic routes. This would also enable the

researcher to calculate the importance of tramping in the port, a topic which has been barely studied, because Antwerp, is known in the literature as a liner port.

The accessibility to a vast hinterland has always been a trump card in the hands of Antwerp, but it does not make it easier to explain the competition and often the coordination between the various transport facilities. Especially for the neighbouring countries, such as the Netherlands, France and Germany, maritime navigation was hampered by the transport of goods overland. This situation partly explains the important role of the British in short-sea shipping, for the British flag was throughout the period at the top of the general Antwerp traffic. Its share was only slightly menaced by Germany towards the eve of the First World War. The limited impact of the Belgian fleet, because of historical developments and the rather uninterested attitude of the government and the possible investors was also typical for short-sea shipping, although most Belgian shipowners engaged their ships in »international coastal shipping«. Indeed, it is a public secret that the Belgian government was never maritime minded. In spite of temporary patriotic enthusiasm and occasional speeches a coherent long-term policy was lacking.

Table 3: Incoming ships by port of departure, 1880 and 1912

	1880			1912		
	tonnage	number	average	tonnage	number	average
U.K.	770,714	1,305	591	1,736,369	2,201	789
North	96,757	151	641	511,777	493	1,038
Baltic Sea	474,739	791	600	482,371	600	804
South Atlantic	194,756	287	679	279,592	314	890
Mediterranean	218,910	274	799	509,888	387	1,318
Black Sea	257,095	145	1,773	592,342	250	2,369
Others	19,258	74	260	42,723	63	678

Table 4: Outgoing ships by port of destination, 1880 and 1912

	1880			1912		
	tonnage	number	average	tonnage	number	average
U.K.	1,379,077	1,915	720	2,437,452	2,619	931
North	134,766	252	535	443,580	473	938
Baltic Sea	235,949	424	556	362,061	474	764
South Atlantic	169,438	279	607	246,605	276	893
Mediterranean	54,541	62	880	551,613	373	1,479
Black Sea	41,353	27	1,532	80,666	39	2,068
Others	17,105	68	252	33,085	54	613

14

MARITIME INFRASTRUCTURE:
THE RESPONSE IN WESTERN EUROPEAN PORTS TO THE DEMANDS OF COASTAL SHIPPING, 1850–1914

LEWIS R. FISCHER

This essay differs somewhat from most of the others in this volume in that it focuses neither upon a national fleet nor for the most part on what is often thought of as coastal shipping. This is because the research on which this chapter is based grows out of a long-term research project on the comparative development of ports around the world. It seemed to me (and to the editors of this volume as well) that it would be useful to have a paper that dealt in a comparative fashion with the interplay between coastal shipping and port infrastructure throughout western Europe. In examining this topic, I am in effect asking how ports responded to a significant increase in traffic. Between 1850 and 1914, for example, the volume of maritime cargo, measured in ton-miles, grew seven-fold. Much of this was intercontinental, but coastal traffic also expanded, roughly doubling in western Europe over this period.[1] This growth in coastal traffic has for the most part been overlooked by economic and maritime historians too often enamoured of newer (and presumably more »glamorous«) transport technologies, such as railways. Yet in an era in which a wave of industrialisation swept over most of the continent, coastal shipping, as John Armstrong has shown, was absolutely crucial.[2]

In asking how ports coped with this growing traffic, I am thus posing a question of more than esoteric interest. On the one hand, the answer is very

---

[1] On this point, see the discussion in Lewis R. FISCHER/Helge W. NORDVIK, Maritime transport and the integration of the North Atlantic economy, 1850–1914, in: Wolfram FISCHER/R. Marvin McINNIS/Jürgen SCHNEIDER (eds.), The Emergence of a World Economy, 1500–1914, Wiesbaden 1986, pp. 519–44. As might be expected, the figures on coastal shipping for western Europe as a whole are only rough estimates that require additional refinement.

[2] Most surveys of the industrial revolution, even those produced by maritime historians, ignore the role of coastal shipping. See, for example, Derek H. ALDCROFT/Simon P. VILLE (eds.), The European economy, 1750–1914: a thematic approach, Manchester 1994; and Simon P. VILLE, Transport and the development of the European economy, 1750–1918, London 1990. Among John ARMSTRONG's works that show why this is a mistake, see especially: The Role of coastal shipping in UK transport: an estimate of comparative traffic movements in 1910, in: Journal of Transport History, 3rd series, 8 (1987), pp. 164–78.

simple, since we know that most port authorities, however constituted, failed to accommodate growth even in deep-sea shipping, let alone to cope with an expanding coastal commerce.[3] Indeed, my research thus far suggests that the fairest generalisation would be that virtually no infrastructure was put in place specifically to handle coasters. Wherever one looks – from Greece to Spain, and from the United Kingdom to the Baltic – conditions for coastal vessels by and large remained almost as primitive as they had been in the early nineteenth century. This is certainly true in some of the bulk short-sea trades, such as the timber trade from ports in the Gulfs of Bothnia, Finland and Riga.[4] In larger ports, however, the pattern to a certain extent was different: there coasters either reaped at least marginal benefits from whatever investments were made to handle deep-sea shipping or they took over facilities deemed to be outmoded for their larger cousins.

If all this is true – and I think it broadly reflects what happened – why bother even asking the question? My response is that unless we actually do the research we cannot know for certain whether these generalisations are valid. Moreover, the whole issue is complicated by the fact that few scholars have written either on coastal shipping or port development, which means that our knowledge base is less firm than most of us would like. In addition, the study that I am conducting has already yielded some suggestive and unexpected (if preliminary) results. In particular, in a few centres it is clear that something was going on that benefitted coasters relatively more than deep-sea vessels, even if at present I cannot explain very much of what this was.

In this brief paper, I wish to do four things. First, I would like to say something about sources, both those that I have used already and those that I think are especially suitable for comparative analysis. Second, I would like to provide a broad overview of infrastructure development in European ports. My third goal is to examine some of the more suggestive evidence, which comes mainly from data on port turnaround times and includes some important material recently collected on the port of Liverpool. Finally, I will make a few general suggestions about coastal shipping and European ports, as well as some observations on the relationship between port efficiency and European economic development.

---

[3] This is a major part of the message in Gordon JACKSON, The History and Archaeology of Ports, Tadworth 1983.

[4] Conditions in the Baltic ports are summarised in Lewis R. FISCHER/Helge W. NORDVIK, Myth and reality in Baltic shipping: the timber trade to Britain, 1863–1908, in: Scandinavian Journal of History 12 (1987), pp. 99–116; L. R. FISCHER, A Flotilla of wood and coal: Shipping in the trades between Britain and the Baltic, 1865–1913, in: Yrjö KAUKIAINEN (ed.), The Baltic as a Trade Route: Competition between Steam and Sail, Kotka 1992, pp. 36–63; and L. R. FISCHER, The Nordic challenge to British domination in the Baltic timber trade to Britain, 1863–1913, in: Lewis R. FISCHER/Helge W. NORDVIK/Walter E. MINCHINTON (eds.), Shipping and Trade in the Northern Seas, Bergen 1988, pp. 74–88.

Before we begin, however, we need to agree on a definition for coastal shipping. In its narrowest form, coastal shipping may be thought of simply as maritime commerce conducted within the territorial waters of a single nation. This definition would exclude interstate trading, and it would also ignore inland transport, such as riverine, lake or canal shipping. In Europe, though, such a narrow definition makes little sense. In part this is because a good deal of domestic shipping has used inland waterways. Second, there is the fact that economic regions in Europe have long overlapped national boundaries. For example, the economies of Belgium and the Netherlands were closely integrated well before the middle of the nineteenth century, and coasters routinely sailed between ports in the two countries.[5] Finally, there is the problem caused by shifting national boundaries. Employing a »strict« definition of coastal shipping would mean that trade between Liverpool and Dublin, for instance, would have been coastal before Irish independence but international thereafter. Yet even a cursory examination of the vessels used in this trade suggests that they were the same before and after this time.[6]

In this essay I therefore want to define coastal shipping more broadly, and I hope more rationally, to include what is often called »short-sea shipping«, by which I mean »pure« coastal shipping plus all non-deep-sea shipping along the European littoral. In proposing this definition I am not trying to engage in semantic games but rather to come up with a functional way of looking at this activity. Indeed, some nations actually adopted this definition as the legal basis of coasting. A good example is the United Kingdom, which defined coasting not only as shipping around the coasts of Britain but also commerce to continental Europe between Brest and the Elbe. Since I am not interested solely in British shipping, I want to be even broader than this, which I why I suggest the definition above. There is another especially compelling reason to do this. Maritime historians have long known that coastal and short-sea vessels were virtually identical, whether judged by tonnage, rig, or type of craft, at least in the tramp sector. What is striking is how interchangeable many of these craft actually were. To make this point, I performed an experiment using the British Empire Agreements and Accounts of Crew described below. I drew a random sample of fifty vessels engaged in the British coastal trade between 1860 and the First World War, and discovered that thirty-eight of these craft

[5] See the discussion in Fernand SUYKENS [et al.], Antwerp: a Port for All Seasons, Antwerp 1986, esp. chapter 3. FISCHER/NORDVIK/MINCHINTON (eds.), Shipping and Trade, pp. 74–88.

[6] On the levels of shipping between the two ports in the middle of the nineteenth century, see Valerie C. BURTON, Liverpool's mid-nineteenth century coasting trade, in: Valerie C. BURTON (ed.), Liverpool shipping, trade and industry, Liverpool 1989, pp. 26–66. I recently conducted an analysis of this using a random sample of 100 ships in the Anglo-Irish trade in the period 1910–13. Of those vessels still afloat in the period 1920–3, more than sixty per cent were still employed in the same trade.

made one or more short-sea voyages. I then took a similarly-sized sample of vessels engaged primarily in the short-sea trades, and found that no fewer than forty-seven at sometime made at least one coastal voyage. These findings matter, since they open up the range of sources available to study this type of shipping.

What, then, are these sources? In this essay I have used three main types: published port guides; British Empire crew agreements; and dock registers. I would like to discuss these in some detail, not only so that readers can understand the strengths and limits of what I have been able to do but also because I think that together they form the basis for some important transnational comparisons.

First, there are the published guides that were designed to inform masters about conditions in ports around the world, which I have used for evidence on infrastructure development in general. These guides provide a wide variety of information on port conditions, including things like port dues, depth of channel and cargo restrictions. They also provide a vast amount of material on infrastructure – everything from cranes to dredging projects, from docks to warehouses, and from quays and moles to interfaces with land transport. There were a variety of these published prior to World War I, but I have found those compiled by G D Urquhart to be the most useful. Urquhart's *Dues and Charges on Shipping*, with separate volumes for British and »foreign« ports, give the best coverage of investments in port infrastructure that I have seen thus far.[7]

I have used these guides to begin to compile a computerised data base using the guides that I have thus far been able to find. This data base includes all information on infrastructure mentioned in the guides, and allows me to see with some precision when port authorities made investments and what priorities they deemed most important. While all the guides I have consulted thus far were compiled and published by Englishmen, their focus is far broader, which makes them especially useful for international comparisons.

There is one drawback to the guides: it is difficult to locate enough guides to construct a complete time series. Despite a good deal of digging in repositories in three countries over the past three years, I have thus far been able to locate only twelve for the period 1850 to 1914. Four of these are in the Urquhart series, although I know that there were at least eleven published in this period. The data set at present contains material taken from guides spanning the years from 1857 to 1911. In a more perfect world, I would like to supplement these

---

[7] G. D. URQUHART, Dues and Charges on Shipping in Foreign Ports: a manual of reference for the use of shipowners, shipbrokers and shipmasters, London 1869. There are ten editions in the British Library in London from 1869 to 1914. From the fourth edition there is a co-author, John Green, and they are published by G. Philip & Son.

with material from port yearbooks and similar publications, but thus far I have been able to find neither the time nor the funds to do so.

While the data set I have compiled thus far has obvious utility, it is still far from complete. Unfortunately, it also has some other drawbacks. The first is that it is apparent that these guides were not always updated as regularly as an historian might have liked. Even when we know from other sources that a port has invested in new infrastructure, it can sometimes take a decade or more for this to be reflected in the guides. A good example of this is the graving dock that was opened in Cristiania (Oslo) in 1862: the first time I can find it mentioned in a guide was forty years later.[8] While I suspect that this probably was atypical, if only because competitive pressures probably provided an inducement for more regular updating, it is nonetheless vexing. An even more bothersome problem is that the guides seldom differentiate between facilities for coasters and deep-sea vessels. Of course, in many ports there were no separate facilities, but in others there were. For the most part I can only tell this inferentially, or when I stumble across evidence from other sources, such as shipping newspapers or the work of another historian. For example, I learned about the opening of Senhouse Dock, a facility specifically for coasters and short-sea vessels in the port of Maryport in northwestern England, only by reading a local history about a small shipping line.[9]

My second principal source, which is the centrepiece of the second section of this paper, is one that I have used and written about extensively: the British Empire Agreements and Accounts of Crew, eighty percent of which are housed in the Maritime History Archive at Memorial University of Newfoundland. These »crew lists«, which have been mandated by British maritime law since 1860, are the actual agreements between masters and crews of all vessels registered in the British Empire. While they are obviously excellent sources for anyone interested in the international maritime labour force, they are also useful for scholars interested in ports. This is because the law mandated that whenever a vessel spent forty-eight hours or more in a foreign port the master had to deposit the articles with either the shipping master or the British consul in that city. This regulation makes the crew agreements a splen-

---

[8] This example is discussed in Lewis R. FISCHER/Helge W. NORDVIK, Management and success in shipbroking: the case of Fearnley and Eger, 1869–1972, in: Simon P. VILLE/David M. WILLIAMS (eds.), Management, Finance and Industrial Relations in the Maritime Industry, Milan 1994, pp. 77–87; and FISCHER/NORDVIK, The Evolution of Norwegian Export Ports, 1850–1910, in: Lars U. SCHOLL [et al.] (eds.), The North Sea: Resources and Seaway, Aberdeen 1996, pp. 11–55.

[9] Herbert and Mary JACKSON, Holme Shipping Line: Maryport, 1873–1913, Maryport 1991. I wish to thank David J. CLARKE for calling this to my attention. It is worth consulting two articles by Clarke on Maryport, both of which discuss infrastructure developments: Maryport: a late coastal switch to steam propulsion, in: David J. STARKEY (ed.), Steam at Sea, Exeter, forthcoming, and Maryport coasters and coaster men, 1855–1889, in: The Northern Mariner/Le Marin du nord 9 (1999).

did vehicle to analyse what happened to British Empire vessels in ports
outside the United Kingdom. The vast majority of agreements for short-sea
voyages have survived, and a reasonable sample was computerised as part of
the Atlantic Canada Shipping Project and for a variety of subsequent research
projects.[10]

I will use these data sets to examine turnaround time, which is one way of
measuring how efficient ports were from the perspective of a shipowner.
Turnaround time is calculated simply by subtracting the date the agreement
was deposited from the date it was returned, with suitable modifications to
compensate for any internal evidence in the documents (such as a desertion)
that suggests that the vessel spent more time in a port than the official dates
would suggest. There are no special problems in using these agreements for
most non-British ports, although smaller harbours, especially in the Baltic,
frequently had no officials to stamp them. These documents are more prob-
lematic for United Kingdom ports. This is because there unfortunately was no
law to require masters to deposit these agreements in home ports, which
means that there is no lengthy time series of evidence on what happened there.
Some masters, however, did deposit the agreements even in domestic ports,
which gives us some idea of what happened in the United Kingdom. If a voyage ended in Britain, the agreements were deposited; by comparing when one
voyage ended and the next one began, it is possible to calculate turnaround
time even in British ports.

There is one other source that I have used in this essay that is worth discussion. The port of Liverpool, the Mersey Docks and Harbours Board began in
the mid-nineteenth century to keep a series of registers for each dock (or each
dock system) in the port. These registers are gold mines of information for
maritime historians, since they systematically provide information on the
name of the ship, its tonnage and cargo, where it is from or bound, and, most
important, the dates of entering a dock, loading and unloading, and departure.
On a less regular basis the registers also provide information on how long a
vessel had to wait in the Mersey for space in a dock.[11]

Although they are among the best sources I have ever seen for studying
some aspects of the functioning of ports, they have almost never been used by
historians. One reason for this is the sheer mass of the records. For this project, I chose to examine a single dock. Computerising the entrances and clearances for a single month at five-yearly intervals between 1850 and 1910 took
four weeks of solid work. Another drawback to the registers is that in Liver-

---

[10] On the crew lists, see especially Lewis R. FISCHER/Eric W. SAGER, An Approach to
the quantitative analysis of British shipping records, in: Business History 22 (1980), pp.
135–51.

[11] These registers are housed in the Maritime Records Centre in the Merseyside Maritime Museum.

pool vessels frequently discharged in one dock and loaded in another. To get from one to another often required a vessel to pass through one or more intermediate docks. In short, there is a serious problem in linking records in this port. For this paper I have tried to limit the discussion only to those vessels that both loaded and unloaded in a single dock, although I cannot be certain that craft that took on a significant amount of cargo elsewhere in the port have been excluded.

For dock registers to be useful for a project concerned with international comparisons requires the existence of similar documents elsewhere. I know that the Antwerp port records are as useful, but beyond that it is difficult to know, since scholars almost never mention them. This may mean that similar records were never compiled or have been destroyed, or it may suggest that historians simply have never used them. If this essay does nothing else, I hope that it will at least induce scholars elsewhere to ascertain whether similar records exist for their nations.

What can these sources tell us about ports, and specifically about the experience of coasters broadly defined in them? We can begin by examining the shipping guides for evidence about infrastructure. The most common view we have of nineteenth-century European ports from historians is that they did not function all that well; the most typical reason adduced for this is lack of investment.[12] Contemporaries agreed. As one anonymous shipowner observed in 1874, »there is a crisis in most European ports caused by a sustained starvation of investment. This must be corrected if the shipping industry is not to collapse«.[13] Similarly, an 1890 article in *Fairplay* quoted a shipowner complaining that »although we continue to buy new ships, ports have not kept pace«.[14] These examples could easily be multiplied ten-fold or more.

Whether these views are correct or not is dealt with below, but it is important to recognise that even if these observations were true, they might not tell us much about the functioning of ports. When it comes to ports, there appears to be a fundamental »law« that goes something like this: ports are bad in all times and all places, but so what? In other words, while historians can always find shipowners complaining about ports, it is important to bear in mind that somehow these inadequate harbours still seemed to manage to handle the interchange of cargoes between ship and shore. The economic growth rates of trading societies in the nineteenth century does not provide much comfort to

[12] Typical is Natividad DE LA PUERTA RUEDA, Management and finance in nineteenth-century Spanish ports, in: The Northern Mariner/Le Marin du nord 7 (1997), pp. 41–9. See also DE LA PUERTA RUEDA, El Puerto de Bilbao como reflejo del desarrollo industrial de Vizcaya, 1857–1913, Bilbao 1994.

[13] Shipping and Mercantile Gazette, 24 November 1874.

[14] Fairplay, 12 July 1890.

the notion that inefficient ports dragged down standards of living to any great extent.[15]

More significantly, our survey of European ports suggests a great deal more modernisation in this period, especially in the provision of infrastructure, than is normally conceded. Further, if there were limits to modernisation it was generally because of a shortage of revenues. This is understandable given the level of competition that existed between ports in western Europe. Given that distances between ports were frequently not that great, and that land-based transport systems improved markedly during the last half of the century, port authorities had to be careful in setting rates lest they drive ships to their competitors. The result of this situation appears to have been that port authorities recognised that they needed to walk a fine line between providing the most desirable facilities and building those that were within their financial means. In other words, it was not that port authorities refused to invest but that the demands for new infrastructure outstripped the funds available. Without going into a mass of confusing detail, the problem in Europe appears to have been that many ports were simply ill-equipped financially to fulfil the wish lists of shipowners.[16]

Regardless of why port authorities in Europe did not do more, it is still impressive just how much investment did occur in this era. While it is impossible to put a dollar figure on it, the data on more than 300 western European ports contained in my data base demonstrates clearly that investment was occurring, particularly in the largest ports. To see this point, I have divided western European ports into two categories: the thirty largest ports – those that handled the overwhelming majority of both coastal and international traffic – and the remainder. If we look at the large ports, we see that in 1857 only forty percent were equipped with mechanical or steam dockside cranes. Yet by 1911, ninety-seven percent were. In the smaller ports, the comparable figures were six percent and fifty-two percent. Further, sixteen of the top thirty ports had multi-storied warehouse facilities in 1857; by 1911, only two lacked such amenities (for smaller ports, this proportion had risen from about five percent to just under one-quarter by 1911). Finally, in 1857 only six of the thirty largest ports had direct railway connections to their hinterland; by 1911, all did (the percentages for small ports had risen from less than five percent to more than half). I could present similar figures for a range of other infrastructure improvements, but the picture would be more or less the same: ports did in

[15] This generalisation is based upon a current project of mine to try to examine systematically the growth rates of various maritime-oriented nations.

[16] Adrian JARVIS, Managing change: the organisation of port authorities at the turn of the twentieth century, in: The Northern Mariner/Le Marin du nord 6 (1996), pp. 31–42, suggests that the structure of port management may also be an important variable. He may be correct, but if so the patterns are not apparent in this survey.

fact invest in infrastructure in the two-thirds of a century before the outbreak
of World War I, regardless of what contemporaries implied.

If ports in general invested in infrastructure, what can we say about facilities
specifically for coasters? Here things get more complicated. In part, the problem is that the shipping guides seldom differentiated between what was available for coasters and deep-sea vessels. In large ports, this distinction might
well have mattered, for various types of craft often used different facilities, but
in many of the smaller ports, this would have been moot: all ships used the
same facilities, although in many ports deep-sea vessels, and especially steamers, were given priority.[17] A cursory glance at my data set suggests the not
surprising conclusion that the vast majority of infrastructure improvements
went to deep-sea vessels. Yet what is remarkable is that a number of ports appear to have invested in facilities that would probably have benefitted coasters
more. Nowhere was this more true than in the coal trade, which prior to World
War I was by far the most important employer of coastal shipping in western
Europe. By 1911 more than half of the ports in non-coal-producing regions of
western Europe had made significant investments in the handling of coal, investments that were likely to benefit deep-sea craft only in the sense of providing more efficient bunkering. Indeed, given the importance of coal as a
cargo for coasters, these investments were far more likely to help coasting
than deep-sea vessels.[18] We will return to this point below.

If it is clear that ports improved their infrastructures in this period, it is, as
we have just seen, less obvious that this affected coasters to the same degree
as deep-sea vessels. To understand this point, we need to look not at ports but
rather at the experiences that various types of vessels had in ports. To do this
for non-British ports I have used the crew agreements described earlier. I am
interested here in both sail and steam, but for practical reasons I have tried to
limit the analysis to tramps rather than liners. This is because liners present a
host of insuperable problems. For starters, many of them had dedicated berths
in ports, facilities which enabled them to load and unload far more rapidly
than would have been the case had they used general berths. The difficulty for
the historian is that it is impossible to determine which liners had dedicated
berths from the available records. Second, as noted above, crew agreements
only had to be deposited with the authorities if the vessel was in port for forty-

---

[17] I cannot tell about priorities in all ports, but by 1911 at least sixteen of the thirty
»large ports« explicitly gave priority to steamers. Since by that date the vast majority of
sailing vessels were engaged in coasting or short-sea shipping, this is the same thing as
giving priority to deep-sea ships.

[18] Of course, these investments might well have benefited coastal liners more than
coastal tramps, given the increasing importance of liners in the carriage of some bulk
goods. If this were the case, it would help us to understand the inducement to modernise: as
coastal liners became increasingly dominated by steam, the amount of capital that they
represented rose proportionally.

eight hours or more. Yet as Gordon Jackson has pointed out, in a port like
Glasgow many of the coastal steamers in the late nineteenth century would
have discharged their cargoes, loaded, and departed with an hour of arrival,
and hence would not even appear in my data sets. While such speed was not
necessarily typical, the problem is apparent: if I picked any of these up by ac-
cident it could easily skew the results of any analysis. Thus, the discussion that
follows is restricted solely to tramps, at least in so far as I have been able to
weed out the liners.

To examine the impact that investments in infrastructure had on the various
types of shipping, I began by augmenting my available data sets to ensure
coverage of at least the major ports; in the end, I had to limit the analysis to
these ports because of the lack of sufficient data for most of the smaller harbours. To make the analysis manageable – and because I was interested in
long-term change – I decided for this paper to examine only three sample
years: 1870, 1890 and 1910. To control for any effects related to seasonality, I
further limited the study only to vessels entering ports in the months of June,
July and August. Despite these limitations, I ended up with a file containing
data on more than 32,000 entrances into western European ports by tramp vessels of various types.

The analysis done on this file yielded some potentially significant findings.
Perhaps the most important was also the least surprising: that despite all the
complaints from shipowners, ports were becoming more efficient by the
measure of turnaround time. In the large ports, turnaround time for deep-sea
sailing vessels declined on average by eleven percent between 1870 and 1890,
and then by another four percent between 1890 and 1910.[19] Steamers did even
better in these ports, with turnaround times declining by thirty-two percent
between 1870 and 1890, and an additional twenty-four percent between 1890
and 1910. While these data do show improvements, the fact that the decline
was steeper before 1890 than after at least provides some credence to shipowner complaints at the turn of the century.

What about the coastal/short-sea sector? Here gains, when they actually accrued, were more modest. Among steamers, turnaround times declined by
eighteen percent between 1870 and 1890, and by sixteen percent from 1890 to
1910. For sailing vessels, however, there was almost no change: turnaround
times actually rose by two percent between 1870 and 1890 and by an additional three percent thereafter. For Europe as a whole, these results thus confirm the general point made earlier: most ports, and certainly the largest ones,
were able to handle deep-sea vessels, and especially steamers, much faster in

---

[19] It is difficult to know how much weight to put on the decline in turnaround time for
sailing vessels. This is because we know that in many fleets, including the British, shipowners appear to have been unconcerned about the rapidity of turnaround for sailing vessels after the 1870s, preferring instead to use these assets as »floating warehouses«.

1910 than in 1870. On the other hand, coasters were left behind, at least in the tramp sector.[20] Although I would have expected greater efficiency gains after 1890, the other trends are not surprising in the least.

Care needs to be taken with this evidence, since sometimes generalisations can obscure important trends. In this case, the global analysis obscures some important differences between ports. Indeed, in six ports there is some startling evidence that suggests, but does not definitively prove, that coasters were being treated relatively better than deep-sea vessels. These ports are Helsinki, Copenhagen, Hamburg, Rotterdam, Le Havre and Barcelona. In Helsinki, coastal sailing vessels showed greater efficiency gains than did deep-sea sailing vessels in the period 1890–1910, although the reverse was true for steamers. This finding may, however, be specious, for while I tried to ensure that vessels heading for Helsinki via intermediate ports were correctly classified as coastal or deep-sea, it is possible that I mislabelled a few. Given that Helsinki had the lowest number of entrances of any of the major ports in my data files, any error would have been magnified. In Copenhagen, the efficiency of coastal sailing vessels improved more rapidly than did deep-sea sail, but only in the period 1870–1890. In Le Havre, on the other hand, coastal steamers earned greater efficiency gains than did deep-sea steam in the 1870–1890 period. I have no easy explanation for either of these findings, especially since they pertain to only one type of propulsion in only one period. I do have confidence in these findings because, unlike for Helsinki, there are more than enough cases, with low standard deviations, for them to be significant.

The really interesting ports are Hamburg, Rotterdam and Barcelona, where both steam and sailing coasters scored greater efficiency gains than deep-sea vessels in both periods. The two northern European ports were among the most efficient harbours for deep-sea vessels in 1870, so it might not be too surprising that efficiency improvements for deep-sea vessels were below the European average: for Hamburg, deep-sea sailing vessels improved their productivity by four and two percent, respectively, while in Rotterdam turnaround time for deep-sea sailing vessels dropped by five and one percent in the periods 1870–1890 and 1890–1910. But in both ports the turnaround time for coastal sailing vessels went against the European trend, declining by seven and two percent in Hamburg and by five and four percent in Rotterdam. In Barcelona, which had a horrible reputation among foreign shipowners, there were healthy gains in efficiency for both deep-sea and coastal sail: twelve and nine per cent, respectively, for deep-sea craft, and fifteen and fourteen per cent for coasters.

---

[20] I would be extremely surprised if there were not significant improvements in the coastal liner sector, although whether they would have equalled those among the deep-sea steamers is something that is much less clear.

Significantly, the results for steam more or less paralleled the findings for sail. In Hamburg, turnaround time for deep-sea steamers fell by seventeen per cent between 1870 and 1890 and by a further ten per cent in the two decades before 1910. Rotterdam's turnaround times fell by twelve and six per cent, respectively. On the other hand, coastal steamers enjoyed even greater efficiency gains: twenty-one per cent, 1890–1910, and sixteen per cent, 1890–1910, in Hamburg; and fifteen and seven per cent for Rotterdam. In Barcelona, the gains for steamers were staggering: forty-nine per cent for deep-sea steamers between 1870 and 1890, and thirty per cent thereafter, while coastal steamers cut their turnaround time by sixty per cent before 1890 and a further thirty-three per cent afterwards.

If we step away from the evidence for a moment, these results may become clearer. While it might be possible to argue in the cases of Hamburg and Rotterdam that the relatively low rates of efficiency growth were caused by the fact that both ports were so efficient in the first place, it is less possible to make this case for the post-1890 period. Indeed, the continuing impressive improvements for these ports suggests that something was going on. While I have searched the standard works on the topic for clues, I must admit that I do not really understand what made these ports so different. Barcelona, on the other hand, had the longest turnaround times of any of the major European ports for both sail and steam in 1870 and therefore had the greatest scope for improvement. There is nothing in the literature to suggest why its gains should be so large, let alone why sail should do relatively better than steam so consistently.[21] Thus far, the specialists whom I have consulted have not been able to shed much light on possible causes, so the mystery remains.

While I have a good deal of confidence in most of this evidence, it might be useful as well to look more closely at the experience of Liverpool. We can compare what happened to coasters and deep-sea vessels there using two sources: the crew list data files already discussed and another data set compiled from the dock registers for the Huskisson Dock system. The crew list files indicate, despite all the problems that Adrian Jarvis has described with port facilities, Liverpool was, by European standards, a fairly typical port as measured by turnaround time. Between 1870 and 1890 turnaround times for deep-sea sailing vessels fell by eleven per cent, exactly the average for all the large European ports, while between 1890 and 1910, turnaround time for such vessels fell by three per cent, slightly under the European average. For deep-sea steam, Liverpool did not perform quite as well as the European average: turnaround time fell by twenty-three per cent between 1870 and 1890, and by

---

[21] On Hamburg and Rotterdam, see the relevant essays in Leo M. AKVELD/Jaap R. BRUIJN (eds.), Shipping Companies and Authorities in the 19th and 20th Centuries: their common interest in the development of port facilities, The Hague 1989. On Barcelona, see Joan ALEMANY LLOVERA, Los puertos espanoles en el siglo XIX, Madrid 1991.

eighteen per cent thereafter. It was for coasters that Liverpool was a special nightmare. Turnaround times for sailing coastal craft rose by six per cent in both periods. Although turnaround times fell for coastal steamers, they did so at less than half the European average for each period: seven per cent between 1870 and 1890 and six per cent between 1890 and 1910.

The data from Huskisson support these trends in a very qualified way. The qualifications stem from one of the problems discussed above: the tendency in Liverpool for a vessel to discharge in one dock and to load in another. This happened frequently enough in Huskisson to render the number of cases marginal for any kind of analysis, especially in 1890. Nonetheless, keeping this problem in mind, the data suggest that for deep-sea sail, turnaround time declined by nine per cent between 1870 and 1890, close to the port average, and by six per cent between 1890 and 1910, almost double the rate for the port as a whole. For deep-sea steam, Huskisson's figures were continually below the port average: a decline of eighteen per cent, 1870–1890, and eleven per cent thereafter. Huskisson was better, however, for coasters than was typical for the port, especially after 1890. For sailing coasters, turnaround times actually fell in Huskisson, by three per cent before 1890 and two per cent thereafter. It was among coastal steamers that Huskisson really stood out: turnaround times for these vessels fell by twelve per cent between 1870 and 1890 and by eight per cent between 1890 and 1910.

Although there are broad similarities between the two sources, the intriguing question is why Huskisson was different for coasters. Part of the answer, probably, is that as it aged, Huskisson more and more became a dock for coasters. Although no evidence has been yet found to suggest that any improvements were made specifically for coasting vessels, it does appear that at the very least dock personnel got increasingly good at handling them. It is also interesting – and potentially significant – that there are almost no instances of coasters being required to wait in the river. At least for Huskisson this information was seldom provided, which might mean that there were almost never backlogs that required a vessel to wait before entering the dock, or it might suggest that the dock masters never bothered to fill in the information in the registers. Regardless, what is striking is that the frequency for coasters declined almost linearly over the period. Just over two per cent of coasters were forced to wait before 1870, but less than half of one per cent in the latter period. What makes this even more suggestive is that the frequency for deep-sea vessels was almost identical in the two eras. Even if Liverpool was not an especially efficient port for coasters in general, it appears as though some of its docks may have been. If similar studies of dock registers in other ports existed, it might be possible to see if the Liverpool experience, where at least one dock appears to be more efficient for coasters than was the port as a whole, was typical or deviant.

This essay concludes by saying something about the relationship between port infrastructure and economic development. If the efficiency gains for the large ports were typical, an admittedly hazardous assumption, and if there were more-or-less continuous gains in efficiency over time, another less than certain premise, then we can calculate by regression that deep-sea gains (steam and sail combined) averaged about 1.2 per cent per annum for deep-sea vessels and 0.7 per cent per year for coasters. To put this into perspective, general European productivity was in the order of 2.3 per cent per annum over the same period. A reasonable conclusion to draw from this data is that ports were in fact a weak link in the transport chain.

Did less than optimally efficient ports constrain economic growth? The answer almost certainly is affirmative, although I doubt that the net effects were very great. A more likely outcome, however, was that the problems in ports retarded the growth of specialisation, especially in the far north and the far south of Europe where, on average, ports were least efficient. While the studies have not yet been done to confirm or deny this speculation, it seems likely that inefficient ports were also those where the highest proportion of work was performed manually. In many of the Baltic timber ports and the harbours of Greece and southern Italy, it is a reasonable hypothesis that the failure to invest in port infrastructure induced men to remain in less productive occupations for longer periods of time. This in turn might well have had a greater impact on economic growth than the fairly low growth rates of maritime efficiency reported above.

If all of this is merely speculation, however, there are some things that we do know. One is that by the outbreak of the First World War, on average Europe's coasters and the ports they served handled more cargoes more rapidly than in the middle of the nineteenth century. Shipowners may have bemoaned what seemed to them unduly slow rates of investment in infrastructure, but as this chapter has shown, port authorities did invest as they could afford to do so. For those countries that were particularly export-dependent, these port investments made special sense. As for coasters, while they may often have been second-class citizens of the maritime world, by the time of the First World War they were certainly more efficient citizens.

15

HAMBURG'S COASTAL SHIPPING
IN THE NINETEENTH CENTURY

ORTWIN PELC

It may seem strange to speak of »coastal shipping« in connection with a port like Hamburg, because Hamburg is situated on a river, the Elbe, about 100 km from its outlet to the North Sea. On the other hand, today Hamburg is the second biggest seaport in Europe and, since the sixteenth century, it has been the largest harbour in Germany. Hamburg is the most eastern of the European Atlantic harbours and is situated on one of the most important German waterways.

In the middle ages Hamburg was a transit harbour for the goods of the Hanseatic League in the trade between western Europe and the Baltic. When trade became overseas trade in the sixteenth century Hamburg became an international seaport. Inland shipping up the Elbe to Brandenburg and Bohemia and their wide hinterland was important too. The economic importance and strength of Hamburg as a seaport in the nineteenth century was based on its overseas trade.[1] No special research has been carried out on Hamburg's coastal shipping. To date there has been research on the topographic and technical development of the harbour, including the conditions of work[2], the history of several shipping companies, the shipping and trade connections to particular countries, among others England[3], Hamburg's important role as an emigration port and the different types of ships.[4] Of course, at all times there

---

[1] Günther MOLTMANN, Hamburgs Öffnung nach Übersee im späten 18. und im 19. Jahrhundert, in: Jörg DUPPLER (ed.), Hamburg zur See, Herford 1989, pp. 73–92; several articles in Volker PLAGEMANN (ed.), Übersee. Seefahrt und Seemacht im Deutschen Kaiserreich, Munich 1988.

[2] Max BUCHHEISTER, Hamburg, sein Hafen und seine Schiffahrt, Hamburg 1902; Arnold KLUDAS/Dieter MAASS/Susanne SABISCH, Hafen Hamburg, Die Geschichte des Hamburger Freihafens von den Anfängen bis zur Gegenwart, Hamburg 1988; Dieter MAASS, Der Ausbau des Hamburger Hafens 1840–1910, Hamburg 1990; Jürgen RATH, Arbeit im Hamburger Hafen, Hamburg 1988.

[3] Otto-Ernst KRAWEHL, Hamburgs Schiffs- und Warenverkehr mit England und den englischen Kolonien 1814–1860, Cologne/Vienna 1977.

[4] Hans SZYMANSKI, Die Segelschiffe der deutschen Kleinschiffahrt, Lübeck 1929; idem, Der Ever der Niederelbe, Lübeck 1932; idem, Deutsche Segelschiffe. Die Geschichte der

was coastal shipping from and to Hamburg, down the Elbe to the coasts of the North Sea and into the Baltic. Especially in the nineteenth century it played an important role, because people in the rapidly growing city – 130,000 inhabitants in 1800, one million in 1913 – needed to be supplied with agrarian products, food, etc. On the other hand harbours, towns and regions to which ships from Hamburg sailed in the North Sea and the Baltic needed manufactured products.

In this chapter I will comment on the geographical aspects of Hamburg's coastal shipping (see map 6 on p. 222), the general development of the harbour and shipping; the statistical sources and data on coastal shipping; and give examples of coastal shipping.

The growth of Hamburg and its economic power in the nineteenth century was based on the expanding shipping of its port. But what part in the worldwide shipping of Hamburg did the coastal trade play and what does »coastal shipping« mean for Hamburg? Limitation to the territory of Hamburg, one of the definitions of »coastal shipping«, is not possible, because until 1871 Hamburg was too small in size as an independent territory, bordering the Danish-, later Prussian-ruled duchy of Holstein in the north, east and west, and the kingdom of Hanover (a Prussian province as of 1866) to the south.

The shipping from Hamburg to the mouth of the Elbe was, strictly speaking, inland navigation, although the river is very wide. On both banks of the Elbe were several harbours whose intensive shipping traffic has been already well researched.[5] A serious competitor on the Elbe was Altona, located near Hamburg and until 1867, when it became a part of Prussia, the second largest city in Denmark. The place with the largest number of ships on the Elbe was the village of Blankenese. Shippers from Blankenese with their small ships were important for the distribution of goods from the harbour of Hamburg to places along the lower Elbe, the North Sea and the Baltic Sea.[6] In the statistics there is a clear difference between the intensive shipping from Hamburg to the harbours on the lower Elbe and shipping to the North Sea and other destinations.

Strictly speaking Hamburg's coastal shipping must refer to the coasts of the North Sea, within the borders of the German Empire of 1871, thus extending to the mouth of the river Ems and the border of the Netherlands in the west and to the Danish border in the north. As a ship which sailed from Hamburg

hölzernen Frachtsegler an den deutschen Ost- und Nordseeküsten vom Ende des 18. Jahrhunderts bis auf die Gegenwart, Berlin 1934.

[5] Hubert KINDT, Die Entwicklung der Elbe als mitteleuropäische Binnenschiffahrtsstraße, Kiel 1990; Gerhard THEUERKAUF, Die Handelsschiffart auf der Elbe. Von den Zolltarifen des 13, Jahrhunderts zur Elbe-Schiffahrts-Acte von 1821, in: Die Elbe, ein Lebenslauf, Berlin 1992, pp. 69–75.

[6] Jörgen BRACKER, Unser Strom. Hamburg und die Niederelbe von Lauenburg bis Cuxhaven, Hamburg 1995; Wilhelm TIMMERMANN, Die Blankeneser Schiffahrt, Blankenese 1925.

through the Schleswig-Holstein Canal to the Baltic Sea also never lost contact with the coast, and since the German Empire extended to East Prussia, the southern shore of the Baltic Sea could be included in Hamburg's coastal shipping as well. If geographical conditions alone are considered, Hamburg's coastal shipping could extend further to the west, to the Netherlands, and to the Baltic, especially to Denmark. In this chapter I will restrict myself to the shipping between Hamburg and the shores of the North Sea, because this is the most stringent definition of coastal shipping.

For shipping around the coast of the North Sea the relatively strong tide played an important role. It caused drastic changes to the coast, influenced the development of harbours and caused the construction of special types of ships which were able to take the ground at low tide. The mud-flats along the German North Sea coast are a five to twenty kilometres wide flatwater parallel to the coast which is bounded to the sea by islands and sandbanks. Since the Middle Ages the coast has been protected by a system of dykes. At its drainage gates, the sluices, small harbours developed. They could only be reached by the flat bottomed sailing ships which were used in the coastal trade behind the islands. Larger seaports were situated on the high and dry country (the *Geest*) near the mouths of the rivers Elbe, Weser and Ems and in the upper parts of these rivers. At the very flat coast of the North Sea in Schleswig-Holstein only relatively small seaports developed which were permanently threatened by mud. Since in the second half of the nineteenth century they were not able to adapt their navigable water and the docks to larger types of ships and to steamships, they more and more lost their economic importance.

Hamburg is situated at the junction of the river Alster with the Elbe. Navigation on the Elbe was and is tidal far above Hamburg. The harbour of Hamburg developed in the Middle Ages at the mouth of the Alster and was always included in the fortification which was widened in the seventeenth century. When overseas trade increased, this inner harbour became too small. From the second half of the eighteenth century numerous large vessels moored at posts in the river Elbe and were loaded and unloaded by lighters. Only the smaller ships of the inland and coastal trade were able to sail into the canals of the town. In 1840 the first quay was built especially for steamships. In 1858 the first basin in the harbour followed, the Sandtorhafen, whose cranes, warehouses and a connecting railway ushered in the beginning of a modern harbour. At the same time, the discussion which started in the 1840s over whether a dock on the English model or a tidal harbour should be planned was decided in favour of a tidal harbour. From the beginning of the 1860s the islands on the other bank of the Elbe were included in the plans for a modern seaport, wharfs and more basins were built there. With the foundation of the Empire in 1871, the Free and Hanseatic city of Hamburg retained the status of a »foreign country« with regard to customs (*Zollausland*). Not until 1888 was Hamburg

included in the German customs zone and simultaneously a toll-free seaport
was founded. This was an important step towards developing a seaport with
worldwide connections. Coastal shipping profited from this indirectly, because
it transported a part of the imported goods around the German coasts. The
directories of Hamburg in the nineteenth century mention a lot of pubs near
the harbour, where the shippers from the lower Elbe and the North Sea coast
met and received transport orders.[7]

If one wishes to do statistical research on the regions and harbours of the
ships which came to and left Hamburg, reliable and detailed data are available
from around 1850. For the years since 1765 there are records of the ships'
registration documents issued by the Hamburg authorities, which give information of the ships and shippers domiciled in Hamburg. Important, too, are
the records of the *waterschout* in Hamburg which from 1760 registered the
enrolling and payment of the sailors. In the records of the Hamburg customs-
yacht (*Zolljacht*) from 1824 one will find information on the ships, their owners and shippers, their freight, origin and destination.[8] But it is not clear how
complete and reliable they are. From the 1840s the official of Hamburg's main
customs-office (*Haupt-Zoll-Comptoir*) collected statistical data which were
first published in 1850. They were followed by more and more detailed annual
publications on the trade and shipping by the bureau of trade-statistics (*Han-
delsstatistisches Bureau*).[9] From this voluminous data, information on coastal
shipping can be extracted, because they mention origin and destination of the
ships, their nationality, if they were sailing or steamships, if they sailed with
cargo or ballast, and the kind of cargo from and to special regions.[10]

Between 1806 and 1814 there was no shipping traffic because of the French
occupation and the English blockade of the Elbe. From 1815 to the beginning
of the First World War the statistics show a rapid growth in shipping traffic, of
course slowing in some years because of political or economic crises. In 1815
in Hamburg harbour there were 2003 ships of about 145,000 tons and in 1903
14,028 ships of 9,155,926 tons, among them 9449 steamships (8,314,084
tons). In 1870 the number of steamships surpassed that of the sailing ships.[11]
Although the ever-larger steamships became more and more important, the
small vessels remained important in the coastal trade.

---

[7] Jörgen BRACKER, Hamburg. Von den Anfängen bis zur Gegenwart, Hamburg 1992,
p. 159.

[8] Walter KRESSE, Materialien zur Entwicklungsgeschichte der Hamburger Handelsflotte
1765–1823, Hamburg 1966, pp. 7–14; idem, Die Fahrtgebiete der Hamburger
Handelsflotte 1824–1888, Hamburg 1972, p. 7.

[9] Tabellarische Übersichten des Hamburgischen Handels im Jahre 1857 (and the following years), zusammengestellt von dem handelsstatistischen Bureau, Hamburg 1858, and the
following years.

[10] On the problems of these data see: Tabellarische Übersichten 1913, p. 7.

[11] Tabellarische Übersichten 1903, pp. 58–59.

Until the 1920s many different types of ships were used in the coastal shipping of the North Sea. There were important differences in construction, measurement and the kind of transport they were used for. The ship types were *Galeass, Schnacke, Tjalk, Ewer, Jolle* and *Jacht*. The *Ewer* was the most important ship on the Elbe used in coastal trade. In the middle of the nineteenth century about 260 *Ewer* used in coastal shipping originated in 47 harbours on the lower Elbe. At the end of the century 460 *Ewer* from 73 harbours were part of the coastal fleet.[12]

In 1864 neighbouring Schleswig-Holstein had 2555 ships with a tonnage of 51,248 Commerzlast (CL).[13] 60 per cent of these ships were very small, below 10 CL, and made up only 14 per cent of the tonnage. Another 30 per cent measured between 10 and 50 CL.[14] At that time the commercial fleets of the neighbouring countries, Hanover and Mecklenburg, had nearly the same tonnage as the ships in Schleswig-Holstein; the fleet of Oldenburg was only half this size; Hamburg and Bremen twice that.[15] Looking only at the number of ships on the west coast of Schleswig-Holstein in 1864 one finds 216 ships with an average tonnage of 9.4 CL. Because of the shallow water only small ships are found here. Beyond it on the lower Eider with 328 ships and on the right bank of the lower Elbe with 1105 ships remarkable larger fleets originated, but both of them did not refer strictly speaking to coastal shipping.

There were important seaports on the west coast of Schleswig and Holstein. The small town Hoyer in the low marshland opposite the island of Sylt had about 1000 inhabitants in 1855. Four ships were based there; in the nearby canal which flows into the North Sea, was a berth.[16] On average 80 to 90 ships landed here every year and sailed to and from Hamburg, Altona, Bremen, Holland and England. From 1852 there existed a regular steamship connection to England.

Husum was the most important seaport on the west coast of Schleswig-Holstein. Agrarian products from the hinterland were exported and industrial

---

[12] SZYMANSKI, Ever, p. 322. In total 1100 *Ewer* originated in 114 harbours on the lower Elbe around 1900.

[13] One Commerzlast (CL) equals about 2.6 metric tons or 2.500 kilogramme. Until 1874 Commerzlast were used in the statistics, from 1875 onwards tons.

[14] Ingwer Ernst MOMSEN, Die Entwicklung der Handelsflotte Schleswig-Holsteins 1745–1865, in: Walter ASMUS (ed.), Die Entwicklung des Verkehrs in Schleswig-Holstein 1750–1918, Neumünster 1996, pp. 77–97, here pp. 79–81; idem, Die Schiffahrt in Scheswig-Holstein um 1840, in: Zeitschrift der Gesellschaft für Schleswig-Holsteinische Geschichte 122 (1997), pp. 75–110; on research into shipping in Schleswig-Holstein see Jürgen BROCKSTEDT, Die Schiffahrt in Schleswig-Holstein 1800–1850, in: Zeitschrift der Gesellschaft für Schleswig-Holsteinische Geschichte 102/103 (1977/78), pp. 139–154.

[15] Walter ASMUS/Andreas KUNZ/Ingwer Ernst MOMSEN, Atlas zur Verkehrsgeschichte Schleswig-Holsteins im 19. Jahrhundert, Neumünster 1995, p. 71.

[16] Johannes von SCHRÖDER, Topographie des Herzogthums Schleswig, Oldenburg 1854, p. 241.

products imported through this harbour. The north Frisian islands too were supplied. Husum's harbour also served for the transit of goods from England and Holland to the Baltic Sea because the overland route to Flensburg was only 35 km long. Constant improvement of the difficult entrance to the harbour and the docks and a railway connection in 1854 enhanced this function.[17] Tönning at the mouth of the Eider developed an important harbour with the construction of the Schleswig-Holstein Canal in 1784. In 1887 Büsum had a fleet of twenty two shrimp cutters which delivered to Hamburg. In 1903 shrimp factories were founded in Büsum. From Friedrichstadt, Süderstapel and Pahlhude (with a large brick-factory) on the Eider there were intensive shipping connections to Hamburg as well.

These were not the only seaports to play a role in the coastal shipping to and from the west coast of Schleswig-Holstein and the north-Frisian islands, but a large number of small landing places too which often consisted of only a wooden pier at a drainage canal or near a ferry. The hamlets of Südwesthörn, Ockholm, Tetenbüllspieker, Katingsiel, Wollersum, Schülpersiel, Warwerort and Wöhrden were places like this. In Schülpersiel near Tönning, for example, there was a drainage canal where around 1830 a wooden pier was erected. Grain and sheep were exported and building material imported. In the second half of the nineteenth century between these small harbours and Hamburg each year two to three ships of 17 to 30 tons sailed. This was not an important trade but a regular one.

From the islands of Sylt, Amrum, Föhr, Nordstrand and Pellworm agrarian products and fish (grain, beans, wool, oysters) were exported to Hamburg. At the southern end of Sylt, Hörnum got a pier for shipping about 1900. In 1903 three steamships of altogether 1154 tons ran there from Hamburg, four sailing ships of 365 tons capacity came in ballast. Near Munkmarsch on the island of Sylt there was no pier. At low tide the ships lay on the mud-flats from where the goods were transferred. In 1903 a sailing ship of 39 tons capacity and two ships of together 59 tons came in ballast from Munkmarsch to Hamburg. Two sailing ships with 64 tons of cargo went there.[18]

Two harbours in this region, Husum and the island of Föhr, maintained shipping connections with Hamburg for a long time. Although, as already mentioned, Husum was one of the more important harbours on the west coast of Schleswig-Holstein, in the 1850s and 1860s ships did not sail every year between the two towns. In 1858 six and in 1862 ten ships were counted, in the years 1860, 1861 and 1865 to 1868 only one or two. Although there were steamships among them, they were no larger than 10 to 23 CL. In the following decades shipping increased, and at the end of the century the traffic was

---

[17] Gert Uwe DETLEFSEN, Häfen-Werften-Schiffe. Chronik der Schiffahrt an der Westküste Schleswig-Holsteins, St. Peter-Ording, 1987, pp. 93–103.

[18] Tabellarische Übersichten 1903, pp. 12, 21.

remarkable: in 1897, for example, 35 ships came to Hamburg, but only seven were loaded, and 62 ships left for Husum, 58 of them loaded with altogether 1964 tons; in 1898 we find nearly the same proportions: 49 ships reached Hamburg, but only nine were loaded, and 63 left it, of which 60 were loaded. The average tonnage indicates that the size of the ships remained small.

The island of Föhr with its old shipping tradition had one harbour, Wyk, but in the statistics sometimes the whole island is mentioned and sometimes only Wyk. In the 1850s and 1860s no more than one to three ships were mentioned as voyaging to and from Hamburg, but the number increased to 26 in 1897, and 18 in 1898. They came empty to Hamburg and left with cargo.

Shipping between the island of Heligoland and Hamburg played a special role. From 1807 the island belonged to England until it was exchanged for Zanzibar by the German government in 1890. At the time of the blockade of the Elbe, from 1806 to 1814, the island saw an immense increase in its trade, because it became a staple place to smuggle goods to the coast. The island was an appropriate place for intermediate trade and was used as a shelter for ships in case of emergency. At all times there existed a lively trade between Heligoland and Hamburg, partly via Cuxhaven, the outpost of Hamburg at the mouth of the Elbe. In the 1850s an average of 40 ships (8,600 tons) sailed between Heligoland and Hamburg annually, at the beginning of the 1890s about 220 ships (73,900 tons). In 1903 138 of 47,183 tons were counted, among them only one sailing ship, the rest were steamships.[19]

For Hamburg's coastal shipping to the west, Bremen was the most important trade partner. Beyond that there were a lot of smaller and medium-sized harbours, among them Bremerhaven, Wilhelmshaven, Norden and Emden, which had regular shipping connections with Hamburg. The statistics of Hamburg additionally mention many places in this region in the interior like Oldenburg, Papenburg, Aurich and Leer, which had connections to the coast via their navigable rivers and which sent their ships to Hamburg. In this case the shipping was strictly speaking a combination of inland and coastal shipping. To add it to the statistics of the coastal trade would paint an inaccurate picture. This applies to Bremen too which, like Hamburg, is a river port. In addition, on the river Weser there were many smaller harbours with shipping connections to Hamburg such as: Vegesack, Lemwerder, Blumental, Elsfleth, Brake, Großensiel and Nordenham.

Little is known about the shipping between Hamburg and Bremen in the eighteenth century. From around 1630 the *Reihefahrt* existed between the two harbours. This was a form of regulated shipping in which each vessel had to take its turn to load at fixed freight rates, rather than allowing the competition of an unregulated market. It is a hint of how intense the shipping was. The

---

[19] Tabellarische Übersichten 1899, pp. 41–43, 1903, p. 21.

shippers from Hamburg who sailed to Bremen were organized in a company which used the model of Amsterdam, and prescribed how the goods traffic should be carried out.[20] The *waterschout* in Hamburg counted between 1786 and 1797 five to seven shippers annually with a cargo of 150 to 190 CL. The ships made several journeys between the two seaports. This kind of regulated freight organisation existed only until the 1790s. It is mentioned for the last time in 1798; attempts to revive it in 1817 and 1819 were not successful.[21]

After the great fire of Hamburg in 1842, shipping from Bremen to Hamburg received an immense boost because building materials were needed to rebuild the city. In 1843, for example, 86 ships with bricks reached Hamburg, in 1844 there were 39. Another 17 ships arriving at Hamburg between 1843 and 1846 carried natural stone, cement, tiles and asphalt from Bremen.[22] Between 1841 and 1845 an average of 403 ships with a combined cargo of 10,380 tons came to Hamburg annually from Bremen and other harbours on the Weser; between 1846 and 1850 this number dropped to 350. In the second half of the nineteenth century the number rose from 471 ships annually in the 1850s to 1180 in the 1890s, and from 15,216 tons to 228,431 tons.[23] A typical example for coastal shipping in the 1820s and 1830s is the Christoffer family from Hamburg. It owned five ships and had, with two to four journeys every year, an intensive trade with Bremen. Other shippers from Hamburg sailed once or twice annually to Bremen and to other coastal regions too.[24]

Although Bremen dominated the shipping with Hamburg, the role of the large number of other harbours and shipping places in the mouths of the rivers, on the coast, and on the east Frisian islands should not be underestimated. These harbours belonged to Bremen, the Kingdom of Hanover, or the Grand Duchy of Oldenburg and were competitors. Bremerhaven was founded by Bremen at the mouth of the Weser to preserve the position of Bremen as a seaport. In its direct neighbourhood the port of Geestemünde was founded by the Kingdom of Hanover about 1845. It never attained the importance of Bremerhaven, but played a role in regional shipping and shipbuilding. A closer look at the statistics shows large fluctuations in the shipping with Hamburg.[25] In 1859 there were 108 arrivals and departures in Hamburg, in 1860 there were 177. In the 1860s this number dropped to 25–30 annually and fluctuated in this range until the 1890s. Maybe these fluctuations were caused

---

[20] Ernst BAASCH, Die Beurtfahrt zwischen Hamburg, Bremen und Holland, Hamburg 1898; an organisation for the interests of coastal shippers was founded by shippers from the Elbe: KRESSE, Materialien, p. 22; idem, Fahrtgebiete, pp. 20, 86–87.

[21] KRESSE, Materialien, p. 22; idem, Fahrtgebiete, pp. 20, 86–87.

[22] KRESSE, Fahrtgebiete, p. 20–21.

[23] Tabellarische Übersichten 1903, p. 42.

[24] KRESSE, Fahrtgebiete, p. 20.

[25] Tabellarische Übersichten 1857–1903.

by the relatively high concentration and the competition of ports at the mouth of the Weser. In 1863 the first two steamships came from Geestemünde to Hamburg, between 1895 and 1898 there were eight to fourteen each year with a capacity of 70 to 480 tons each.

The east Frisian islands of Wangerooge, Langenoog and Juist are seldom mentioned in the statistics of the harbour of Hamburg, but there were shipping connections to Norderney, also with steamships. Relatively often one can find shipping to the towns of Nordenham, Varel, Wilhelmshaven, Norden and Emden as well as to smaller harbours like Ellenserdamm and Hooksiel near Wilhelmshaven and to the east Frisian villages Neuharlingersiel, Bensersiel and Greetsiel. The variety of the goods shipped from there to Hamburg was considerable: paper, grain, tobacco, glass, spirits, hemp, butter, machines, train oil, building materials, tea, peat, fur and ironmongery.[26]

The small sluice-harbours (*Sielhäfen*) like Bensersiel nearly exclusively concentrated on shipping. They exported agrarian goods from their hinterland and imported building materials and fuel. These harbours, which were often only 30 to 50 meters wide, were constantly threatened by mud. From 1857 between Bensersiel and Hamburg, for example, nearly every year ships sailed to and fro. They were small, 10 to 15 CL, and normally only 1 to 4 arrivals and departures were counted. In 1858 one ship of 17 CL arrived empty in Hamburg, five ships with altogether 69 CL of cargo left Hamburg. In 1863 three ships with 35 CL sailed to Bensersiel, in 1866 four with 56 CL, and in 1867 one with 9 CL. In the 1890s ships seldom sailed to and from Bensersiel, only six in 1895 and 1897 and seven in 1898.[27] From around 1870 the sluice-harbours on the North Sea coast lost much of their importance, because ships became larger and steamships were not able to reach the small harbours. Additionally, overland transport by train became easier.[28]

Another example is the important east Frisian harbour of Emden at the mouth of the river Ems, whose shipping tradition and connections to Hamburg go back to the Middle Ages. In the 1850s and 1860s each year between fourteen and thirty five arrivals and departures were registered in Hamburg. In individual cases the ships might have been larger then from Bensersiel, but their average was 10–15 CL. The 25 ships registered in 1865 had altogether 325 CL, an average of 13 CL. In the 1890s 60–80 much-bigger ships from Emden were counted in Hamburg. Some of them were now steamships, in 1893 three out of 80 with 1401 tons, in 1898 four out of 72 with 1292 tons.[29]

---

[26] Tabellarische Übersichten 1857, p. 25.

[27] Tabellarische Übersichten 1857–1903.

[28] Heide BARMEYER, Die Sielhafenorte in der oldenburgisch-ostfriesischen Küstenmarsch zwischen Weser und Ems, in: Deutsches Schiffahrtsarchiv 1 (1975), pp. 11–23.

[29] Tabellarische Übersichten 1857–1903.

One can also find in coastal shipping the transition from fishing to cargo shipping. For example fishing boats (*Ewer*) transported herrings from Emden to Hamburg and oysters from the islands of Amrum and Sylt. A cargo ship carried on twelve occasions between 1840 to 1842, mussel shells from Süderwatt for lime factories in Hamburg.[30]

Some research has focused on the shipping connections between Hamburg and the region of Wursten (Land Wursten).[31] Wursten lays to the north of Bremerhaven at the mouth of the Weser. It is protected by dykes. The settlements were on hills, the roads on embankments and the marsh is crossed by drainage ditches. Shipping was made difficult by shallow water, sands, the tide, storms and fog. The harbours were only shallow openings in the marsh. Nevertheless the Frisian peasants living there were at the same time shippers. Until the end of the nineteenth century they carried out nearly the whole of their trade by ships alone, because it was the cheapest form of transport. The first information on trade with Hamburg dates from the beginning of the fifteenth century: barley and horses were brought to Hamburg, beer, salt, hops and wood were shipped to Wursten. According to the customs lists of Stade in the years 1840 to 1860, 330 ships arrived from Wursten in Hamburg.[32] Nearly all of these ships came from the Dorumer Tief, only 31 came from the Wremener, Cappeler or Wedewardener Tief. Except for eight from Hamburg and five from Holland all shippers originated from here. An average of about 16 ships came each year to Hamburg, normally they had a crew of two and a capacity of 6.5 CL. These ships (*Ewer*) were very wide and flat, 9–10 meters long, 4.5 meters wide and had a draught of 1.2 meters. They were smaller than the *Ewer* of the Elbe. They carried wheat, beans and wood from Bremerhaven, rice and tiles from Bremen, and paraffin oil from Geestemünde to Hamburg. From Hamburg they took groceries and industrial products. At the beginning of the 1890s the shipper Johannes Stelling transported the first cargo of chile saltpetre from Hamburg to Wursten. In the 1890s shipping in Wursten declined, because the railway, which was opened in 1881 along the lower Elbe, got a connection from Cuxhaven to Geestemünde. The inhabitants of Wursten then switched to fishing.

Shipping to the seaside resorts was not cargo shipping but nevertheless part of the coastal trade, especially to Heligoland. In 1816 in Cuxhaven the first German seaside resort on the North Sea coast was opened. In the same year the first steamship from England came to Hamburg via Heligoland. The regular service of the *Lady of the Lake* between Cuxhaven and Hamburg was not

---

[30] KRESSE, Fahrtgebiete, p. 21.

[31] Erich von LEHE, Handel und Schiffahrt zwischen Hamburg und Land Wursten in sieben Jahrhunderten (1238–1938), in: Jahrbuch der Männer vom Morgenstern 31 (1948), pp. 89–127.

[32] LEHE, Handel, pp. 105–108, 120–125.

profitable and was stopped in the same year. In 1824 a regular service between London and Hamburg via Heligoland was established by an English company, which was followed in the next year by Dutch ships from Amsterdam to Hamburg via Cuxhaven.[33] When in 1826 a seaside resort was opened on Heligoland, passenger transport increased. From 1829 there was a regular Dutch service between Hamburg and the island.

Fishermen tried to use the increasing demand for passenger transport between the mainland and the islands for additional income. In 1828 the fisherman J. Fock sailed his *Ewer* twice to Norderney, but he was not successful, maybe his fare was too dear or his boat still smelt too strongly of fish. In 1832 he was more successful with four journeys. Other fishermen were encouraged to carry tourists from Hamburg to Norderney; in 1833 15 journeys were counted. Steamship competition then became too severe and no more of these trips by fishermen took place.[34]

From the 1830s several companies tried with differing success to run passenger services to the mouth of the Elbe and to the islands in the North Sea. Because of increasing demand, ever larger ships had to be used. At the beginning of the twentieth century the Hamburg-based HAPAG shipping line dominated the traffic to the seaside resorts. Traffic increased when in 1881 the railway from Harburg, near Hamburg on the south bank of the Elbe, to Cuxhaven was opened and travellers from throughout Germany could use the connecting steamship.

At all times in the nineteenth century there was constant shipping between Hamburg and the harbours on the North Sea coast which ranged from one journey a year to the small harbours to dozens of journeys to the large seaports. Short term changes in shipping could be caused by events like the great fire in Hamburg in 1842. The long term development was influenced by the technical conditions of the harbours, the advent of steamships, which could not be used in shallow water, and the building of railways to the coast. The latter could have a positive or negative influence on coastal shipping: positive, when they opened a hinterland to the harbours, negative when they took over the transport capacity of the ships. In any case, coastal shipping was just one part of a wider traffic network. The coastal ports were simultaneously the termini for inland navigation and overland transport. There was a link between overseas shipping, European shipping, North Sea and Baltic Sea shipping, coastal shipping and inland navigation. Coastal shipping supplied Hamburg's population with agrarian products and carried products from all over the world to the consumers on the coasts of the North Sea. In the nineteenth century it

---

[33] Theodor SIERSDORFER, Hamburg-Cuxhaven-Helgoland. Eine kleine Chronik der Niederelbe-Bäderdampfer, Norderstedt 1974, pp. 3–38; Gerhard KROLL, Zur Dampfschiffahrt auf der Niederelbe, MS., Hamburg 1951, pp. 56–64, 84–89, 120–122.

[34] KRESSE, Fahrtgebiete, p. 21.

never lost its importance, although the railway appeared as a competitor. Sometimes coastal shipping even led to the foundation of industries in small harbours.

In a larger study more detailed information could be given on the relations between Hamburg and particular places on the coast if statistical material on shipping could be found in their archives. More information could then be given on the homeport of the ships and shippers. As far as we know, coastal shippers from Hamburg not only sailed to the coast of the North Sea but, depending on the kind of ships and changing economic demands, to Holland, England and also into the Baltic.

Map 6: Hamburg's coastal shipping links c. 1850
(Ports, islands, rivers, etc. shown are those mentioned in the text)

Map: IEG-Maps (http://www.ieg-maps.uni-mainz.de).
Cartography: Joachim Robert Moeschl

16

COMPETITION AND CO-OPERATION IN SPANISH TWENTIETH-CENTURY COASTAL LINER SHIPPING[*]

JESÚS M. VALDALISO

Conferences and other colluding practices in coastal trade have received little attention in Spain as in other European countries. A comparative study on transport in Europe stated that railway competition prevented coastal shipping collusion.[1] By way of contrast, Armstrong has recently demonstrated the pervasive existence of conferences in British coastal shipping during the nineteenth century, and the extent of cooperation with other modes of transport.[2] As I will show in the following pages, conferences and pooling agreements were also widespread in Spanish coastal liner shipping from its origins around the middle of the nineteenth century to its decline in the late 1960s. One of these agreements, that of 1930 signed by the three most important companies in the Spanish coastal liner trade, Ybarra y Cía., Cía. Naviera Sota y Aznar (later Naviera Aznar) and Cía. Trasmediterránea, resulted in setting up the most powerful and long lasting pool in the history of Spanish coastal trade, Servicios Mancomunados de Cabotaje (SMC).

This paper is in three parts. The first shows the evolution of cooperation and competition in Spanish coastal liner shipping up to the 1930s. The second, which draws heavily on the records of SMC, focuses on the pool's management, namely the establishment of freight rates and deferred rebates, the evolution of traffic and profits, the relations among the constituent firms, the mechanisms of detecting cheating and the commercial relations with shippers, and the possible threats to the pool, those coming from other challengers and those stemming from state intervention. The last section examines the main

[*] I thank Carneb Unzeta and May Garcia Uranga from the Archivo Foral de Bizkaia, for the facilities given to work on the Sota and Aznar papers (henceforth AFB, FSA).

[1] Simon VILLE, Transport and the Development of the European Economy, 1750–1918, London 1990, p. 95.

[2] John ARMSTRONG, Conferences in British nineteenth-century coastal shipping, in: The Mariner's Mirror 77 (1991), pp. 55–65, and Railways and coastal shipping in Britain in the later nineteenth century: cooperation and competition, in: Chris WRIGLEY/John SHEPHERD (eds.), On the Move. Essays in Labour and Transport History Presented to Philip Bagwell, London 1991, pp. 76–103.

causes of the decline of coastal liners in Spain, viz., the rise of inter-modal competition, that of railways and of road transport.

Coastal liner shipping in Spain from its beginnings up to 1914

Liner shipping in the Spanish coastal trade started in the 1840s, linked to the diffusion of the steamship. At the risk of excessive simplification, two types of liner service were offered in those years: short-haul lines, which frequently ran a mixed service – cargo and passengers – between two or three nearby ports; and long-haul ones. The latter sometimes extended their service to foreign ports, like Marseille, London or Liverpool, in order to attract a large enough volume of cargo to run the line at a profit. Liner firms appeared in many ports, but Barcelona, Bilbao and Seville contained the most important companies, that is those which ran long-distance lines.

From their origins, liner firms employed competitive as well as cooperative strategies. The reservation of coastal trade to the Spanish flag – in force since 1829 – not only encouraged the creation of shipping firms but also eased the establishment of agreements among them. Generally speaking, a great number of firms entered and quit the market in the period from 1850 to 1914. Shipping firms cooperated frequently by means of cartels, but the absence of a dominant firm and »cheating« or »free-riding« problems caused most of them to disappear after a few years of existence. Around the mid-1890s, there were about ten firms which offered long-haul liner services in the Spanish coastal trade, apart from other companies employed in the traffic between Spanish ports and the Balearic and Canary Islands.[3]

There is not a clear relationship between coastal liner shipping and railways in the second half of the nineteenth century. On the one hand, railways diverted traffic from coastal trade by applying discriminatory rates; but on the other, some shipping firms signed agreements of inter-modal cooperation with railway companies. From the mid-1890s coastal trade increased considerably, in spite of the diffusion of coastal railroads, but shipping firms' complaints about railway competition continued. The scarce data available on this question suggest that, as happened in Britain[4], both competition and collaboration were strategies employed by railway companies and shipping firms in the Spanish coastal trade.

---

[3] See Jesús M. VALDALISO, La navegación regular de cabotaje en España en los siglos XIX y XX: guerras de fletes, conferencias y consorcios navieros, Bilbao 1997. The evolution of coastal trade is traced in Esperanza FRAX, Puertos y comercio de cabotaje en España, 1857–1934, Madrid 1981, and El mercado interior y los principales puertos, 1857–1920, Madrid 1987, and Antonio GOMEZ MENDOZA, Transportes y comunicaciones, in: Albert CARRERAS (ed.), Estadísticas Históricas de España, Madrid 1989.

[4] ARMSTRONG, Railways and coastal shipping.

Business concentration and the creation
of the first shipping pools (1914 – 1935)

In 1916 most of the firms which ran coastal liner services agreed to merge in a new company, the Cía. Trasmediterránea. Among the aims of this combination, its promoters intended to improve coordination of the traffic of the participant companies, rationalization of fleet deployment which would eliminate redundant and costly services, stronger bargaining position with the railway companies and other shippers, and the achievement of economies of scale in the management and running of the business.[5] The creation of Trasmediterránea brought about a new duopolistic structure, with only two big firms working long-haul routes, Ybarra y Cía., which was in this trade from the 1860s and the Trasmediterránea.

State intervention in this sector began during the First World War. Even as a neutral power, Spain had to take quasi wartime economic measures. The large rise in freight rates diverted a great part of coastal trade to railway transport, thus causing heavy congestion.[6] In order to solve this problem and to facilitate a better coordination between railways and coastal shipping, the government established maximum tariffs in 1917 (which meant an increase of 40 per cent over the average freight earnings per ton of Ybarra y Cía.) and made compulsory the employment of a mixed form of transport – coastal plus railways – for a great variety of cargoes.[7] The government also created the Comité de Tráfico Marítimo, a state office in charge of regulating coastal liner shipping and ascribing firms and tonnage to liner services.[8] The Comité ceased work after the war, but maximum freight tariffs were still in force, at least officially.

Competition resumed in Spanish coastal trade after the end of the war, with the onset of a crisis in international maritime transport. Many ships, formerly employed in international trades, came back to the coastal trade, which was reserved to Spanish-registered ships, and this increased competition and reduced freight rates to pre-1917 levels. In order to face the challenge of these

---

[5] Jesús M. VALDALISO, Explaining the structure and the boundaries of Spanish shipping firms (c. 1860–c. 1930). Contractual versus Competence Theories, The London School of Economics, Business History Unit, Occasional Paper 1996/1.

[6] Coastal trade deviation to railway lines aggravated the so called railway problem in Spain. About the latter, see Miguel ARTOLA, La acción del Estado, in: Miguel ARTOLA (Dir.), Los ferrocarriles en España. 1844–1943. I. El Estado y los ferrocarriles, Madrid 1978, chapter 4; and Pedro TEDDE DE LORCA, Las compañías ferroviarias en España (1855–1935), in: ARTOLA, Los ferrocarriles, p. 99. British coastal shipping underwent a similar problem during those years, see Derek ALDCROFT, The eclipse of British coastal shipping, 1913–21, in: Journal of Transport History 6 (1963), pp. 24–38.

[7] Gaceta de Madrid, 26/10/1917, pp. 210–11; 19/12/1917, pp. 628 and ff.

[8] R.O 20/12/1917, in M. MARTÍNEZ ALCUBILLA, Diccionario de la Administración Española, Apendix for 1917, p. 652.

outsiders, Ybarra and Trasmediterránea, together with Ramón A. Ramos, a firm which had started a liner service between Barcelona and Malaga during the war, signed a pooling agreement in 1922. The consortium coordinated the traffic of the participant firms and fixed market shares and freight rates.[9]

Cooperation among the three constituent firms worked well during the following years, but not for long. In 1928 a new and powerful challenger entered the trade, the Cía. Naviera Sota y Aznar, which started a line between Pasajes and Barcelona, using four new ships. In order to avoid cut-throat competition, Ybarra and Trasmediterránea offered Aznar equal participation in the pool, but the offer was rejected. As a consequence, a fierce rate war raged throughout 1929, which resulted in a rate reduction close to fifty per cent, and some retaliation measures of Ybarra against Aznar's subsidiary shipyard.[10] The hostilities ceased in January 1930, with the signature of an agreement which created the most effective and long-lived consortium in the history of the Spanish coastal liner trade.

The first written agreement was signed by Ybarra, Aznar and Trasmediterránea for a 15 year period. The three participant firms agreed to determine jointly the liner services offered, their routes and prices in the transport of general cargo, and not to alter them without joint consultation; to bring to the pool every contract still in force with shippers; to share cargoes, costs and freights in the following proportion: Ybarra 50 per cent, Aznar thirty per cent, and Trasmediterránea 20 per cent; and, finally, to avoid competition in the trades other than those included in this agreement, where each firm was already established.[11]

The pool had to deal with three problems on its constitution: the outbreak of a severe crisis in world maritime transport, which in the end also affected the Spanish coastal trade[12]; inter-modal competition (that of the railways); and price regulation by the state. Between February 1930 and February 1935 the volume of cargo carried by the pool decreased over forty per cent; the number of ships in service diminished from thirty-seven to twenty-eight. After consulting with the other two participants, Trasmediterránea quit the pool in 1935 and suspended its Pasajes-Barcelona line, maintaining only its sovereignty lines, which were state subsidised and exclusive to it, and short-haul routes. However, a great deal of cooperation continued among the three firms,

[9] F. GOSEASCOECHEA, Historia de la Naviera 'Ybarra' de Sevilla. Años 1846–1957, unpublished manuscript, c. 1957, pp. 62–3.

[10] Ybarra cancelled some contracts it had placed with this shipyard. GOSEASCOECHEA, Historia de la Naviera »Ybarra«; Eugenio TORRES, Ramón de la Sota. Historia económica de un impresario, Madrid 1989, pp. 1152 and 1172–3; and Jesús M. VALDALISO, Los navieros vascos y la marina mercante en España, 1860–1935. Una historia económica, Bilbao 1991.

[11] AFB, FSA, File 2704/2.

[12] VALDALISO, Los navieros vascos, pp. 167–9.

because the new agreement, signed in 1935, not only maintained a common pricing policy, but also avoided competition in other trades, and a promise by both Ybarra and Aznar to acquire the tonnage used by Trasmediterranea in the 1930 pool.[13]

The outbreak of the Spanish Civil War in 1936 interrupted the liner services, which were resumed in August 1937, however, with a single line, that of Ybarra but with vessels of the two participant companies.[14] The pool kept on serving the same line that Ybarra had been running from the mid-nineteenth century, from Pasajes to Barcelona and return, stopping in more than thirty intermediate ports in both directions.[15] Up to 1936, each firm had run its own lines, although sharing cargoes, costs and freight earnings. Joint liner operations were maintained from 1937 onwards, thus permitting the pool to offer a steadier supply of tonnage to shippers, giving at the same time a more flexible deployment to its merchant tonnage.[16] This change was the first step to a more far-reaching reorganization of the pool's operations, which took place in 1939 once the war was over.

SMC as the »dominant firm« in the sector (1939–1968).

The 1935 agreement was modified in 1939 with the aim of improving joint operations by the participants. Its most outstanding clauses were: the creation of a traffic office in Seville, formed by the managers of both companies; a monthly managers' meeting in Madrid; new shares on freights and cargoes (Ybarra sixty per cent, Aznar forty per cent); a change in the accountancy system to prevent and detect cheating; and the attempt to fix a common policy with shipping agents. A month later, the managers agreed to set up a permanent office in Seville, with the name of Servicios Mancomunados de Cabotaje (SMC), which would be in charge of the coastal liner services. The office would be managed by two delegates, one from each company, and all its staff and administrative costs would be paid by the participant firms in the same proportion they had in the pool.[17]

The 1939 agreement was prolonged for a twenty five year period without any change. Generally speaking, the pool worked well throughout that time. As microeconomic theory points out, collusion is expected to be more suc-

---

[13] VALDALISO, La navegación regular, pp. 47–8.

[14] AFB, FSA, File 2915/13.

[15] AFB, FSA, File 2477/13.

[16] Both Aznar and Ybarra employed the surplus tonnage of its coastal line in the coastal tramp trade, see Naviera Aznar and Ybarra y Cía., Memorias; and AFB, FSA, File 3520/5.

[17] AFB, FSA, Files 2704/2 and 2477/13.

cessful when sellers are few and buyers are many[18] and that was the case of
SMC. Apart from that, there were other factors which help to explain why
cheating problems did not appear: a good relationship among the two families
who controlled the management and proprietorship of each company, Ybarra
and Aznar, respectively; joint management of the pool at the Seville office; a
previous experience of almost ten years collaboration in the same trade; and
the long-standing cooperative strategy developed by Ybarra in the coastal
trade, which gave it a masterful competence in detecting or preventing cheating.[19] Deviations from the fixed shares existed, but they usually did not
exceed five per cent. Moreover, penalties for not fulfilling cargo quotas were
not applied until the late-1950s or if so, they were unimportant. Only then did
they rise considerably, due to Aznar insistence, which between 1935 and 1966
surpassed its quota twenty-five times, for only eight times by Ybarra. In any
case, this did not seem to cause any serious problem to the pool's running.[20]

A new, and last, agreement was signed at the end of 1964 for a five year
period. Among its new clauses it modified the former companies' shares,
giving each a fifty per cent participation in both cargo volume and freight
earnings. The new agreement also increased penalties; and it stipulated that
the Seville office be closed in 1966, it being replaced by a managers' meeting
in Madrid every two months.[21] The closing of the Seville office was the
starting point for the dismantling of the pool and of the liner service. In its
1966 report Ybarra pointed out that »Coastal liner shipping has finished«.
That year Ybarra sold two of its vessels used in coastal liner services. Another
three were still in service until 1968, when they were sold and the Sevillian
firm quit a trade which it had been working for more than a century.[22] In 1968
Aznar maintained a single ship in the coastal line to fulfill previous commit-
ments and started selling its coastal fleet, which was completely sold the next
year.[23]

There is statistical data for some basic performance indicators of SMC and
its previous pools from 1932 to 1966, such as tons carried, gross freight earnings, costs, bonuses and net freight earnings. Measured by the cargo carried,
the »golden years« of SMC were those from 1939 to 1947, as is shown in
figure 1, when it transported almost one million tons every year. It was in

---

[18] F. M. SCHERER, Industrial Market Structure and Economic Performance, Boston 1980,
pp. 199–200; and A. JACQUEMIN/M. E. SLADE, Cartels, collusion, and horizontal merger,
in: R. SCHMALENSEE/R. D. WILLIG (eds.), Handbook of Industrial Organization, Amsterdam
1989, vol. 1, p. 421.

[19] Some problems appeared in the early 1940s, but they were quickly detected and
solved, on these see VALDALISO, La navegación regular, pp. 49–50.

[20] Ibid., p. 50.

[21] AFB, FSA, File 2704/2.

[22] Ybarra y Cía., Memoria 1966, p. 7; Memoria 1968, p. 3.

[23] Naviera Aznar, Memoria 1968, p. 8; and AFB, FSA, File 3636/3.

these years that the pool's market power was highest, close to two thirds of the whole Spanish coastal liner trade, including trade with the Balearic islands, and the reserved traffic of Trasmediterránea.[24] From 1954 onwards the volume of cargo decreased steadily, almost without interruption. Both gross freight earnings and costs rose more or less uniformly up to 1958, and began to drop from 1959 because of the heavy decline in cargo carried.

Figure 1: Tons carried, gross freight earnings and costs of SMC (and prior arrangements), 1932–1966

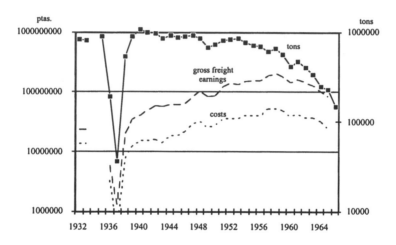

Source: based on AFB, FSA, Signatures 2704/2, 2911/22 and 3404/2.

Figure 2 shows average gross freight earnings and costs per ton, in current prices and deflated. With regard to the former, its trend in deflated pesetas is almost flat, although it decreases slightly from 1932 to 1953 and rises

[24] To calculate SMC's market power we need to know, first, the volume of the Spanish coastal liner trade, and this is not always possible due to the changing criteria of the state offices in charge of compiling official statistics. Nevertheless, the Lista Oficial de Buques offers from 1941 to 1953 the volume of cargo carried by Spanish ships distinguishing »coastal liner shipping«, which is the data I have employed. The cargo carried by SMC directly (that shown in figure 1) accounted for more than 50 per cent of coastal liner trade to 1947, and was close to 40 per cent in the following years. However, this is a minimum, because to that we must add the cargo transported by its subsidiary firm, Naviera Valenciana, and that transported by SMC or its subsidiary in the pools they had established with Ramón A. Ramos and Naviera Mallorquina. I have been able to collect data for almost all this traffic in 1946 (excepting that jointly shared with Mallorquina), and the total cargo controlled by SMC accounted for 68 per cent of the whole coastal liner trade. There is no reason to think that percentages in other years varied considerably. »Coastal liner shipping« includes all the traffic carried by Trasmediterránea on the sovereignty lines (reserved and subsidized traffic), so the calculation of SMC's market power is biased downward. On this, see VALDALISO, La navegación regular, pp. 52–3.

moderately from 1954 to 1964. As to the latter, also in deflated pesetas, it shows a downward overall trend for the whole period which includes four different phases: decreases in 1936–42 and in 1949–53, and increases in 1943–48 and 1954–65.

Except for the 1930s, costs never surpassed forty per cent of gross freight earnings, being close to thirty per cent, see figure 3. From 1938 onwards, net freight earnings represented near sixty per cent of gross earnings except for 1943 and 1944. Bonuses to shippers accounted for the rest. Discounts of gross freight earnings experienced a steady rise: from two to three per cent in 1939–47, to five to nine per cent in 1948–54, to ten to twelve per cent from 1955 onwards. The extent of these bonuses indicates clearly SMC's decreasing bargaining position with its customers, and indirectly, increasing intra-modal and/or inter-modal competition.

Both Aznar and Ybarra plied other routes which were open to competition, apart from the collusive coastal liner trade. Aznar ran several lines between Spanish ports and the United Kingdom and South America. It also had a tramp fleet employed in the international and coastal shipping market. Ybarra ran a line between Spain, Brazil and Argentine. The coastal shipping pool's profits accounted for a substantial part of their total earnings (twenty-six per cent of Aznar gross freight earnings between 1937 and 1965, and thirty-two per cent

Figure 2: SMC (and previous pools):
　　　　　　gross freight earnings and total costs per ton, 1932–1965

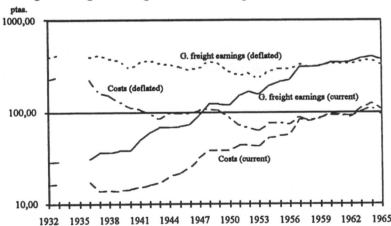

Source: see Figure 1. For the price index employed as a deflator, see A. Ojeda, *Indices de precios en España (1913–1986)* (Madrid, 1987), pp. 72–3.

Figure 3: SMC's gross freight earnings distribution, 1932–1965

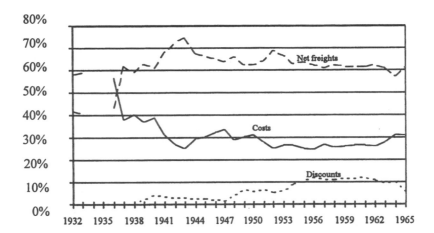

Source: see Figure 1.

of Ybarra's between 1952 and 1966).[25] Coastal liner gains allowed both companies to renew part of their tonnage, above all that employed in their transatlantic lines, where competition appeared to be particularly strong.[26] Neither Ybarra nor Aznar made substantial investments in their coastal liner tonnage throughout most of the pool's life. Ybarra pointed to the low level of coastal freight rates as the reason not to invest.[27] Even if one admits that the Sevillian firm was right, it seems that the main reason lay in the lack of intra-modal competition in this market.

Threats to SMC's market power: potential challengers

The coastal liner fleet accounted for seven per cent of the number and four per cent of the tonnage of the Spanish merchant marine in 1960. Of that, SMC (Ybarra and Aznar) owned thirty-five per cent of the number and eighty per cent of the tonnage. SMC's fleet consisted of big steam vessels, twenty-five years old and over. Below them, there were two companies of relative import-

[25] Data on gross freight earnings come from the annual reports of each company. For a more detailed analysis, see VALDALISO, La navegación regular, p. 56.

[26] Ybarra y Cía., Memoria 1953, pp. 3–4 and 9; Memoria 1954, p. 7. Ybarra explicitly acknowledged the role played by coastal liner profits in its Memoria 1958, p. 9.

[27] Subsecretaría de la Marina Mercante, Estudio sobre los problemas actuales del tráfico de cabotaje presentado por la Naviera Ybarra, S. en C., Madrid 1951.

ance, Vapores Suardíaz and Naviera Mallorquina, owners of a numerous fleet
of small and newer motor ships, constructed in the 1940s and 1950s. The rest
of the shipowners in this trade, with the exception of Naviera Astur-Andaluza,
employed small motor vessels. The coastal liner fleet as a whole had in 1960
one of the oldest age structures of the entire Spanish merchant fleet, with
seventy-seven per cent of its tonnage older than thirty years. Only steam colliers and timber carriers in the tramp coastal trade and inter-island sovereignty
lines used older tonnage.

Table 1: Fleets of Spanish shipping firms deployed
in coastal liner trade in 1960

Firm	No.	%	GRT	%
Ybarra y Cía.	12	20.3	30,655	47.8
Naviera Aznar	9	15.2	20,763	32.4
Vapores Suardíaz	22	37.3	4,665	7.3
Naviera Mallorquina	9	15.2	4,392	6.8
Naviera Astur-Andaluza	1	1.7	2,516	3.9
Fos Hermanos	3	5.0	624	1.0
Sociedad Hnos. Varela	1	1.7	247	0.4
Jose V. Moncho Alecreu	1	1.7	156	0.2
Francisco Rama Isla	1	1.7	138	0.2
Total	59	100.0	64,156	100.0

Source: author's estimates from *Lista Oficial de Buques 1961.*

During the 1940s and 1950s SMC had to confront the competition of
smaller and newer motor vessels, not only owned by liner firms, but also by
outsiders employed in the tramp business.[28] These competed occasionally with
liner firms, above all with SMC services.[29] The smaller motor ship offered a
quick and non-stop service with closed holds, while SMC's vessels had to call
at many intermediate ports, thus slowing it down and broadening the scope for
fraud and pilferage of cargoes, a very frequent problem in those years.
Moreover, the motor ship's small size was not a hindrance to capturing a part
of the general cargo which did not need great transport capacity. The
challenge of outsiders did not affect the hegemony of SMC but, as it diminished the cargo available to SMC's fleet, cut its freight earnings.[30]

[28] All of these ships were constructed with the help of state funds. In this way, the state
lowered entry barriers to the coastal trade. See AFB, FSA, File 3727/3.

[29] It is quite revealing of that competition that the government had to publish a law in
1942 stating that official tariffs authorised for SMC ruled for all the ships that effected that
traffic.

[30] Subsecretaría Marina Mercante, Estudio, pp. 11 and 13; and Fairplay, 10 May 1951,
p. 1040.

SMC put into practice three different strategies against its competitors (liner firms or outsiders): compete, cooperate and/or buy them. The competitive response consisted of, on the one hand, price discrimination and deferred rebates offered to shippers; and, on the other, to compete with the same type of small vessel by means of a subsidiary firm, the Cía. Naviera Valenciana, of which Aznar and Ybarra controlled fifty-one per cent of its share capital.[31] Valenciana started two regular services between Spanish Mediterranean ports in the 1940s (Valencia-Barcelona in 1941; Valencia-Majorca in 1946), precisely the trade segment where competition from smaller ships was most intense. Apart from that, the subsidiary company occasionally entered the coastal tramp trade.[32] Valenciana competed fiercely with Trasmediterránea on the Valencia-Barcelona line in the early 1940s, but an agreement was reached after Ybarra's rmediation.[33] Another strong challenger in the 1950s was Vapores Suardíaz, which operated a line between Barcelona, Malaga and Seville. Cut-throat competition with Suardíaz put Valenciana into the red. Finally, the subsidiary firm was liquidated, its fleet being sold to a friendly company, Naviera Malloquina.[34]

SMC and its subsidiary firm pursued a cooperative strategy with Naviera Mallorquina on the Barcelona-Palma and Valencia-Barcelona routes; and with Ramón A. Ramos (and his successors) on the Malaga-Motril-Almeria-Barcelona route. SMC signed in 1940 an agreement to collaborate with the former for ten years, which was renewed for another five at Mallorquina's initiative.[35] Ybarra had a long-term relationship with Ramos, one of the SMC participants dating back to 1922. Their pooling agreements on that route were periodically renewed.[36] SMC also established agreements on cargo transshipment in different ports with the above mentioned companies and others, like Trasmediterránea, Cabo Hermanos and Cía. Española de Navegación Marítima.[37]

The last strategy used to reduce competition was to buy part or the whole of the challenger's fleet. SMC put it in practice occasionally, only against outsiders which had captured some of its former clients. Its degree of success varied considerably.[38]

---

[31] AFB, FSA, File 3677/28.

[32] AFB, FSA, File 3727/3.

[33] AFB, FSA, Files 3756/7, 2476/8 and 3727/3.

[34] AFB, Files 2477/17 and 3663/1. Data on the fleet's sale come from Lista Oficial de Buques 1957, p. 516.

[35] AFB, FSA, File 3727/1.

[36] AFB, FSA, File 3404/2.

[37] AFB, FSA, File 2703/4.

[38] VALDALISO, La navegación regular, pp. 66–7.

SMC benefited from its market power in the liner coastal trade to reach agreements with shippers. Usually, SMC signed formal contracts with the most important shippers, offering bonuses over official freight rates and deferred rebates in order to maintain their loyalty.[39] While the distribution of some products (rice and grain, for example) was monopolized by the Cooperativas Nacionales (state-supported syndicates of producers) or by state-owned firms (in the case of tobacco) SMC managed to get not only control over transport, but over the insurance, and loading-unloading business as well.[40] When, very occasionally, SMC had to compete in open auctions for the carriage of a given amount of cargo, it also benefited from »first-mover« (that is a better knowledge of freight rates for that merchandise) or »scale« advantages (a stronger financial power and a larger fleet) which finally gave it the contract.[41]

In conclusion, it seems clear that the only serious competition that SMC had to confront in the 1940s and 1950s was that of Suardíaz on the Seville-Barcelona route and, occasionally, of some outsiders. Given the facts presented, we could equate SMC's position in the coastal liner trade to that of »dominant firm« defined by industrial economics, with a few other liner firms running shorter-haul and less important routes, and the competition of outsiders. It is revealing that the only ships of the Spanish merchant fleet which were excluded from the shipowners agreement that had created OFICEMA in 1951, were those »ascribed to national coastal liner services«, those which Trasmediterránea employed in the Spanish sovereignty lines, and finally those owned by non-shipping firms dedicated to carrying their own goods.[42] OFICEMA (acronym of Oficina Central Marítima, central maritime office) was a state-supported cartel, with disciplinary power to fix freight rates, regulate transport markets and even to establish pooling agreements. It also became the pressure group of Spanish shipowners. The exclusion of coastal liner tonnage thus indicated, it should be stressed again, that competition in this trade had already been regulated.[43]

[39] See SMC's ratebook in AFB, FSA, File 2703/4. Coastal liner companies in Britain put in practice a similar policy, see ARMSTRONG, Conferences, and idem, Freight pricing policy in coastal liner companies before the First World War, in: Journal of Transport History 10 (1989), 180–97.

[40] See AFB, FSA, File 2477/17 on rice, and AFB, FSA, File 3606/4 on tobacco.

[41] AFB, FSA, File 2477/17.

[42] Archive of the Asociación de Navieros Vascos (Bilbao), File n° 4.

[43] Ibid., and Santos PASTOR, El transporte marítimo en España, Madrid 1982, pp. 474–78. Moreover, Aznar and Ybarra played an hegemonic role in OFICEMA throughout its existence, see PASTOR, El transporte marítimo, p. 480.

Threats to SMC's market power: state intervention

Price-fixing arrangements in the Spanish coastal liner trade were limited by state intervention. The 1930 pool agreed to charge the maximum freight rates established by the state in 1917, but the first republican government suspended its application in 1931. By the law of 29 April 1931 the government justified state intervention in the coastal trade on account of its reservation to the Spanish flag, saying that price regulation could not be left exclusively in the hands of shipowners.[44] Another law in 1932 decreed a new tariff of freight rates which was considerably lower than that of the 1930 agreement, see table 2. The government published a new official tariff of maximum coastal freight rates in 1943, which showed a rise of between sixty and eighty per cent with regard to the 1932 level. Four years later SMC's pressures on the government succeeded in getting a further price increase, far above the rise requested, by means of a nominal charge of twenty-two pesetas on every general cargo ton.[45] As a result, SMC's earnings rose during the 1940s well above costs, see table 2.

The collaborating companies applied for a further fifty-one per cent rise in freight rates in 1951. The Subsecretaría de la Marina Mercante, a state organisation dependent on the Department of Industry and Trade, published the shipowners' memorial and various ambiguously favourable reports. However, this increase finally lacked official support by the Industry and Trade Department, and SMC had to negotiate its application with every customer.[46] State policy regarding freight rates in coastal liner shipping did not change substantially in the following years. The government fixed maximum freight rates in the coastal trade for entire cargoes in 1952, but it did not say a word about general cargo, so SMC continued to need the permission of Subsecretaría to each increase.[47] The state liberalized freight rates in 1963, with the exception of state-trade and crude oil, although it compelled liner shipping firms to communicate any change in their charges and fares. Finally, a new law in 1966 re-established for Spanish liner firms the requirement of state approval of its freight rates and charters.[48]

---

[44] ARANZADI, Repertorio Cronológico de Legislación 1931, R. 104. State intervention in price-fixing had a long tradition in railroad transport, see ARTOLA, La acción del Estado, chapter 3.

[45] AFB, FSA, File 2477/17. For more detail, VALDALISO, La navegación regular, pp. 70–1.

[46] On this, see VALDALISO, ibid., p. 72.

[47] ARANZADI, Repertorio Cronológico de Legislación 1952, R. 376; and 1960, R. 701.

[48] ARANZADI, Repertorio Cronológico de Legislación 1963, R. 743; and 1966, R. 1754.

Table 2: Official freight tariffs and average freights and costs per ton carried
by SMC, 1917–1948 (1932 = 100)

	1917	1932	1943*	1947*
A) Official freight tariffs				
Bilbao to Seville or Barcelona (3ª)	120	100	168	212
Barcelona to Seville (3ª)	125	100	175	230
Olive oil from Seville to Bilbao	150	100	147	257
Iron goods from Bilbao to Seville or Barcelona	150	100	192	247
B) SMC				
Gross freights per ton		100	239	434
Costs per ton		100	131	265
Net freights per ton		100	384	661

Source: author's estimate from A) *Gaceta de Madrid 19/12/1917* and *3/7/1932;* and
Aranzadi, Repertorio Cronológico de Legislación 1943 (R. 287) and 1947 (R. 1013).
B) See Figure 1.

* 1944 and 1948 for SMC (when new tariffs had already come into force).

Therefore, state intervention by means of price regulation continued to exist
almost throughout the life of SMC and its previous agreements. Industrial
economics emphasises two problems associated with this mechanism of
control which appeared here: on the one hand, the difficulty of price-fixing in
a sector with a multiplicity of routes and cargoes; on the other, the lack of
incentives to the colluding firms, given that they could pass on cost increases
in the final price, and the widespread possibility that they did not declare their
true costs.[49] SMC lost any discretionary power over freight rates, and had to
justify to the government any petition for an increase. This method, apart from
being slow and complicated meant that SMC had to renegotiate its contracts if
it wanted them adjusted to every new freight rate tariff. Some shippers did not
agree and SMC was forced to maintain its former contracts at the risk of heavy
losses; others were convinced only after promise of a discount which also
meant a cut in SMC profits. If shippers had another means of transport
available, such as railways or trucks, the bargaining power of SMC became
almost non existent. Let us look at some examples.

SMC signed freight charters with Tabacalera in 1942 and 1946, in both
cases a year before new coastal liner tariffs were approved. As a result of this,
tobacco freight rates charged to this company were during the 1940s always
below the official level: SMC's proposal to Tabacalera in 1946 asked for a
freight charter which was for between fifty and eighty per cent of the 1943

[49] Julio SEGURA, Teoría de la economía industrial, Madrid 1993, pp. 115–117.

official rate; the new tariff agreed in 1952 established freight rates which did not exceed those fixed by the government in 1947.[50] With regard to Solvay, a big chemical firm, SMC succeeded in applying the new rates in 1947 and a further increase of 50 per cent in 1951, but it had to offer, confidentially, a twenty per cent discount on the total bill.[51] The same happened in 1947 with a long-standing customer, Altos Hornos de Vizcaya, which received a fifteen per cent discount. This firm rejected the proposed fifty per cent increase in 1951. That rise was vital to SMC, because confidential reports showed that rates in force only covered fifty-four per cent of its total costs. SMC played aggressively and retaliated with the suppression of bonuses, but Altos Hornos de Vizcaya did not make up its mind. Quite the opposite, it suspended the contract and began to transport its iron by rail or road. That response was somehow premonitory of what was going to happen with coastal liner trade later on.[52]

Inter-modal competition and the decline of coastal liner shipping in the 1950s and 1960s

The substitution of railway and road transport for coastal shipping was a threat that SMC increasingly began to hear from shippers in the 1940s.[53] However, inter-modal competition did not become really effective until the 1950s. Between 1950 and 1970, according to official statistics, road transport multiplied by almost ten times, while railway transport and coastal shipping multiplied by 1.3 and 2.7, respectively[54], see figure 4. The latter's overall growth rate hides a profound change in the type of cargo carried: an increase in tramp cargoes like ores and, above all, oil, and a heavy decrease of general cargo, the bread and butter trade for coastal liner shipping, that also took place in other European countries.[55] Inter-modal competition explains the decline of general cargo in the 1950s and 1960s and, in the last resort, the disappearance of liner shipping between the ports of peninsular Spain.

---

[50] AFB, FSA, File 3606/4.

[51] AFB, FSA, File 2703/4.

[52] The whole commercial correspondence regarding these negotiations in AFB, FSA, File 2477/18. A more detailed study is in VALDALISO, La navegación regular, pp. 74–6.

[53] AFB, FSA, Files 2476/9 and 2477.

[54] Ministerio de Transportes, Turismo y Comunicaciones, Estadísticas de Transporte. Series cronológicas (1950–1980), Madrid 1983. In 1951, shipping, railways and road transport accounted for, respectively, 36, 38 and 21 per cent; in 1960 for 33, 21 and 45 per cent; ten years later for 28, 12 and 59 per cent.

[55] PASTOR, El transporte marítimo, p. 1235.

Figure 4: Internal cargo traffic in Spain, 1950 – 1970 ('000 ton-km)

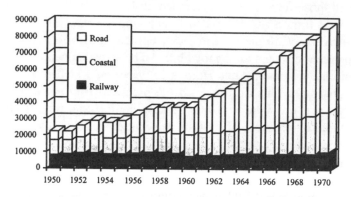

Source: see footnote 54.

Two further sources allow us to understand better that process of intermodal competition for the carriage of general cargo. The first one is a memorial about the problems of coastal shipping, submitted by Ybarra y Cía. to the Subsecretaría de la Marina Mercante at the beginning of 1951, to which a careful comparative study on transport costs, shipping and railway, is appended. The second one is the correspondence between SMC and its shipping agents in Valencia in 1950–2, in which detailed reports on the market situation, transport costs and prices for Valencian rice can be found.

Ybarra y Cía's report attempts to explain the decline of general cargo in coastal liner shipping since 1947. Apart from generic reasons, like droughts or economic isolation, which applied to all industries in those years, the Sevillian firm blamed for price increases in shipping »the higher cost of loading and unloading operations ... taxes, cargo insurance ... [and] thefts and cheating, as well as deficient cargo handling«.[56] That explains, as table 3, shows, that although the price of maritime transport was far below railway fares (between twenty-five and fifty per cent, and close to seventy per cent in short-hauls), total transport cost (insurance, taxes, loading-unloading and other expenses included) was much higher in coastal shipping than in railways (between ten and fifty per cent in long-hauls; between ninety and one hundred and forty per cent in short-hauls and particular traffic, like that of cotton goods and rice).

As tables 3 and 4 show, freight rates accounted for, approximately, one fifth of total shipping costs, while railway fares' percentage was much higher, between two thirds and three quarters of total railway costs, sometimes more. According to Ybarra's report, that was explained by two causes: in the first

[56] Subsecretaría Marina Mercante, Estudio, pp. 7–8.

Table 3: Transport costs of some products by railway and
coastal shipping in 1950 (ptas per metric ton)

	Coastal shipping freight rate (ptas.)	Railway				
		Total costs (marit.) (ptas.)	Fares (ptas.)	Total costs (railway) (ptas.)	Freight/ railway fares (%)	Maritime/ railway (%)
Canned fish from Vigo to Valencia	169.0	776.2	535.0	644.6	31.6	145.1
Industrial oil from Vigo to Coruña	81.4	434.5	118.1	179.3	68.9	242.3
Ironmongery from Bilbao to Seville	113.0	869.6	441.1	587.9	25.6	147.9
Paper from Bilbao to Seville	176.0	451.5	368.3	436.5	47.8	103.4
Olives from Seville to Barcelona	164.8	713.7	512.1	643.8	32.2	110.9
Soap from Seville to Cadiz	69.6	343.2	97.9	140.2	71.1	244.8
Cotton cloths from Barcelona to Seville	274.0	2,178.1	601.3	1,004.3	45.6	216.9
Paints and varnish from Barcelona to Vigo	164.8	867.4	509.6	654.2	32.3	132.6
Rice from Valencia to Barcelona	74.4	442.4	159.3	239.9	46.7	184.4
Tinned foods from Valencia to Sevilla	109.0	448.8	439.5	505.7	24.8	88.7
Wine from Valencia to Vigo	134.0	502.6	363.3	419.1	36.9	119.9

Source: author's estimates from Subsecretaría de la Marina Mercante, Estudio, pp. 18 – 25.

Table 4: Cost structure of coastal shipping and
railway transport in 1950 (in percentage)

	Canned fish from Vigo to Valencia		Rice from Valencia to Barcelona		Olive oil from Seville to Bilbao	
	Coastal shipping	Railway	Coastal shipping	Railway	Coastal shipping	Railway
Loading, unloading & others	21.1	1.7	24.0	4.5	21.1	2.7
Taxes	3.1	5.8	4.9	2.0	6.7	5.1
Insurance	54.1	9.5	54.2	27.1	45.3	8.6
Freight or transport charges	21.8	83.0	16.8	66.4	26.8	82.9
Total	100.0	100.0	100.0	100.0	100.0	100.0

Source: author's estimates from Subsecretaría de la Marina Mercante, *Estudio*, pp. 33 – 43.

place, freight rates had risen less than railway fares, which were state-subsidized (railways had been nationalized in 1941, and their operation was delegated to a state-owned company, RENFE)[57]; secondly, the heavier weight of insurance and loading-unloading costs in shipping, which accounted for nearly seventy per cent of total costs.[58] Other sources corroborated that explanation, pointing out two further causes: lower taxes on road transport, and excessive red-tape in coastal shipping.[59]

The transport of rice from Valencia to other Spanish ports was almost wholly controlled by SMC in the 1940s. The coastal pool began to suffer railway competition from 1949 onwards. That year, the state transported its entire quota (near thirty to thirty-five per cent of the total harvest) by RENFE.[60] The rest of the harvest was marketed by the Cooperativa Nacional del Arroz until 1950, and by private producers from 1951 onwards. According to SMC shipping agents in Valencia, the total cost of maritime transport was slightly cheaper (five to six per cent) than that of the railways in 1950. However, railways offered two advantages, security and speed, which clearly offset lower shipping costs. SMC shipping agents said confidentially that 300 tons of rice from Valencia needed fifteen days to reach Bilbao by ship, but there was widespread theft in loading, at intermediate stops and when unloading; by railway, the same cargo was in Bilbao in four days with no theft. The extent of pilferage drove up cargo insurance costs sharply making maritime transport increasingly unable to compete with railways on total costs. SMC could counteract those disadvantages while the distribution of rice was controlled by the Cooperativa, which was offered discounts on freight rates and loyalty bonuses. Since competition for cargoes opened up from 1951 SMC tariffs simply could not compete with railway fares. Its subsidiary firm, Naviera Valenciana, attempted to offer a more competitive rate, including loading and unloading and insurance costs, but its best price still exceeded railway fares and, moreover, did not allow the shipping firm to cover insurance costs and make a profit.[61]

To solve this competitiveness problem, Ybarra y Cía. asked the state for help: tax relief for coastal shipping, a reinforcement of security in ports to avoid theft (and diminish insurance costs), free contracting of stevedores (to

[57] Miguel MUÑOZ RUBIO, Renfe (1941–1991). Medio siglo de ferrocarril público, Madrid 1995.

[58] Subsecretaría Marina Mercante, Estudio, pp. 11–15. About the data employed by Ybarra and its estimation procedures, see VALDALISO, La navegación regular, pp. 82–5.

[59] Fairplay, 8 October 1959, p. 43; and 12 January 1961, pp. 157–8. See also Ramón CHAPA, Problemas del tráfico de cabotaje, in: Información Comercial Española, 470 (1972), pp. 89–93.

[60] AFB, FSA, File 2477/17.

[61] The correspondence regarding this cargo can be found in AFB, FSA, Files 2477/9 and 2477/17. A more detailed analysis is in VALDALISO, La navegación regular, pp. 87–8.

diminish costs and improving cargo-handling), a better coordination with RENFE (which actually meant the establishment of cargo reservation for coastal shipping), a regulation of intra-modal competition (from liner firms and outsiders), and finally, a new law of protection and encouragement of shipping industries. Except for the latter, none of the rest were effectively put into force by the state.

Apart from seeking state aid, without success, SMC attempted to face road and railway competition by cutting costs and offering a better service. In order to achieve a faster and more efficient liner service, SMC cut out some intermediate stops in secondary ports in 1957. Four years later, it started up a »special fast service«, broadened in the following years.[62] In 1967, a year after the closing of the Seville office, Naviera Aznar stated in its annual report that »general cargo has disappeared, [coastal] traffic being sustained only with bulk cargoes. If things do not change, one must think that coastal trade is going to disappear completely«.

After the disappearance of SMC in the late 1960s, new liner firms entered the market, with new and very specialized tonnage (container, multi-purpose and ro-ro vessels).[63] None of these firms established, however, any regular service between peninsular ports exclusively (like those run by SMC). They served regular lines between peninsular ports and the Balearic or Canary Islands, or the Spanish possessions in North Africa, or inter-island services.[64] Taking into account demand structure, that fleet deployment is not striking: in 1975 general cargo traffic between peninsular ports accounted for only four per cent of general cargo moved in coastal shipping as a whole. The rest of the traffic was between mainland Spain and its islands and foreign possessions (eighty six per cent) and the inter-island traffic (ten per cent).[65] Inter-modal competition, therefore, had limited the employment of shipping to its »natural traffic« in the Spanish coastal liner trade.

Inter-modal competition did not occur only in coastal liner shipping. It also affected the coastal tramp trade, the carriage of general cargo to and from Europe, and the export of some perishable products like fruit and vegetables. Oranges, for example, were increasingly carried by railways in the 1940s and 1950s, and by road transport from the late 1950s. In this trade, shipping still offered a lower price, but it could not compete on quality (higher speed and better cargo handling) with railways and trucks. In the mid-1960s, shipping

---

[62] About this, see the annual reports of Naviera Aznar for 1957 and 1958 and for 1961 to 1965; and of Ybarra y Cía. for 1955, 1956 and 1963.

[63] S. BUHIGAS, Consecuencias de una nueva política marítima en el tráfico de cabotaje, in: Jornadas sobre transporte marítimo y política económica, Madrid 1984, pp. 138 and 152.

[64] VALDALISO, La navegación regular, pp. 92–3.

[65] BUHIGAS, Consecuencias, pp. 129–61.

was almost wholly confined to the carriage of oranges to Scandinavian countries.[66] In the coastal tramp trade, the replacement of shipping by railways and road transport in the carriage of bulk dry cargo reduced demand for ships, thus increasing intra-modal competition despite OFICEMA efforts to regulate it.[67] Coastal shipping in the 1960s could be characterized as a »sick industry«, where idle capacity and the difficulty of alternative deployment for surplus tonnage resulted in a decrease in prices far below a minimum rate of profit.[68] Even OFICEMA could not regulate competition in this trade, and a new cartel was created in 1967.[69]

Conclusions

In the history of coastal liner shipping in Spain, since its beginnings around the mid-nineteenth century to its decline in the late 1960s, phases of pure competition in the sector were scarce and short-lived. On the contrary, collusive arrangements were pervasive, from conferences which fixed freight rates and established a regular schedule of sailings to pooling agreements.[70] Spanish coastal liner shipping became more concentrated in the 1914–1935 period. With the exception of Ybarra y Cía. all the firms which served this trade merged in the Cía. Trasmediterránea in 1916. Both firms, together with another less important one formed during the war years, Ramón A. Ramos, signed in 1922 the first pooling agreement in the trade's history. In the late 1920s a new challenger entered the market, the Cía Naviera Sota y Aznar. After a freight rate war, a new pooling agreement was signed by the »big three«, Trasmediterránea, Ybarra and Aznar in 1930, leaving Ramos outside (which, notwithstanding, established a particular agreement with the big three for the Malaga-Barcelona service). Trasmediterránea quit the consortium, called SMC, in 1935, but Ybarra and Aznar kept it working until the late-1960s, when it disappeared.

Traditional explanations of conferences which note the high proportion of fixed costs in a shipping liner firm's total costs[71], maintain a considerable explanatory power. Nevertheless, it has also to be taken into account, that its

[66] E. BAGES, Citrus export and shipping. An example of sea/land competition, in: Fairplay, 24 June 1965.

[67] On this problem, see VALDALISO, La navegación regular, pp. 90–1.

[68] SCHERER, Industrial Market Structure, pp. 212–3.

[69] About the cartel of 1967 see VALDALISO, La navegación regular, pp. 90–1.

[70] The extent of market collusion in the coastal liner trade did not differ substantially from other Spanish industries, see Francisco COMÍN and Pablo MARTÍN ACEÑA, Los rasgos históricos de las empresas en España: un panorama, Madrid 1996, p. 27. The particularity of the coastal liner trade lay in the widespread use of pools and in its great stability.

[71] S. G. STURMEY, British Shipping and World Competition, London 1962.

setting up entailed a certain degree of regulation in a sector with a notorious excess of capacity.[72] SMC also benefited from two characteristics emphasized by industrial economists to explain cartels' stability, the small number of colluding firms and the multiplicity and dispersion of its customers.[73]

The analysis of SMC's market power, estimated both by its market and tonnage share, shows that it played the role of »dominant firm« in coastal liner shipping as industrial economics points out. Between 1939 and 1966 SMC controlled the peninsular coastal trade, capturing in the best years (1940s) more than two thirds of the market; its fleet accounted for more than 80 per cent of the total employed in this traffic; its freight tariffs ruled the whole trade; and the competition of other liner firms, was reduced to short-haul routes. All of this helps to explain why the coastal liner trade, together with sovereignty lines, were the only trades that OFICEMA, the Spanish shipping cartel created in 1951, did not control. Nevertheless, entry barriers against outsiders were very low, which explains why small tramp firms entered this trade from the 1940s onwards, although only for a small share of the market. In this sense, the Spanish coastal liner trade in the 1940s could be defined as »contestable«[74], a characterization which would help to explain the downward trend of freight rates in real terms during that decade. The threat of those potential challengers was not so great as to oblige SMC to renew its fleet, which was the oldest in the sector. Contestability continued in the 1950s and 1960s, but now the reason was inter-modal, more than intra-modal competition.

Up to the First World War, state intervention was limited to reserve coastal trade to the Spanish flag and to give subsidies to some mail services between the peninsula and the Balearic and Canary islands and the Spanish possessions in North Africa. From 1917 onwards, due to war circumstances, the government fixed maximum freight rates and regulated competition between the coastal trade and railways. From then to the late 1940s, the state role was focused on tariff regulation. Price regulation, notwithstanding the problems that its application entails, limited SMC's discretionary power. During the 1950s, the state maintained its regulative capacity, but somewhat softened. Average freight rates per ton increased, although cargo transported diminished considerably due to the increasing importance of inter-modal competitors, railways and trucks. In the last resort, inter-modal competition caused the

---

[72] B. M. DEAKIN, Shipping Conferences. A Study of their Origins, Development and Economic Practices, Cambridge 1973; S. G. STURMEY, Shipping Economics. Collected Papers (London, 1975); and J. O. JANSSON/D. SHNEERSON, Liner Shipping Economics, London 1987.

[73] SCHERER, Industrial Market Structure, and JACQUEMIN/SLADE, Cartels.

[74] On contestability, see J. E. DAVIES, Competition, contestability and the liner shipping industry, in: Journal of Transport Economics and Policy 20 (1986), pp. 299–312.

decline and disappearance of SMC particularly, and of the Spanish coastal
liner trade between peninsular ports in general. Firms that kept to the trade
after SMC had disappeared or, more frequently, started up after that, were created to serve traffic where maritime transport had a »natural monopoly«, the
routes between the Iberian peninsula and the Balearic and Canary Islands, the
inter-island traffic or the trade with Spanish possessions in North Africa.
Tramp coastal trade was also affected by inter-modal competition. Demand
reduction limited the cartel's effectiveness, strengthened competition and
freight rates plummeted. With the exception of a few cargoes, shipping had
stopped being an economic alternative for transport between Spanish peninsular ports.

17

CONCLUSION

JOHN ARMSTRONG AND ANDREAS KUNZ

One important purpose of any social science is to try and draw generalisations about the way the world works or worked. This study is in that tradition. One of the explicit aims of the workshop in Hamburg and the research and briefing that preceded it was to try to be able to generalise throughout western Europe on some aspects of the history of the coastal trade. Among the questions posed were what research has been carried out; how good were the potential sources for research in this area; what sources existed; how important was the coastal trade to industrialisation and urbanisation; what sort of growth rates did coastal trade experience. This conclusion tries to assess how much progress was made on these topics.

Sadly, most of these questions remain unanswered despite the workshop. We thought members of the workshop would be able to search the existing secondary literature on their country and largely in their language, draw this together, and write it up in English for a wider audience than simply readers of the particular language. This, we thought, would be a valuable exercise in making existing knowledge more widely known. As it turned out this was not so easy. In most European countries there is not an extensive or flourishing literature on the coastal trade. Indeed, as was true of Great Britain until the 1980s, it has largely been ignored, despite the controversies over the role of railways in economic development in the 1960s and of horse-drawn road transport in the 1970s. Thus most of the contributors were breaking new ground when they researched the coastal trade. Despite these setbacks some conclusions can be drawn.

Perhaps the first and most obvious is that already discussed, namely, that research in the coastal trade has been curiously neglected in most European countries. Despite a thriving tradition of maritime history in Europe and numerous journals and conferences, overseas trade or naval history remain the areas of most research and the coastal trade has been greatly overlooked. The reasons for this neglect do not overly concern us here, but might include the greater glamour of overseas trade, the piecemeal and scattered nature of the records of the coastal trade, the mundane ports, commodities and communities involved compared to the exotic cultures, cargoes and cities of foreign trade.

The second point that emerges clearly is the great diversity, even within Western Europe, of practices and experiences related to coastal shipping. This can be traced in at least three ways. Firstly, and most simply, the definition of what is meant by the coastal trade varies enormously between countries, as explained in the Introduction. It ranges from Belgium's post 1879 all-inclusive definition of any trade within Europe, to Britain's usage as domestic or internal trade, via France's petit and grand cabotage. The most common usage seems to have been that of internal trade and certainly adopting that definition aids analysis by making a clear distinction from short-sea and overseas trade. Although this may be the commonest and most convenient, the wide range of definitions points up the problems of doing comparative research and the richness of European experience. A complication on top of this definitional problem is that measuring coastal trade may be very difficult and rather imprecise because of the overlap between coastal, short sea, riverine and even canal traffic, with no clear cut distinction between them.

A second point of divergence in European experience is the quantity and quality of statistics which were collected about the coastal trade. In order to carry out research on a trans-European basis we need comparable statistics, as explained in the Introduction. Sadly, it is rarely the case that any country has collected all the statistics that ideally one needs on a consistent basis for any length of time. The basis of recording should have remained unchanged over time, or where there were changes, a period of overlap should have existed to allow splicing of the series. Given that such an ideal is never likely to be available, the recording of such or similar statistics on a consistent basis would be a desirable outcome. In practice there is a wide variety in the statistics available. In Spain and Italy there seem to be rich veins to be mined, with details of ships and cargoes so that, given time or generous research funding, a fairly comprehensive picture of the coastal trade could be built up. The UK is somewhere in the middle with national statistics broken down by port, of ship movements, but no similar details of cargoes carried and no information on from where the ships came or to where they were going. At the other extreme in some countries no statistics were collected of the coastal trade, because it was not considered as a separate entity. Belgium is the most extreme example of this, perhaps aggravated by the small extent of its coastline, in which no separate statistics were kept of the coastal trade. The historian therefore, has a severe uphill struggle to reconstruct any trends in the coastal trade of such countries with which to make trans-European comparisons.

The third area in which there was wide diversity was in the role which government played in the coastal trade. At the most extreme, governments left almost everything to the play of market forces, offering neither subsidy nor protection from foreign competition. At the other end of the spectrum, many governments reserved the coastal trade to ships registered in that country and flying the national flag. Some also paid a subsidy for operating the routes where there appeared to be pressing social reasons or where some form of competition to the otherwise all devouring railway seemed a good check on the latter's tendency to charge monopolistic prices. Although the practice varied throughout Europe, from the British and Belgium approach after mid century of free entry and trade, to the Greek and Italian, protection and subsidy in the Italian case the norm was closer to the protective end of the continuum, with most countries restricting the trade to national flag carriers. These countries with least restrictions had particular circumstances for being so free, namely the tiny size of Belgium's coastline and the huge technological lead which Britain enjoyed in both shipping and shipbuilding on a world-wide basis which led her correctly to believe that she had little to fear from foreign intrusion.

One way in which a number of European governments aided the coastal trade was through port improvements and other infrastructural developments. The young Italian government placed much emphasis on this and spent much money albeit not very efficiently it would seem. Spain too spent public money on upgrading ports and harbours. Even where such activities were not directly aimed at improving conditions for the coaster they had some effect, even if only in a hand-me-down way. At the extreme, the Italian government took over some coastal shipping lines after 1904 but this was a rare case of direct government intervention.

The importance of coastal shipping in forwarding industrialisation and urbanisation is the key issue that needs to be addressed. We still lack the systematic empirical base of quantities moved, details of cargoes carried, costs, prices, speeds and frequencies which would allow us to base generalisation on firm evidential foundations. We can however attempt some tentative conclusions in the hope that future research will provide more data with which to support or refute these preliminary hypotheses.

Here there is much more congruence between the experiences of different European countries. The basic economics of coasting held throughout maritime Europe. Essentially before the railway, the coaster, like the canal barge and river lighter, was particularly suited to carrying bulky goods over long distances, especially when compared to land transport by horse-drawn waggon or packhorse. The difference in carrying capacity and the lower manning levels per ton on the coaster gave it a huge cost advantage over horse-powered road transport. This advantage was particularly high where end points of the transport service were close to navigable water, but was negated where there was considerable distance between port and final destinations. Thus countries with long shorelines, combined with extensive navigable rivers, had a natural proclivity to coastal transport as coasters could double up as river barges, or offload into lighters. On the contrary, where centres of activity were resolutely inland the coaster was likely to play a smaller role and when this was combined with a large land mass unbroken by estuaries, bays and rivers the coaster's role might be anticipated to be diminished. On this basis one can understand Britain using coastal shipping on a large scale, as by the early nineteenth century, thanks to river improvements and canal construction nowhere in Britain was more than fifteen miles from navigable water. On the contrary Spain with an inland capital was less able to benefit from coastal activity. On this basis one might expect countries like Italy, Norway and Sweden to have a thriving coastal trade which would have helped industrialisation in those countries, whereas countries like Spain, Germany and France would have derived relatively less benefit from coasters.

Although the coaster had a particular edge in carrying bulky low value commodities, it also carried many higher value goods like groceries, textiles and manufactured goods, especially where both despatching and receiving towns were on the coast or a navigable river. Cost was the main advantage. Industrialisation and urbanisation required huge amounts of bulky low-value goods to be moved, either for consumption by growing urban populations, or to build the urban and industrial infrastructure (houses, roads, sewers, factories and offices) or as industrial inputs.

Industry was increasingly located in towns and consumed large quantities of coal, iron ore, salt, limestone and other bulky products. These could not have been carried solely by horse transport. The cost would have been prohibitive. Thus without the coaster industrialisation and urbanisation would have been much retarded if not impossible. The various chapters have stressed the role of the coaster in moving bricks to urban centres. Bricks and tiles went from Flensburg to many Danish towns, from Sonderburg to Rostock, and from Bremen and Pahlhude to Hamburg. Grain to feed urban populations was equally important, as in the case of grain coming from all over the Ottoman Empire to Istanbul and from many parts of Denmark to Copenhagen in the eighteenth century. Warming the urban population was also crucial, hence firewood being carried to Copenhagen from east Jutland, from Finland to Stockholm and St Petersburg, and coal being moved to various small Scottish ports or from Newcastle to London.

The coaster helped provide the essential pre requisites to industrialisation. As in the Ottoman Empire it encouraged the commercialisation of agriculture, monetisation and market growth. It did this partly by providing additional forms of employment for the small peasant mainly engaged in extractive industries such as agriculture, fishing or forestry. By working their own small boats such small-scale farmers found additional markets for their produce, or were able to cut and market firewood, catch and sell fish and other seafood, or in the Scottish case, gather and process kelp for despatch by coaster to the Glaswegian chemical works. These activities could often take place in periods when agricultural work was unnecessary, for example in winter for firewood collecting. In this way it reduced underemployment, which was a normal part of peasant agriculture. Some countries recognised this, for example France, where *Navigation de bornage* was accepted as short distance, small boat trade by peasants, or Finland where such »peasant shipping« was given special status. This was also a route into longer distance trade and larger ships, even where it was strictly not allowed, and hence a further step in economic development. The other crucial role which the coaster played in industrialisation was in promoting overseas trade by assembling manufactured and other goods for export and distributing from the major importing ports the foreign luxury goods. In this way there was a »hub and spoke« system in which smaller ships carried the goods to smaller ports which was much more efficient than the large foreign-going ship making a number of calls to discharge. Given that overseas trade grew faster than industrial output in the nineteenth century, and trade was perceived as an engine of growth, it was crucial to facilitate the flow of goods, both inward and outward, and this the coaster did in many European countries. Thus we have the example of French wine, Dutch tobacco and southern European fruits being imported into Copenhagen and then some of these luxuries being distributed to the small Danish ports by coaster. Similarly Edinburgh and Glasgow acted as hubs for receiving imports and distributing them by coaster to numerous small Scottish ports, and in similar vein, Glasgow particularly, they acted as assemblers of coaster-carried local goods for export. Lorient in Brittany performed a similar role in bringing together French goods for export to the East Indies. Through this activity and the opening up of local markets, the coaster encouraged regional specialisation and hence lower cost production and contributed in a small way to the international division of labour.

Before the railway and the steam coaster the sailing ship carried high value goods, such as the Bordeaux wine trade, as a matter of course, except perhaps when war or piracy were particularly predatory. That speeds were low, by modern standards, did not matter because so was the horse drawn alternative. Reliability was also rather low but there was a greater tolerance of this because all forms of transport worked in days rather than hours and a generous degree of leeway was accepted. The offsetting virtue was the relatively low freight rates and large scale of consignment. The arrival of the steamer improved reliability, but at a cost of a higher price, so much coastal traffic remained sail-borne. The greatest use of the early steamer was for passengers and parcels, as in Finland, or for carrying high value perishables, such as salmon and lobster to market as in Scotland. In this way the steam coaster created traffic rather than simply diverting it from the sailing ship.

The advent of railways impinged on coastal trade in most countries, not to kill it off but to encourage radical realignments. Those goods which needed fast, predictable travel times and were prepared to pay premium prices went by rail, especially where the destinations were at some remove from navigable water. The passenger traffic was almost entirely taken over by the railways, as travellers valued speed and reliability and were willing to pay for them.

The coaster responded to railway competition in two ways. It became cheaper to operate by economising on crew costs and the amount of coal it consumed, if a steamer, and through economies of scale by building bigger ships. We do not need to go through these in detail as they have been explored in the essay on Britain. To a large degree the two forms of transport – railway and coastal steamer – were complementary offering different sorts of services for different types of commodities and routes. This is particularly evident in Spain, where the star like configuration of the railway network meant direct competition was almost impossible except on a few routes, from north to south. Even here they passed through Madrid and involved trans-shipment which reduced the railway's attractiveness. Similarly, in Finland railway routes were different from those of the steamer and did not directly compete. The result was that in most countries, where statistics are available the tonnage of coastal trade continued to expand up until the First World War and was a crucial element in both industrialisation and urbanisation.

The essays in this volume cover a wide geographical range, from Finland to Spain and Scotland to the Ottoman Empire. They also exhibit a broad temporal spread from the early eighteenth-century to the mid-twentieth century. Eleven different European countries are specifically dealt with, and a good variety of topics are addressed but, despite this, we have made only an initial impression on the overall subject. We still need a sound quantitative and empirical base for most countries, as well as local studies to show in detail how coastal trade operated and how it impinged on regions and countries. This study is a start but it has only scratched the surface. Much remains to be done.

SELECT BIBLIOGRAPHY

ANDERSON-SKOG, Lena and Olle KRANTZ (eds.), Institutions in the Transport and Communications Industries: State and Private Actors in the Making of Institutional Patterns, 1850–1990, Canton, Mass. 1999.

AKVELD, Leo M. and Jaap R. BRUIJN (eds.), Shipping Companies and Authorities in the 19th and 20th Centuries: their common interest in the development of port facilities, The Hague 1989.

ARMSTRONG, John (ed.), Coastal and Short Sea Shipping, Aldershot 1996.

BARKER, T. C. and C. I. SAVAGE, An Economic History of Transport in Britain, London 1974.

BUTEL, Paul, Européens et espaces maritimes (vers 1690–vers 1790), Bordeaux 1997.

DEVOS, Greta, German Ocean Shipping and the Port of Antwerp 1875–1914, in: Proceedings of the International Colloquium »Industrial Revolutions and the Sea« (Brussels 28–31 March 1989) (= Collectanea Maritima V), Brussels 1991.

DYOS, H. J. and D. H. ALDCROFT, British Transport. An economic survey from the seventeenth century to the twentieth, Leicester 1969.

FANFANI, T. (ed.), La Penisola italiana e il mare. Costruzioni navali trasporti e commerci tra XV e XX secolo, Naples 1993.

FELDBAEK, Ole, Dansk Soefarts Historie, vol. 3, Copenhagen 1997.

FISCHER, Lewis R. and Helge W. NORDVIK, Maritime transport and the integration of the North Atlantic economy, 1850–1914, in: Wolfram FISCHER et al. (eds.), The Emergence of a World Economy, 1500–1914, Wiesbaden 1986.

FISCHER, Lewis R. et al., (eds.), Shipping and Trade in the Northern Seas, Bergen 1988.

FRANGAKIS-SYRETT, Elena, The Commerce of Smyrna in the Eigtheenth Century, 1700–1800, Athens 1992.

FRAX, Esperanza, Puertos y comercio de cabotaje en Espana, 1857–1934, Madrid 1981.

FRAX, Esperanza, El mercado interior y los principales puertos, 1857–1920, Madrid 1987.

FREEMAN, Michael J. and Derek H. ALDCROFT (eds.), Transport in Victorian Britain, Manchester 1988.

Frutta di Mare. Evolution and Revolution in the Maritime World in the 19th and 20th Centuries, Amsterdam 1998.

GERSTENBERGER, Heide and Ulrich WELKE (eds.), Das Handwerk der Seefahrt im Zeitalter der Industrialisierung, Bremen 1995.

GÓMEZ-MENDOZA, Antonio, Transportes y communicaciones, in: Albert Carreras (ed.), Estadisticas Históricas de Espana, Madrid 1987.

JACKSON, Gordon, Trade and Shipping of Dundee, 1780–1850, Dundee 1991.

JEANNIN, Pierre, The sea-borne and the overland trade routes of northern Europe in the XVIth and XVIIth Centuries, in: Journal of European Economic History 11 (1982).

KAUKIAINEN, Yrjö, A History of Finnish Shipping, London/New York 1993.

KAUKIAINEN, Yrjö, Sailing into Twilight. Finnish Shipping in an Age of Transport Revolution 1860–1914, Helsinki 1991.

KRANTZ, Olle, Transporter och kommunikationer 1800–1980 [Transport and Communications 1800–1980], Lund 1986.

KUNZ, Andreas and John ARMSTRONG (eds.), Inland Navigation and Economic Development in Nineteenth-Century Europe, Mainz 1995.

KUNZ, Andreas, (ed. and comp.), Statistik der Binnenschiffahrt in Deutschland 1835–1989, St. Katharinen 1999.

LEAGUE OF NATIONS (ed.), Enquiry into the Scope of the Idea of Coastal Shipping in the Various Countries, Geneva 1931.

Les Grandes Voies Maritimes dans le Monde, XVe–XIXe Siècles, Paris 1965.

MOLLER, Anders Monrad, Dansk Soefarts Historie, vol. 4, Copenhagen 1998.

MOLLER, Anders Monrad, Henrik Dethlevsen and Hans Chr. Johansen, Dansk Soefarts Historie, vol. 5, Copenhagen 1998.

PELTONEN, Matti T., Liikene Suomessa 1860–1913 [Transport and Communication in Finland], Helsinki 1983.

PINKNEY, David H., Cabotage, France's forgotton common carrier, in: French Historical Studies, vol. XVI (1989).

SCHOLL, Lars U. et al.(eds.), The North Sea: Resources and Seaway, Aberdeen 1996.

SMOUT, T. C. (ed.), Scotland and the Sea, Edinburgh 1992.

Third European Research Roundtable Conference on Shortsea Shipping, Delft 1996.

VALDALISO, Jesús M., La navegación regular de cabotaje en España en los siglos XIX y XX: guerras de fletes, conferencias y consorcios navieros, Bilbao 1997.

VILLE, Simon P., Transport and the development of the European economy, 1750–1918.

CONTRIBUTORS

JOHN ARMSTRONG is Professor of Business History at Thames Valley University, London, UK.

GRETA DEVOS is Professor of Contemporary History at Antwerp University, Belgium.

LEWIS R. FISCHER is Professor of Economic History at the Memorial University of Newfoundland, Canada.

ELENA FRANGAKIS-SYRETT is Professor of History at Queens College, City University of New York, USA.

ANDREA GIUNTINI lectures in economic history at the University of Florence, Italy.

ANTONIO GÓMEZ-MENDOZA is Professor of Economic History at the Complutense University of Madrid, Spain.

GORDON JACKSON recently retired from Strathclyde University, Glasgow, UK.

HANS CHRISTIAN JOHANSEN is Professor of Economic History at the University of Copenhagen, Denmark.

YRJÖ KAUKIAINEN is Professor of History at the University of Helsinki, Finland.

OLLE KRANTZ is Professor of Economic History at Umeå University, Sweden.

ANDREAS KUNZ is Deputy Director in the World History Section at the Institute of European History, Mainz, Germany.

JARI OJALA lectures in economic history at the University of Jyväskylä, Finland.

ORTWIN PELC is conservator for port history at the Museum for Hamburg History, Hamburg, Germany.

DANIEL A. RABUZZI is a historian and acting CEO at Kentucky Virtual University, USA.

JESÚS M. VALDALISO is Professor of Economic History at the University of Bilbao, Spain.

PETER VOSS was Research Fellow at the Institute of European History, Mainz, Germany.

GENERAL INDEX

This index concentrates on geographical names, transport-related concepts, names of shipping companies, and historical persons. It refers to the text only; notes, tables and maps have not been referenced. Geographical names have been indexed as they appear in the text. Ports indexed under country headings are minor ports, while major ports appear under their individual names.